3 0250 09065 4398

CURRICULUM
COLLECTION

Curr
LB
1573
H684
v.6:1
gr.4
1988
cop.2

D0604394

HOUGHTON MIFFLIN LITERARY READERS

BOOK 4

HOUGHTON MIFFLIN COMPANY   BOSTON

Atlanta   Dallas   Geneva, Illinois   Palo Alto   Princeton   Toronto

Program Authors

William K. Durr, John J. Pikulski, Rita M. Bean, J. David Cooper, Nicholas A. Glaser, M. Jean Greenlaw, Hugh Schoephoerster, Mary Lou Alsin, Kathryn Au, Rosalinda B. Barrera, Joseph E. Brzeinski, Ruth P. Bunyan, Jacqueline C. Comas, Frank X. Estrada, Robert L. Hillerich, Timothy G. Johnson, Pamela A. Mason, Joseph S. Renzulli

Senior Consultants

Jacqueline L. Chaparro, Alan N. Crawford, Alfredo Schifini, Sheila Valencia

Program Reviewers

Donna Bessant, Mara Bommarito, Yetive Bradley, Patricia M. Callan, Clara J. Hanline, Fannie Humphery, Barbara H. Jeffus, Beverly Jimenez, Sue Cramton Johnson, Michael P. Klentschy, Petra Montante, Nancy Rhodes, Julie Ryan, Lily Sarmiento, Ellis Vance, Judy Williams, Leslie M. Woldt, Janet Gong Yin

Acknowledgments

For each of the selections listed below, grateful acknowledgement is made for permission to adapt and/or reprint original or copyrighted material, as follows:

"About Elephants," an adaptation of *Seven True Elephant Stories,* by Barbara Williams. Copyright © 1978. Reprinted by permission of Hastings House Publishers, Inc.

". . . and now Miguel," an adaptation of *. . . and now Miguel* by Joseph Krumgold (Thomas Y. Crowell). Copyright, 1953 by Joseph Krumgold. Reprinted by permission of Harper and Row, Publishers, Inc.

"Anna, Grandpa and the Big Storm," adapted from *Anna, Grandpa and the Big Storm* by Carla Stevens. Copyright © 1982 by Carla Stevens. Reprinted by permission of Clarion Books/ Ticknor & Fields, a Houghton Mifflin Company.

"The Ants at the Olympics" from *Animal Alphabet* by Richard Digance. Copyright © 1980 by Richard Digance. Reprinted by permission of Michael Joseph, Ltd.

"The Arrival of Paddington," from *Paddington on Stage* by Alfred Bradley and Michael Bond. Copyright © 1974 by Alfred Bradley and Michael Bond. Adapted and reprinted by permission of Harvey Unna & Stephen Durbridge, Ltd. and Houghton Mifflin Company. Illustrations from *A Bear Called Paddington* by Michael Bond. Illustrated by Peggy Fortnum. Copyright © 1958 by Michael Bond. Reprinted by permission of Houghton Mifflin Company and Collins Publishers.

Continued on page 453.

Copyright © 1989 by Houghton Mifflin Company.
All rights reserved.

No part of this work may be reproduced or transmitted in any form or by any means, electronic or mechanical, including photocopying and recording, or by any information storage or retrieval system without the prior written permission of the copyright owner unless such copying is expressly permitted by federal copyright law. With the exception of non-profit transcription in Braille, Houghton Mifflin is not authorized to grant permission for further uses of copyrighted selections reprinted in this text without the permission of their owners. Permission must be obtained from the individual copyright owners as identified herein. Address requests for permission to make copies of Houghton Mifflin material to Permissions, Houghton Mifflin Company, One Beacon Street, Boston, MA 02108.

Printed in the U.S.A.

ISBN: 0-395-47701-8

HIJ-D-96543210

Contents

1. Learning from Nature

Houghton Mifflin Literature
Appearances

2. Sharing

Houghton Mifflin Literature
Blackberries in the Dark

3.   Accepting Challenges

5. Facing the Truth

Houghton Mifflin Literature
The Real Thief

6. Discovering Myself

Houghton Mifflin Literature

A Likely Place

1

Learning
from Nature

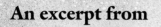

Anna, Grandpa, and the Big Storm

by Carla Stevens

Illustrated by Nancy Edwards Calder

Anna's grandfather Jensen was visiting her in New York City in 1888. He was bored with city life and said he didn't like the city too much. For something to do, he offered to take Anna to school as it had started to snow very hard. Anna was eager to get to school because she was doing well in spelling and hoped to win that day's spelling bee. So they set out.

Anna followed Grandpa up the long flight of steps to the Fourteenth Street El station. No one was at the ticket booth so they ducked under the turnstile to the platform. They stood out of the wind at the head of the stairs. Anna could see only one other person waiting for a train on the uptown side.

Anna looked at her rosy-cheeked grandfather. Snow clung to his moustache and eyebrows and froze. They looked like tiny icebergs.

"Here comes the train!" Grandpa shouted.

A steam engine, pulling two green cars, puffed toward them. When the train stopped, Anna and Grandpa hurried across the platform and stepped inside. There were lots of empty seats. They sat down behind a large woman. She took up most of the seat in front of them.

Anna pulled off her hat. Her pom-pom looked like a big white snowball. She shook it, spraying the floor with wet snow. The conductor came up the aisle and stopped at their seat.

Grandpa said, "No one was at the station to sell us a ticket."

"That will be five cents," the conductor said. "Each."

"You mean I have to pay for her, too?" Grandpa's eyes twinkled.

"Grandpa," Anna whispered, tugging at his arm. "I'm almost eight years old."

Grandpa and the conductor laughed. Anna didn't like to be teased. She turned away and tried to look out, but snow covered the windows.

Grandpa leaned forward. "Quite a storm," he said to the woman in the seat in front of them. "Nothing like the Blizzard of '72, though. Why it was so cold, the smoke froze as it came out of the chimney!"

There he goes again, Anna thought. Why does Grandpa always talk to strangers?

A woman holding a basket sat across from them. She leaned over. "In Poland, when I was a little girl, it snowed like this all winter long."

The woman in the seat ahead turned around. "This storm can't last. First day of spring is less than two weeks away."

"That's just what I was telling my daughter this morning!" Grandpa said.

Anna could see that Grandpa was growing more cheerful by the minute.

Suddenly the train stopped.

"What's the trouble?" the woman from Poland asked. "Conductor, why has the train stopped?"

The conductor didn't reply. He opened the car door and stepped out onto the platform. No one inside said a word.

Then Grandpa stood up. "I'll find out what's the matter."

Anna tugged at his coat sleeve. "Oh, please sit down,

Grandpa." He didn't seem to understand how scared she felt. How she wished she had stayed home!

The door opened again and the conductor entered the car. He was covered with snow. "We're stuck," he said. "The engine can't move. Too much snow has drifted onto the tracks ahead. We'll have to stay here until help comes."

"Did you hear that, Anna?" Grandpa almost bounced up and down in his seat. "We're stuck! Stuck and stranded on the Third Avenue El! What do you think about that!"

When Anna heard the news, she grew even more frightened. "Mama will be so worried. She doesn't know where we are."

"She knows you are with me," Grandpa said cheerfully. "That's all she needs to know." He leaned forward again. "We might as well get acquainted," he said. "My name is Erik Jensen, and this is my granddaughter, Anna."

The woman in the seat ahead turned around. "Josie Sweeney," she said. "Pleased to meet you."

"How-dee-do," said the woman across the aisle. "I'm Mrs. Esther Polanski. And this is my friend, Miss Ruth Cohen."

Someone tapped Anna on her shoulder. She turned around. Two young men smiled. One man said, "John King and my brother, Bruce."

A young woman with a high fur collar and a big hat sat by herself at the rear of the car. Anna looked in her direction. "My name is Anna Romano," she said shyly.

"I'm Addie Beaver," said the young woman. She smiled and wrapped her coat more tightly around her.

It was growing colder and colder inside the car. When the conductor shook the snow off his clothes, it no longer melted into puddles on the floor.

"We'll all freeze to death if we stay here," moaned Mrs. Sweeney.

"Oooooo, my feet are so cold," Addie Beaver said.

Anna looked at her high-button shoes and felt sorry for Addie Beaver. Even though Anna had on her warm boots, her toes began to grow cold, too. She stood in the aisle and stamped her feet up and down.

Suddenly Anna had an idea. "Grandpa!" she said. "I know a game we can play that might help keep us warm."

"Why Anna, what a good idea," Grandpa replied.

"It's called, 'Simon Says'."

"Listen everybody!" Grandpa shouted. "My granddaughter, Anna, knows a game that will help us stay warm."

"How do we play, Anna?" asked Mrs. Polanski. "Tell us."

"Everybody has to stand up," said Anna.

"Come on, everybody," Grandpa said. "We must keep moving if we don't want to freeze to death."

Miss Beaver was the first to stand. Then John and Bruce King stood up. Grandpa bowed first to Mrs. Sweeney, then to Mrs. Polanski and Miss Cohen. "May I help you, ladies?" he asked. They giggled and stood up. Now everybody was looking at Anna.

"All right," she said. "You must do only what Simon tells you to do. If *I* tell you to do something, you mustn't do it."

"I don't understand," Mrs. Sweeney said.

"Maybe we'll catch on if we start playing," Grandpa said.

"All right," Anna said. "I'll begin. Simon says, 'Clap your hands'."

Everybody began to clap hands.

"Simon says, 'Stop'!"

Everybody stopped.

"Good!" Anna said. "Simon says, 'Follow me'!" Anna marched down the aisle of the car, then around one of the poles, then back again. Everyone followed her.

"Simon says, 'Stop'!"

Everyone stopped.

Anna patted her head and rubbed her stomach at the same time.

"Simon says, 'Pat your head and rub your stomach.' Like this."

Everyone began to laugh at one another.

"Simon says, 'Swing your arms around and around'."

"Ooof! This is hard work!" puffed Mrs. Sweeney.

"Now. Touch your toes!"

Mrs. Sweeney bent down and tried to touch her toes.

"Oh! Oh! You're out, Mrs. Sweeney!" Anna said.

"Why am I out?" She asked indignantly.

Anna giggled. "Because *Simon* didn't say to touch your toes. *I* did!"

Mrs. Sweeney sat down. "It's just as well," she panted. "I was getting all tired out."

"Is everyone warming up?" Grandpa asked.

"Yes! Yes!" they all shouted.

Snow was sifting like flour through the cracks around the windows. Just then, the door opened. A blast of icy cold air blew into the car. Everyone shivered. It was the conductor coming back in again.

"Get ready to leave," he said. "The firemen are coming!"

Everyone rushed to the door and tried to look out. The snow stung Anna's eyes. The wind almost took her breath away.

The conductor closed the door again quickly. "The wind is so fierce it's going to be hard to get a ladder up this high. We're at least thirty feet above Third Avenue."

Ladder! Thirty feet! Anna shivered.

"Oh, Lord help me," groaned Mrs. Sweeney. "I'll never be able to climb down a ladder." She gave Grandpa a pleading look.

"Oh, yes you will, Mrs. Sweeney," he said. "Once you get the hang of it, it's easy."

"In all that wind?" Mrs. Sweeney said. "Never!"

"Don't worry, Mrs. Sweeney. You won't blow away," said Grandpa.

Anna looked at Grandpa. "I'm scared too," she said.

"And what about me?" asked Mrs. Polanski. "I can't stand heights."

The door opened and a fireman appeared. He shook the snow off his clothes. "We'll take you down one at a time. Who wants to go first?"

No one spoke.

"Anna," said Grandpa. "You're a brave girl. You go first."

"I'm afraid to climb down the ladder, Grandpa."

"Why Anna, I'm surprised at you. Don't you remember how you climbed down from the hayloft last summer? It was easy."

"You can do it, Anna," said Miss Cohen.

"Pretend we're still playing that game. Simon says, 'Go down the ladder'," said Mrs. Sweeney.

"So go now," Miss Cohen said. "We'll see you below."

"I'll be right below you to shield you from the wind. You won't fall," said the fireman.

Anna shook with fear. She didn't want to be first to go down the ladder. But how could she disappoint the others?

Grandpa opened the door. The conductor held her hand. Anna put first one foot, then the other, on the ladder. The fierce wind pulled her and pushed her. Icy snow stuck to her clothes, weighing her down.

The fireman was below her on the ladder. His strong arms were around her, holding her steady. With her left foot, Anna felt for the rung below.

Step by step by step, she cautiously went down the ladder. Thirty steps. Would she never reach bottom? One foot plunged into snow and then the other. Oh, so much snow! It covered her legs and reached almost to her waist.

"Stay close to the engine until the rest are down," the fireman said.

Anna struggled through the deep snow to the fire engine. The horses, whipped by the icy wind and snow, stood still, their heads low. Anna huddled against the side of the engine. The roar of the storm was growing louder.

First came Mrs. Polanski, then Ruth Cohen. Then Bruce and John King. Then Addie Beaver. One at a time, the fireman helped each person down the ladder. Now only Grandpa and Mrs. Sweeney remained to be rescued.

Anna could see two shapes on the ladder, one behind the other. The fireman was bringing down someone else.

"Oh, I hope it's Grandpa," Anna said to Addie Beaver.

Suddenly she gasped. She could hardly believe her eyes. One minute the two shapes were there. The next minute they weren't!

Everyone struggled through the deep snow to find out who had fallen off the ladder.

Anna was first to reach the fireman who was brushing snow off his clothes. "What happened?" she asked.

"Mrs. Sweeney missed a step on the ladder. Down she went, taking me with her," the fireman replied.

Mrs. Sweeney lay sprawled in the snow nearby. Her arms and legs were spread out, as if she were going to make a snow angel.

"Are you all right, Mrs. Sweeney?" Grandpa asked. Anna had not seen Grandpa come down the ladder by himself. Now he stood beside her.

"I'm just fine, Mr. Jensen. I think I'm going to lie right here until the storm is over."

"Oh no you're not!" Grandpa said. He and a fireman each took one of Mrs. Sweeney's arms. They pulled her to her feet.

Anna couldn't help giggling. Now Mrs. Sweeney looked like a giant snow lady!

"Climb onto the engine," said a fireman. "We must get the horses back to the firehouse. The temperature is dropping fast."

"We live only two blocks from here," Mrs. Polanski and Miss Cohen said. "We're going to try to get home."

"We'll see that you get there," John King said. "We live on Lafayette Street." The young men and the two ladies linked arms and trudged off through the snow.

"What about you, Miss Beaver?" Grandpa asked. She looked confused.

"Hey, this is no tea party! Let's go!" said the fireman.

"You come with us then, Miss Beaver," Grandpa said. "You too, Mrs. Sweeney."

Anna's fingers were numb with cold. She could hardly hold onto the railing of the engine. Often she had seen the horses racing down the street to a fire. Now they plodded along very, very slowly through the deep snow.

No one spoke. The wind roared and shrieked. The snow blinded them. One fireman jumped off the engine and tried to lead the horses forward.

Anna huddled against the side of the engine, hiding her face in her arms. It was taking them forever to reach the firehouse.

Just then, the horses turned abruptly to the left. The next moment they were inside the stable, snorting and stamping their hooves.

Several men ran forward to unhitch the engine. Everyone began brushing the icy snow off their clothes.

Suddenly Grandpa became very serious. "The thermometer says five degrees above zero, and the temperature is still dropping. We must get home as fast as possible. Mrs. Sweeney, you and Miss Beaver had better come with us."

"Here, Miss," a fireman said. "Put these boots on. You can return them when the storm is over."

"Oh, thank you," Addie Beaver said.

Anna had forgotten about Addie's high-button shoes.

"Whatever you do, Anna, you are *not* to let go of my hand." Grandpa spoke firmly.

"Mr. Jensen, would you mind if I held your other hand?" asked Mrs. Sweeney.

"Not a bit," said Grandpa. "Anna, you take hold of Miss Beaver's hand. No one is to let go under *any* circumstances. Do you all understand?"

Anna had never heard Grandpa talk like that before. Was he frightened too?

They plunged into the deep snow, moving slowly along the south side of Fifteenth Street. The wind had piled the snow into huge drifts on the north side of the street.

When they reached Broadway, the wind was blowing up the avenue with the force of a hurricane. Telephone and telegraph wires were down. Thousands of them cut

through the air like whips. If only they could reach the other side, Anna thought. Then they would be on their very own block.

No one spoke. They clung to one another as they blindly made their way across the avenue. Mrs. Sweeney lost her balance and fell forward in the snow. For a moment Anna thought she was there to stay. But Grandpa tugged at her arm and helped her get to her feet.

They continued on until they reached the other side. Now to find their house. How lucky they were to live on the south side of the block. The snow had reached as high as the first-floor windows of the houses on the north side. At last they came to Number 44. Up the seven steps they climbed. Then through the front door and up more stairs.

A moment later, Mr. Romano opened their apartment door. "Papa, you're home," Anna cried, and fell into her father's arms.

Several hours later, Anna sat in the kitchen watching a checkers game. Mrs. Sweeney, wearing Grandpa's bathrobe, was playing checkers with Grandpa, while Miss Beaver, in Mama's clothes, chatted with Mama. Outside, the storm whistled and roared. Tomorrow would be time enough to study her spelling, Anna decided. Now she just wanted to enjoy the company.

Suddenly Grandpa pushed his chair back. "You win, Mrs. Sweeney. Where did you learn to play checkers?"

"I belong to a club," Mrs. Sweeney replied. "I'm the champ. We meet every Tuesday. Maybe you will come with me next Tuesday, Mr. Jensen?"

"Why, I'd like that," answered Grandpa.

Anna said, "I think Grandpa likes the city better now."

Mrs. Romano smiled. "It took a snowstorm to change his mind."

"You call this a snowstorm?" said Grandpa. He winked at Anna. "When you are an old lady, Anna, as old as I am now, you will be telling your grandchildren all about our adventure in The Great Blizzard of 1888!"

The Great Blizzard of 1888

There really *was* a great blizzard in 1888. It began to snow early Monday morning, March 12th. Before the snow stopped on Tuesday, four to five feet had fallen in New York City. Seventy inches fell in Boston and in other parts of the east.

The winds blew at 75 miles an hour and piled the snow in huge drifts. Everywhere, people were stranded. In New York City, about 15,000 people were trapped in Elevated trains. Like Anna and Grandpa, they had to be rescued by firemen with ladders.

By Thursday of that same week, the sun was out again. The snow began to melt. Anna went to school and won the spelling bee. And Grandpa walked down to Sullivan Street to play checkers again with Josie Sweeney.

New York City, 1888.

Author

Carla Stevens grew up in New York City, where she rode the Third Avenue Elevated as a child. Riding on the El was always a great adventure for her. Mrs. Stevens has been a teacher as well as a writer. Another of her books that is set in the past is *Trouble for Lucy*.

HOW THE
FOREST GREW

by William Jaspersohn

Illustrated by Chuck Eckart

Have you ever wondered
where forests come from,
and how they grow?
This book is about a hardwood
forest in Massachusetts.
It could be about a forest
anywhere because most forests
grow the same way.
To find out how
this Massachusetts forest grew,
we must go back in time.
We must see how
the forest land looked
two hundred years ago.

Two hundred years ago
the land was open and green.
But then the farmer and his family
who owned the land,
and who had cleared it,
moved away.
Changes began.
The wind blew seeds across the fields.
Birds dropped seeds from the air.
The sun warmed the seeds.
The rain watered them,
and they grew.

In a few years the land was filled
with weeds—with dandelions
and goldenrod and chickweed.
And milkweed with its pods of fluff.
And ragweed and black-eyed Susans.
Each spring new plants took root.
The land began to look different.
Burdock and briars
grew among the weeds,
making the land moist and brushy.

Blackberries grew.
Birds came to eat them—
song sparrows, bobolinks,
and catbirds.
Meadow mice
and cottontail rabbits
made their nests
in the tall grass.
Woodchucks, moles, and shrews
dug their tunnels in the ground.
Snakes came to feed
on the small animals.
Hawks and owls
hunted over the land
for their food.
Time passed.

And then one summer
five years after the farm family left,
a tree seedling sprouted.
It wasn't a cedar or a birch seedling,
or a poplar or an aspen seedling,
though it could have been
because these trees like full sunlight.
No, it was a white pine seedling,
another sun-loving tree.
The wind had blown its seed
from a nearby forest.
The seed sprouted.

That same summer
more white pine seedlings sprouted.
The land was speckled
with tiny dots of green.
Year after year,
through weeds and low brush,
the little trees pushed their way up.
Tree scientists call the first trees
that take hold on a piece of land
pioneer trees.
That is what these white pines were.
No other sun-loving tree
grows in such numbers,
or so fast.

As the pine trees grew,
brush-dwelling birds
moved onto the land.
They replaced the field dwellers.
Towhees, warblers, and field sparrows
made their homes in the thickets.
But so did weasels and foxes
who caught mice, rabbits, and birds
for their dinner.

Twenty years after
the first pine seedling sprouted,
the land was covered with white pines.
Their branches blocked the sun's rays.
The old weeds and grasses
died from want of light.
But what the pines did
to the old weeds,
they also did to their own kind.
When new white pine seedlings
tried to grow,
they couldn't get sunlight,
and they died.

Only those seedlings
that liked the shade
grew beneath
the stands of white pines.
Ash trees, red oak, red maple,
and tulip trees—
these were the trees
that the white pines
helped the most.
In less than fifteen years
the new trees were crowding
the white pines for space.
A struggle had begun,
only the strongest
trees would survive.
Scientists call this change
from one kind of tree or animal
to a new kind *succession*.
They say that one kind of tree
or animal succeeds another.

As the new trees on the land
began to succeed the old pines,
the animal life on the land
changed, too.
The meadow mice moved because
their food supply was gone,
and there was no more grass
for them to build their nests.
White-footed mice took their place.
They made their nests
in hollow stumps and logs.
They ate seeds
from the trees and shrubs.

For the first time
deer came to live on the land.
Now there were places
for them to hide
and tender shoots
for them to eat.

Cardinals perched in the trees.
So did redstarts,
ovenbirds, and ruffed grouse.
Squirrels and chipmunks
brought nuts onto the land.
Some of these sprouted
with the other seedlings.

Forty years had passed since
the farmer and his family had left.
And then one summer afternoon,
fifty years after the farm family had gone,
a storm broke over the land.
Lightning struck the tallest pines,
killing some of them
and damaging others.
Strong winds uprooted more pines,
and lightning fires scorched branches.

But this is how forests grow.
The death of some of the pine trees
made room for new and different trees
that had been sprouting
on the forest floor.
As time passed, insects and disease
hurt the other pines.
Every time one of them died,
a red oak, white ash,
or red maple tree
took its place.

The forest grew.
By the year 1860,
more than eighty years
after the farm family had left,
the weeds were all gone.
The pioneer white pines
were nearly all gone.
Red oaks, red maples,
and ash trees were everywhere.
The forest had reached
its *middle stage*.

Now on the forest floor
came the last of the new seedlings.
These were the beeches
and the sugar maples,
trees that like the deep shade.
The other seedlings—
the red oak, red maple,
and ash seedlings—needed more light.
And some of them needed more water,
and different kinds of soil to grow in.
So they died, and the beech
and the sugar maple seedlings
took their place.

Every autumn
the trees lost their leaves.
They fell to the ground
with dead twigs and branches.
All of these things decayed
and made a rich layer of stuff
called *humus*.
Then slowly,
bacteria, worms, and fungi
turned the humus into soil
from which the trees
got food and water.
Sometimes an animal
or an insect died, and its body
became part of the humus, too.

One hundred years had passed
since the farm family had moved.
Now, whenever a red oak, red maple,
or white ash tree died, it made room for
the smaller beeches and sugar maples.
These formed a layer below the older trees
called an *understory*.

Every winter, snow blanketed
the forest floor.
Every spring, the ground
was covered with wildflowers.
Year after year,
the beeches and sugar maple trees
pushed their branches toward the sky.
Hemlocks grew in their shade.
Slowly, one by one,
most of the red oak, red maple,
and ash trees disappeared.

By the year 1927,
which was one hundred and fifty years
after the forest had begun,
the beeches and sugar maples
were the kings of the forest.
Today a family owns the land
and they love the peaceful forest.
They build their house on the same spot
where the farm family once built theirs.
But they do not clear
the land this time.
Instead, they listen and look.
What was once open fields
is now a magnificent forest.
It is home for many wild animals—
for foxes, bobcats, wood turtles,
chipmunks, bears, deer, squirrels,
mice, porcupines,
and many other creatures.

Its tree roots hold water
and keep the soil from washing away.
Birds of many kinds
nest in its branches.
Its humus enriches the earth's soil.
All through the world
other forests are growing
like the one in Massachusetts.
The kinds of trees in each forest
may be different, but the way they
grow is very much the same.
Nothing in a forest ever stands still.
Old trees are dying and making room
for new trees every day.

THE NEXT TIME
YOU GO INTO A FOREST

Think how long it took to grow.

Try and learn the names
of the different trees.

Most forests
have three stages of growth:
↪   the pioneer stage
     the middle stage
     the final, or climax stage
See if you can tell which stage
of growth the forest is in.

A full-grown forest has five layers:
↪   the canopy
     the understory
     the shrub layer
     the herbal layer
     the forest floor layer.
Can you find all five?

If you find a tree stump
and count its growth rings,
you will know the tree's age.

Fungi live on rotting
trees and plants.
Look for them on fallen
logs and stumps.
Can you find signs of insects
that have hurt trees?
Can you find signs of woodpeckers?

Know the different signs
of animal life in a forest:

- tracks
  scat
  feathers, fur, or snakeskins
  nests, burrows, dens
  bones, skeletons

Do you know the poisonous plants
in a forest?

- poison ivy
  poison oak
  poison sumac

Some rules of the forest:

- Never light fires in a forest without adult supervision.

Never go into a forest alone, or at least without telling someone where you are going.

- Never eat any wild plants, berries, or mushrooms without knowing first if they are safe to eat.

- Never pull the bark off a tree. The bare spot may bring disease and insects.

- Never "girdle" a tree. You will kill it.

Remember: trees are living things. Treat them as such.

Author

William Jaspersohn knows New England well. It is the setting for his third children's book, *How the Forest Grew*. This book won the Boston Globe-Horn Book Award.

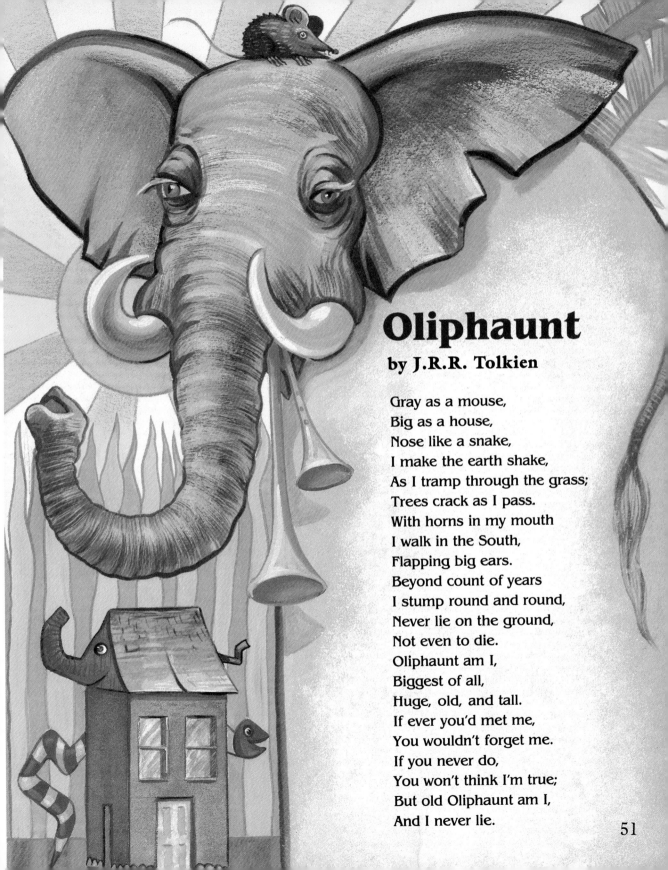

Oliphaunt

by J.R.R. Tolkien

Gray as a mouse,
Big as a house,
Nose like a snake,
I make the earth shake,
As I tramp through the grass;
Trees crack as I pass.
With horns in my mouth
I walk in the South,
Flapping big ears.
Beyond count of years
I stump round and round,
Never lie on the ground,
Not even to die.
Oliphaunt am I,
Biggest of all,
Huge, old, and tall.
If ever you'd met me,
You wouldn't forget me.
If you never do,
You won't think I'm true;
But old Oliphaunt am I,
And I never lie.

51

About Elephants

From the informational selection by Barbara Williams

A big stack of mail was waiting for Abraham Lincoln when he became President in 1861. One interesting letter was from the King of Siam. The king had learned some shocking news. Someone had told him there were no elephants roaming wild in American "jungles." No elephants to help farmers till the soil. No elephants to move the heavy logs to lumber mills. Not even any elephants to ride into battle.

The king was sure no country could last without elephants. So he offered to help. He would send a few elephants to America. President Lincoln could turn them loose in the hot American "jungles." In time, the elephants' children and grandchildren could be caught and tamed.

This may sound silly. But the king was quite serious. To him and other Asians, the elephant was as important as the horse has been to Americans.

Americans have never used elephants for work. But Americans love elephants. At any zoo, people crowd around the elephant cages. At any circus, the audience claps and cheers when the elephant act begins.

An Asian elephant with a rider. In some parts of Asia, elephants are used as work animals.

What Is Unusual About Elephants' Feet?

Elephants are bigger than any other land animal. Some grow to be 12 feet at the shoulder and weigh 12,000 pounds. Hunters can tell the size of an elephant by its footprints. They measure all around one footprint. Then, they multiply by two. That gives the elephant's height at its shoulder.

When you look at it, the elephant's foot seems flat and clumsy. But you don't see the real foot. You see a cushion of flesh around it. Inside this cushion, the elephant walks gently on its toes.

Elephants walk very fast — up to 25 miles an hour. They move with ease through thick forests, up steep hills, along winding jungle paths. Ambling along, an elephant can keep up with our fastest track stars.

But an elephant cannot run. Nor can it jump. For this reason farmers who live near jungles sometimes dig ditches around their land. An elephant can knock down almost any fence. But it cannot jump across a ditch.

The forty thousand muscles and tendons in an elephant's trunk make it strong and flexible — and very useful!

Why Are Elephants' Trunks Important?

To hold up its big head and heavy tusks the elephant needs a strong neck. But its neck cannot turn very well from side to side. If it wants to see something on one side, the elephant must turn its whole body. So the elephant needs another sense to tell it if it is in danger. It learns what it needs to know by smelling the world with its trunk.

An elephant can smell a person several miles away. It can even smell water. The leader of a herd of elephants will wave her trunk in the air for a few seconds. Then she will trudge off. The rest of the herd will follow single file.

Munching leaves as they walk, they will go straight to the water hole.

The trunk is more than a nose for smelling and breathing. It is an instrument for squealing and trumpeting. It is a weapon for fighting. It is a tool for lifting and breaking. It is a snorkel for swimming. It is a paddle for spanking. It is a hand for eating.

A baby elephant isn't born knowing how to use its trunk. A newborn will wave its trunk in the air like a rubber hose, not knowing quite what to do with it. It may sit down and put the tip in its mouth to suck like a thumb. Or it may accidentally hit itself on the back.

At the tip of its trunk, an elephant has either one or two points, which work like fingers. In fact, the points are sometimes called the elephant's fingers. With them, an elephant can pick a blade of grass, crack a peanut, or steal a cube of sugar from its trainer's pocket.

One unusual way the elephant uses its trunk is to take a shower. The elephant will suck up about two gallons of water in its trunk. Then it will lift the trunk above its head.

These young bull elephants in Samburu, Kenya, are using their trunks in a contest of strength.

With a gush, two gallons of water run down the elephant's back. By putting the tip of the trunk in its mouth instead, the elephant will get a cool drink. It needs up to 50 gallons of water a day.

Showers keep an elephant cool. If an elephant gets too hot, it will die. In the heat of day, it just stands still in the shade. When there is a wind, it spreads its big ears to catch a breeze. When the air is still, it flaps its ears like fans. When there is no shade, no wind, and no water, the elephant can do a surprising thing. It can put its trunk deep down its throat and draw water from its stomach to spray on itself.

How Are Elephants' Teeth and Skin Special?

Hidden behind the elephant's trunk is a very large mouth. Just one tooth can be the size of a person's foot and weigh up to ten pounds. During its life the elephant gets six sets of teeth. First come the baby teeth. These are replaced by new ones at ages 2, 6, 9, 25, and 60. Scientists

An African elephant enjoys a bath in a waterhole at Etosha National Park in Namibia, Africa.

studying elephants have been able to look at their teeth and guess how old they are.

Some people believe that elephants live to be over one hundred years old. They think an elephant's wrinkles prove how old it is. But the truth is that elephants live only about sixty or seventy years.

If an elephant does not meet up with a hungry lion, or fall down a mountain, or sink into a bog, or come within shooting range of a man, it may die of tooth wear. When its very last tooth is ground down, an elephant cannot eat the food it must have to go on living.

An elephant needs such big teeth and so many sets of them because it is always eating. Twenty hours out of every twenty-four, an elephant munches, munches, munches. It needs from 200 to 1,000 pounds of food every day, depending on its size and how hard it works. Elephants like grass, leaves, twigs, grain, nuts and especially fruit. They do not eat meat.

With all this eating, an elephant's stomach constantly

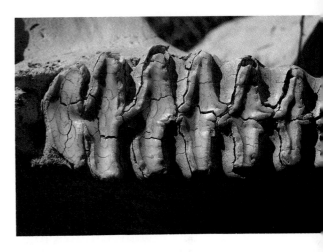

These elephant molars belong to one of the six sets of teeth an elephant has in its lifetime.

growls. Hunters sometimes hear the growling stomachs before they see the elephants. Twenty or thirty growling elephant stomachs can sound like thunder.

The two big teeth which grow out from the elephant's upper jaw are called tusks. Elephants have no other teeth in front. With the sharp points of its tusks, an elephant can strip the bark off trees to eat. It can also fight.

The elephant's most dangerous foe is the hunter. Often, the hunter is after tusks. Elephant tusks are made of ivory, which people have prized for centuries. From it, they carve beautiful boxes, statues, jewelry and even piano keys.

Elephant skin is thick and wrinkled, like the bark of a cottonwood tree. The hide is so thick it makes up about one sixth of the elephant's weight — or about 2,000 pounds. Even so, elephants are ticklish. They hate crawling insects like flies and mosquitoes.

Elephants are gray but they don't always look gray. The color of an elephant's skin depends on what it has been doing. If it looks white, the elephant has probably been moving through the forest, raising clouds of white dust. If it looks red-brown, the elephant has been splashing in a mud pool. But if it looks gray, the elephant has just had a bath.

What Are the Kinds of Elephants?

There are two kinds of elephants. One kind comes from Asia, the other, from Africa. African elephants are sometimes called *loxodonts*.

Some people say that African elephants are bigger than Asian elephants. This is not exactly true. Here is the reason. In Africa, some elephants live in open spaces where low bushes grow. Others live in the forest where high trees grow. The bush elephants are bigger than Asian elephants. But the forest elephants are smaller.

It is not hard to tell the difference between Asian and African elephants. African elephants have big ears that look like the two sides of a giant valentine heart. Asian elephants' ears are smaller and shaped more like a triangle. African elephants have sloping foreheads and sway backs. Asian elephants have foreheads that go straight up and down. Their backs are rounded at the top.

Among both Asian and African elephants, males are called bulls. Females are called cows. Babies are called calves. In Asia, only bulls grow tusks. In Africa, both bulls *and* cows grow tusks. African elephants have rings around their trunks and two "fingers" at the tips. Asian elephants have smoother trunks and one "finger" at the tips.

How Do Elephants Help Each Other?

Elephants are good mothers. They take good care of their babies. When a cow is about 10 years old, she has her first calf. After that, she usually has one about every four years. She does not often have more than ten babies. And she almost never has twins.

The cow carries the baby inside her about 22 months. During this time, a strange thing happens. Another cow senses that the first is going to be a mother. The second cow, known as the "auntie," starts to take care of the mother. She helps during the birth. And she helps the mother raise the baby. If the mother dies, the auntie adopts the baby and raises it as her own.

When the time of birth is close, the mother and auntie choose a good spot. The best

The Asian elephant (top) has smaller ears than the African elephant (bottom). What other differences do you notice?

place is under a tall tree near a river. The tree will give them shade. The river will give them water to drink.

The birth itself is simple. Usually, it takes only a few hours. The new baby elephant

59

has red, wavy hair and a short trunk. Its head has a squashed look. And its belly looks like a crumpled paper bag. Its two ears hug its body like leaves around the heart of a lettuce. The baby weighs about 200 pounds.

The mother uses her trunk to nudge the baby to its feet. This may take several hours. Then, the mother helps it get milk. For a while, the calf has trouble drinking because its floppy trunk keeps getting in the way.

A baby elephant needs its

This baby African elephant will be well taken care of by its mother and auntie.

mother's milk for about two years. And it needs a lot of it — about 21 and a half gallons a day! During that time, the baby stands and walks under its mother's fat stomach. As it grows older, it roams farther away.

Even a calf one day old can walk. With weak and wobbly legs, it balances on its soft round pads. After two days in the world, a baby can keep up with its family, walking about three miles a day in search of food.

Cow elephants and their calves live in groups called herds. They travel together and take care of one another. Sometimes there are as many

as 50 elephants in a herd. Each herd has a leader, or several leaders. They are the oldest cows who have had the most calves.

When danger is near, the herd forms a circle. The cows push the calves to the center where they can't be seen. All the mothers make a tight ring, facing out. Then the cow leader tries to scare off the enemy.

The bulls roam in very small groups, or by themselves. Sometimes, the males will help a herd if it is in danger. But, usually, they stay away. When it is time to mate, a bull joins the herd to "court" one of the cows. Then he leaves again. As a rule, baby elephants do not know their fathers.

As danger approaches, these elephants form a tight defensive circle, with the calves safely hidden in the middle.

Elephants have always appealed to people's imaginations, and many stories have been told about them, some true, some false. This has been a true story.

Author

When Barbara Williams started reading to her own children, she found out how interesting children's books could be. Then she began writing for young readers.

Barbara Williams has written more than thirty books. Two of her picture books have won awards. "About Elephants" is from her book *Seven True Elephant Stories.*

61

LITTLE HOUSE IN THE BIG WOODS

by Laura Ingalls Wilder

Illustrated by Garth Williams

"Two Big Bears" is part of a book called Little House in the Big Woods *by Laura Ingalls Wilder. The author really is the girl Laura in the story.*

In 1872 Laura Ingalls and her family lived in the Big Woods of Wisconsin. Laura lived with her mother and father, her sister Mary, and her baby sister Carrie in a little log house that was miles from any stores, houses, or other people. The family provided their own food from what they could grow and catch. Sometimes life was scary because bears and wolves roamed the woods. There were also wonderful, happy times when friends and relatives gathered for a sugaring off party or a holiday feast. "Two Big Bears" tells about one of the exciting times Laura had living in the Big Woods.

Two Big Bears

One day Pa said that spring was coming.

In the Big Woods the snow was beginning to thaw. Bits of it dropped from the branches of the trees and made little holes in the softening snowbanks below. At noon all the big icicles along the eaves of the little house quivered and sparkled in the sunshine, and drops of water hung trembling at their tips.

Pa said he must go to town to trade the furs of the wild animals he had been trapping all winter. So one evening he made a big bundle of them. There were so many furs that when they were packed tightly and tied together they made a bundle almost as big as Pa.

Very early one morning Pa strapped the bundle of furs on his shoulders, and started to walk to town. There were so many furs to carry that he could not take his gun.

Ma was worried, but Pa said that by starting before sun-up and walking very fast all day he could get home again before dark.

The nearest town was far away. Laura and Mary had never seen a town. They had never seen a store. They had never seen even two houses standing together. But they knew that in a town there were many houses, and a store full of candy and calico and other wonderful things — powder, and shot, and salt, and store sugar.

They knew that Pa would trade his furs to the store-keeper for beautiful things from town, and all day they were expecting the presents he would bring them. When the sun sank low above the treetops and no more drops fell from the tips of the icicles they began to watch eagerly for Pa.

The sun sank out of sight, the woods grew dark, and he did not come. Ma started supper and set the table, but he did not come. It was time to do the chores, and still he had not come.

Ma said that Laura might come with her while she milked the cow. Laura could carry the lantern.

So Laura put on her coat and Ma buttoned it up. And Laura put her hands into her red mittens that hung by a red yarn string around her neck, while Ma lighted the candle in the lantern.

Laura was proud to be helping Ma with the milking, and she carried the lantern very carefully. Its sides were of tin, with places cut in them for the candle-light to shine through.

When Laura walked behind Ma on the path to the barn, the little bits of candle-light from the lantern leaped all around her on the snow. The night was not yet quite dark. The woods were dark, but there was a gray light on the snowy path, and in the sky there were a few faint stars. The stars did not look as warm and bright as the little lights that came from the lantern.

Laura was surprised to see the dark shape of Sukey, the brown cow, standing at the barnyard gate. Ma was surprised, too.

It was too early in the spring for Sukey to be let out in the Big Woods to eat grass. She lived in the barn. But sometimes on warm days Pa left the door of her stall open so she could come into the barnyard. Now Ma and Laura saw her behind the bars, waiting for them.

Ma went up to the gate, and pushed against it to open it. But it did not open very far, because there was Sukey, standing against it. Ma said,

"Sukey, get over!" She reached across the gate and slapped Sukey's shoulder.

Just then one of the dancing little bits of light from the lantern jumped between the bars of the gate, and Laura saw long, shaggy, black fur, and two little, glittering eyes.

Sukey had thin, short, brown fur. Sukey had large, gentle eyes.

Ma said, "Laura, walk back to the house."

So Laura turned around and began to walk toward the house. Ma came behind her. When they had gone part way, Ma snatched her up, lantern and all, and ran. Ma ran with her into the house, and slammed the door.

Then Laura said, "Ma, was it a bear?"

"Yes, Laura," Ma said. "It was a bear."

Laura began to cry. She hung on to Ma and sobbed, "Oh, will he eat Sukey?"

"No," Ma said, hugging her. "Sukey is safe in the barn. Think, Laura — all those big, heavy logs in the barn walls. And the door is heavy and solid, made to keep bears out. No, the bear cannot get in and eat Sukey."

Laura felt better then. "But he could have hurt us, couldn't he?" she asked.

"He didn't hurt us," Ma said. "You were a good girl, Laura, to do exactly as I told you, and to do it quickly, without asking why."

Ma was trembling, and she began to laugh a little. "To think," she said, "I've slapped a bear!"

Then she put supper on the table for Laura and Mary. Pa had not come yet. He didn't come. Laura and Mary were undressed, and they said their prayers and snuggled into the trundle bed.

Ma sat by the lamp, mending one of Pa's shirts. The house seemed cold and still and strange, without Pa.

Laura listened to the wind in the Big Woods. All around the house the wind went crying as though it were lost in the dark and the cold. The wind sounded frightened.

Ma finished mending the shirt. Laura saw her fold it slowly and carefully. She smoothed it with her hand. Then she did a thing she had never done before. She went to the door and pulled the leather latch-string through its hole in the door, so that nobody could get in from outside unless she lifted the latch. She came and took Carrie, all limp and sleeping, out of the big bed.

She saw that Laura and Mary were still awake, and she said to them: "Go to sleep, girls. Everything is all right. Pa will be here in the morning."

Then she went back to her rocking chair and sat there rocking gently and holding Baby Carrie in her arms.

She was sitting up late, waiting for Pa, and Laura and Mary meant to stay awake, too, till he came. But at last they went to sleep.

In the morning Pa was there. He had brought candy for Laura and Mary, and two pieces of pretty calico to make them each a dress. Mary's was a china-blue pattern on a white ground, and Laura's was dark red with little golden-brown dots on it. Ma had calico for a dress, too; it was brown, with a big, feathery white pattern all over it.

They were all happy because Pa had got such good prices for his furs that he could afford to get them such beautiful presents.

The tracks of the big bear were all around the barn, and there were marks of his claws on the walls. But Sukey and the horses were safe inside.

All that day the sun shone, the snow melted, and little streams of water ran from the icicles, which all the time grew thinner. Before the sun set that night, the bear tracks were only shapeless marks in the wet, soft snow.

After supper Pa took Laura and Mary on his knees and said he had a new story to tell them.

The Story of Pa and the Bear in the Way

"When I went to town yesterday with the furs I found it hard walking in the soft snow. It took me a long time to get to town, and other men with furs had come in earlier to do their trading. The storekeeper was busy, and I had to wait until he could look at my furs.

"Then we had to bargain about the price of each one, and then I had to pick out the things I wanted to take in trade.

"So it was nearly sundown before I could start home.

"I tried to hurry, but the walking was hard and I was tired, so I had not gone far before night came. And I was alone in the Big Woods without my gun.

"There were still six miles to walk, and I came along as fast as I could. The night grew darker and darker, and I wished for my gun, because I knew that some of the bears had come out of their winter dens. I had seen their tracks when I went to town in the morning.

"Bears are hungry and cross at this time of year; you know they have been sleeping in their dens all winter long with nothing to eat, and that makes them thin and angry when they wake up. I did not want to meet one.

"I hurried along as quick as I could in the dark. By and by the stars gave a little light. It was still black as pitch where the woods were thick, but in the open places I could see, dimly. I could see the snowy road ahead a little way, and I could see the dark woods standing all around me. I was glad when I came into an open place where the stars gave me this faint light.

"All the time I was watching, as well as I could, for bears. I was listening for the sounds they make when they go carelessly through the bushes.

"Then I came again into an open place, and there, right in the middle of my road, I saw a big black bear.

"He was standing up on his hind legs, looking at me. I could see his eyes shine. I could see his pig-snout. I could even see one of his claws, in the starlight.

"My scalp prickled, and my hair stood straight up. I stopped in my tracks, and stood still. The bear did not move. There he stood, looking at me.

"I knew it would do no good to try to go around him. He would follow me into the dark woods, where he could see better than I could. I did not want to fight a winter-starved bear in the dark. Oh, how I wished for my gun!

"I had to pass that bear, to get home. I thought that if I could scare him, he might get out of the road and let me go by. So I took a deep breath, and suddenly I shouted with all my might and ran at him, waving my arms.

"He didn't move.

"I did not run very far toward him, I tell you! I stopped and looked at him, and he stood looking at me. Then I shouted again. There he stood. I kept on shouting and waving my arms, but he did not budge.

"Well, it would do me no good to run away. There were other bears in the woods. I might meet one any time. I might as well deal with this one as with another. Besides, I was coming home to Ma and you girls. I would never get here, if I ran away from everything in the woods that scared me.

"So at last I looked around, and I got a good big club, a solid, heavy branch that had been broken from a tree by the weight of snow in the winter.

"I lifted it up in my hands, and I ran straight at that bear. I swung my club as hard as I could and brought it down, bang! on his head.

"And there he still stood, for he was nothing but a big, black, burned stump!

"I had passed it on my way to town that morning. It wasn't a bear at all. I only thought it was a bear, because I had been thinking all the time about bears and being afraid I'd meet one."

"It really wasn't a bear at all?" Mary asked.

"No, Mary, it wasn't a bear at all. There I had been yelling, and dancing, and waving my arms, all by myself in the Big Woods, trying to scare a stump!"

Laura said: "Ours was really a bear. But we were not scared, because we thought it was Sukey."

Pa did not say anything, but he hugged her tighter.

"Oo-oo! That bear might have eaten Ma and me all up!" Laura said, snuggling closer to him. "But Ma walked right up to him and slapped him, and he didn't do anything at all. Why didn't he do anything?"

"I guess he was too surprised to do anything, Laura,"

Pa said. "I guess he was afraid, when the lantern shone in his eyes. And when Ma walked up to him and slapped him, he knew *she* wasn't afraid."

"Well, you were brave, too," Laura said. "Even if it was only a stump, you thought it was a bear. You'd have hit him on the head with a club, if he *had* been a bear, wouldn't you, Pa?"

"Yes," said Pa, "I would. You see, I had to."

Then Ma said it was bedtime. She helped Laura and Mary undress and button up their red flannel nightgowns. They knelt down by the trundle bed and said their prayers.

> "Now I lay me down to sleep,
> I pray the Lord my soul to keep.
> If I should die before I wake,
> I pray the Lord my soul to take."

Ma kissed them both, and tucked the covers in around them. They lay there awhile, looking at Ma's smooth, parted hair and her hands busy with sewing in the lamplight. Her needle made little clicking sounds against her thimble and then the thread went softly, swish! through the pretty calico that Pa had traded furs for.

Laura looked at Pa, who was greasing his boots. His mustaches and his hair and his long brown beard were silky in the lamplight, and the colors of his plaid jacket were gay. He whistled cheerfully while he worked, and then he sang:

> "The birds were singing in the morning,
> And the myrtle and the ivy were in bloom,
> And the sun o'er the hills was a-dawning,
> 'Twas then that I laid her in the tomb."

It was a warm night. The fire had gone to coals on the hearth, and Pa did not build it up. All around the little house, in the Big Woods, there were little sounds of falling snow, and from the eaves there was the drip, drip of the melting icicles.

In just a little while the trees would be putting out their baby leaves, all rosy and yellow and pale green, and there would be wild flowers and birds in the woods.

Then there would be no more stories by the fire at night, but all day long Laura and Mary would run and play among the trees, for it would be spring.

Author

Laura Ingalls Wilder was born in 1867 in the Big Woods of Wisconsin. She went by covered wagon to the Dakota Territory. In the "Little House" books, an award-winning series of eight books for children, she told the story of her childhood and of growing up in the early West. Mrs. Wilder wrote her first pioneer story in 1932. Her *Little House on the Prairie* was adapted for television in 1975.

BROTHER TO
THE WIND
Mildred Pitts Walter

THE CAT
WHO THOUGHT
SHE WAS A DOG
AND
THE DOG
WHO THOUGHT
HE WAS A CAT
I. B. Singer

APPEARANCE
APPEARANCES

Houghton Mifflin Literature

The selections you have just read from *Learning from Nature* illustrate one important lesson to be learned from nature: Things are not always what they appear to be.

Now you will read two folktales, *Brother to the Wind* and *The Cat Who Thought She Was a Dog and the Dog Who Thought He Was a Cat*. Both of these selections, as well as the three poems you will read, show that "seeing" is not the same as "understanding."

2

Sharing

The Gift

by Helen Coutant

Illustrated by Mai Vo-Dinh

Anna left the house at the usual time that morning. It would take her five minutes to run down the hill to where the school bus waited. If she was fast, she could stop by old Nana Marie's house. By now, Nana Marie might be back from the hospital. She had disappeared without warning more than a week ago. For two days, no one had answered when Anna knocked on the door after school. By the third day, Anna could scarcely eat she was so worried. Had they taken Nana Marie to one of those homes for very old people? But the next afternoon the daughter-in-law, Rita, who took care of Nana Marie, had opened the door an inch. It was just enough so that Anna could hear her voice over the blare of the TV. "You here to see Nana Marie? She's in the hospital." That was all Anna found out.

Now, rounding a bend in the road, Anna could see Rita standing by the gate in front of Nana Marie's house. Rita's loud voice rang out. "She's coming home today! Home from the hospital! Nana Marie!"

Nana Marie was coming home. Anna's heart gave a joyful leap.

"We're throwing a little party," Rita went on. "Just a few neighbors on the hill to welcome her back, cheer her up. Drop by after school. She'll be looking for you."

A party. That meant Anna would have to share Nana Marie with everyone else. Rita's voice, suddenly lower, caught Anna's attention.

"She won't really be looking for you, Nana Marie won't. But come to see her anyway. She'll need your company now that she's blind. . . ."

Blind? Rita's voice rattled on, but Anna heard nothing more. Her heart seemed to have stopped on the word

blind. How could Nana Marie suddenly be blind? There had been nothing wrong with Nana Marie's eyes. In fact, it was those extraordinary warm eyes, a cornflower blue, that had drawn Anna to Nana Marie in the first place. A small, choking noise escaped from Anna's throat.

Rita cocked her head and looked down, waiting for Anna to speak; then resumed her monologue. "Just happened, just like that," she said, shaking her head. "It's a pity. It's terrible. But you come by this afternoon for the party. We'll cheer her up, give Nana Marie some little presents to help her forget. Can I count on you?"

Count on her! Had Anna ever missed a chance to visit Nana Marie in the last six months, ever since the two had discovered each other one balmy September afternoon?

"So you come!" Rita repeated, her voice rising.

Anna couldn't answer. She pulled back, nodding, and turned away. She walked carefully around the puddles in the road. Her whispered "good-bye" floated up unheard by Rita, who was already going in the house, shivering from the February cold.

When the door banged, Anna took off, propelled by anger and sorrow. Her heart was pumping "blind, blind, blind" faster and faster. Blind without any warning. How could it happen? And yet it had.

She got to the foot of the hill just in time to see the school bus disappear around the curve. It had gone without her. The tears she had been holding back came to her eyes. There was no way she could get to school. Her mother was already at work. Not wanting to go back to the empty house, Anna headed for her favorite path, which led upward into the woods. The day was hers to do as she pleased.

There must be something she could do for Nana Marie. Rita had said something about a present. But what present could ever console a person who had become blind?

Anna remembered a time she had imagined being blind. Once in the middle of the night she had opened her eyes thinking it was morning. The unexpected blackness pressed down on her. She turned her head this way and that and saw nothing, as if she had been buried. Just when she was ready to scream, her hand shot out and touched the light, nudging it on. The brightness, which then appeared so suddenly, dazzled her eyes. The patchwork quilt shone. The yellow walls glistened as if they had been freshly painted, and the air rushed out of her lungs in relief. Now she wondered how Nana Marie had felt waking up blind.

Anna broke into a trot. Ahead was a place she often came, a small, deep spring in the woods. When she knelt to gaze into the bottomless pool, at first she saw nothing but darkness. Then as the sun came out, the water seemed to open up, reflecting the bark of silver beeches, shining like armor. The reflection of luminous silver reminded her of Nana Marie. She sat back on her heels, remembering.

Six months ago, at the end of summer, Anna and her parents moved to the house just up the hill from Rita's. A week later Anna started school. She didn't know anyone and found it hard to make friends with the other fifth graders. She was very lonely until one afternoon when she had looked up and saw Nana Marie's welcoming smile.

There was a small moving van outside Rita's house that day. From a safe distance, half concealed by bushes,

Anna watched it being unloaded. There were only a half dozen pieces of furniture, all a lovely dark wood, highly polished. Rita stood by, directing the operations. Anna could see the simple delight on Rita's face and wondered where this furniture was coming from.

As Anna watched, Rita's husband got out of his car, walked around it, and opened the door by the front seat. Then there was a long wait. Finally a white head emerged. Haltingly, as though every movement took a great deal of thought, a very old woman rose and holding on to her son's arm, began to walk toward the house. Halfway to the steps, she paused for breath. Then, as if she felt Anna's eyes on her, the old woman looked up. Their eyes met, and Nana Marie smiled.

The next afternoon when Anna came home from school, she saw Nana Marie sitting in a rocking chair on the front porch. Slowly Anna approached, her school shoes raising little puffs of dust. The moment Nana Marie saw her she smiled, and the next thing Anna knew she was sitting cross-legged at Nana Marie's feet. Then they began to talk as if they had known each other for years. On and on till supper time they talked, "like old friends reunited," Nana Marie said. They even found out they had birthdays the same month and only two days apart.

Every day after that, when the school bus let Anna off at the bottom of the hill, she raced up to Rita's house to keep Nana Marie company. As long as the afternoons were warm they sat on the porch until twilight. They never ran out of things to talk about. Nana Marie pointed out the fat groundhog scavenging for corn in the stubble of the field below Rita's house, and the flock of wild geese whose perfect "V" cut the sky as they flew south with

haunting cries. And always, if she told Anna to listen,
from far away would come the hollow *clack-clack* of a
woodpecker at work on a tree. Anna would linger,
enchanted, until there was just enough light left for her
to run home. Sometimes an autumn moon, perfectly
round, lit her way.

When cold weather arrived, Anna climbed the steep
stairs to Nana Marie's room. Sitting by the window, they
could see the world just as well as from the porch. They
watched the trees on the top of the mountain turn bare
and black, while there was still a wide strip of deep yellow
at the foot of the mountain. Day by day this strip shrank
until one day, after heavy rains, it was gone. Next came
the snow, pure magic seen from Nana Marie's window.

Although most of Nana Marie's polished furniture was downstairs in Rita's living room, it was still cozy in Nana Marie's room. There was a bed, a table, a large chest of drawers, and a trunk. As soon as Anna arrived, she would put her books on the trunk and boil water on the hot plate in one corner. Then the two of them would have tea and share the events of the day. As the weeks passed, Anna learned that every object in Nana Marie's room had a meaning and a story. One by one, Anna learned the stories.

The silver hairbrush and matching hand mirror that lay on the chest of drawers had been an engagement present from Nana Marie's husband. A large *MK* with many curlicues was engraved on the back of each piece. Next to the hairbrush was a battered red and yellow cigar tin that said *The Finest Turkish*. When Anna opened the lid, she found a large round watch that dangled from a chain. The watch ticked once or twice when Anna moved it, then stopped. It had belonged to Nana Marie's father. An Indian goddess carved out of wood gazed thoughtfully at the box. On the trunk was a very shiny bright-blue clay bowl overflowing with odds and ends. One side of the bowl was crooked, and it tipped when Anna touched it. It had been a present from Nana Marie's grandson when he was seven. Boxes of letters and photographs completely covered the table. Anna loved best the teapot with its two Chinese pheasants. Its spout was stained brown from all the tea that had been poured, and Nana Marie said the teapot was six times as old as Anna.

Finally, what at first had seemed to Anna only a small, cluttered room expanded to become a history of Nana

Marie's life, of her joys and sorrows and memories stretching over almost a century.

Gazing deep into the shining pool again, Anna decided that Nana Marie was like this spring. Each day of her old age she had quietly caught and held a different reflection. Stored in her depths were layers of reflections, shining images of the world. Many of these she had shared with Anna. But now that she was blind, would these images be gone, the way water became dark when there was no light? What would her days be like?

Anna's thoughts moved to the party that Rita would hold in the afternoon. She knew what the neighbors were likely to bring: candy, scarves, flowers. She could do the same, yet none of these gifts would express what she felt for Nana Marie. And could any of them really make Nana Marie feel better?

Lost in thought, Anna continued to follow the path up the mountain. Even though her sneakers were wet from the soft thawing soil of the woods, she decided to stay there until school was out. Maybe by then she would know what to bring Nana Marie.

Slowly the world about her drew Anna in, just as if she had been with Nana Marie. The wan February sun was swallowed by a thick mist, which the mountain seemed to exhale with each gust of wind. Although the air was damp, it had an edge of warmth that had been absent in the morning. It felt almost like the beginnings of spring. As the hours passed, Anna picked up objects she thought Nana Marie would like: a striped rock, a tiny fern, a clump of moss, an empty milkweed pod. None of them, on second thought, seemed a proper gift for Nana Marie. Other days, she would have loved them. But now

Anna thought they could easily make her sad, for in touching them, Nana Marie would be reminded of the things she would never see again. There had to be a way to bring the whole woods, the sky, and the fields to Nana Marie. What else would do? What else would be worthy of their friendship?

Suddenly Anna knew what her gift would be. It would be like no other gift, and a gift no one else could bring. All day long Anna had been seeing the world the way Nana Marie had shown her. Now she would bring everything she had seen to Nana Marie.

Her wet feet, her damp jeans and jacket, no longer mattered. Eagerly she turned and began the long trudge back to Nana Marie's house. Her hands were empty in

her pockets. But the gift she carried in her head was as big as the world.

Just as the sun went over the mountain, Anna emerged from the woods. Ahead of her was the road and Nana Marie's house. She looked at Nana Marie's room, the window directly over the front door. A light should be on by now. But the blinds were down as they had been all week, and the window was so dark it reflected, eerily, the reddish glow of twilight. Everyone must be downstairs at the party. Probably Rita hadn't even bothered to go upstairs and raise the blinds. Yet downstairs the windows were dark too. What had happened? Where was Nana Marie?

Anna stopped to catch her breath. Her entire body was pounding. She ran around Rita's car to the kitchen door. She hesitated, biting her lip, before she rapped softly on the glass part of the door. There was no answer. She could see a light in the living room, the TV set was turned on. She knocked again, louder, then put her hand on the doorknob. It opened from the other side, and Rita stood there in her bathrobe. The kitchen table was covered with the remains of the party: tissue paper, stacked plates and cups. So the neighbors had come and gone. Anna was too late for the party, but Nana Marie must be there!

"Well, here at last," Rita said. "I figured you went home and forgot. The party ended half an hour ago. I told Nana Marie it wasn't any use waiting up for you longer. I expect she's asleep by now. She was real disappointed you didn't come, though she got lots of nice things from everybody. Why don't you come back tomorrow when she's rested."

"Please, I can't," Anna said. She bent, tearing at her wet shoelaces. "I have a present for Nana Marie. It won't take long. I'll take my shoes off and go upstairs to her room."

Rita shrugged. She seemed anxious to get back to her TV show. At the door to the living room she called back, "Don't go waking her up. I just got her settled. You can leave the present on her table. I'll tell her about it tomorrow."

Nodding, Anna headed for the stairs on tiptoe. The world of Rita dropped away as she climbed toward Nana Marie's room. The landing at the top of the stairs was dark, and the door to Nana Marie's room was closed. Anna paused and let her breath out slowly. What did blind people look like? What if the doctors had taken out Nana Marie's eyes and only two black holes were left? Anna's hand hesitated on the doorknob.

Then she opened the door and shut it behind her.

Nana Marie's room was pitch black. There was no sound at all. Was the room empty? The window was straight ahead. Anna ran to it, groping for the cords. The blinds clattered up, crashing in the darkness. Rita was sure to come up. Then a faint light flowed into the room. Outside, in the winter twilight, a small frozen moon was wandering upward.

"Anna," Nana Marie was calling her name. She was not asleep after all. "Anna," Nana Marie said, and now there was surprise and joy in her voice. Nana Marie was sitting in her rocking chair. Her eyes were open and as blue as they had always been, like the sky on a summer morning.

"Oh, Nana Marie!" Anna exclaimed. She patted the old warm skin of Nana Marie's cheek.

"You came," Nana Marie said. "I thought maybe you were getting tired of having such a very old lady for a friend."

"I brought you a present," Anna said. "I'm late because it took me all day to get it."

"Gracious," said Nana Marie. "You shouldn't have done that! All the nice people who came this afternoon brought me presents as if I could see and were still of some use to someone!" She chuckled, gesturing toward the table and a new stack of boxes.

"Mine is different," Anna said. "I brought you a last day."

"A last day. . . ." Nana Marie's voice trailed off. At the hospital someone had arranged her hair in soft waves. She put her hand up as if to touch them, but halfway there her fingers stretched out, reaching for Anna. She took Anna's hand and held it firmly.

"You didn't have a last day to look at the world," Anna said. "So I brought it to you. Everything I saw today. Just as if you saw it with me. The way you would see it. And tomorrow I'll bring you another — and the next day another. I'll bring you enough seeing to last forever. That's my present, Nana Marie."

Nana Marie was silent for a minute. Then she added softly, almost to herself, "Bless you, child, how did you ever think of that?" She leaned back in the rocking chair. One hand held on to Anna's. With the other she gestured toward a chair. "Pull it up right here, Anna," she said, "so we can look out over the valley and the moonlight together. The moon is out, isn't it, Anna? I can feel it." She closed her eyes.

Anna pulled Nana Marie's hand into her lap and held it with both of her own as she described the silver beeches reflected in the spring, the yellow mist breathing in and out, the pale sun — everything she had seen that day.

When Anna was finished, Nana Marie sat up and turned toward her. Nana Marie's blue eyes shone with contentment. "Thank you, Anna," she said. "That was beautiful." She paused briefly and when she continued it was almost as though she was speaking to herself. "*This* is a day I'll always remember."

Anna sat holding on to Nana Marie's hand until the moon disappeared over the house. Even though something as terrible as going blind had happened to Nana Marie, she really hadn't changed. She could still marvel at the world, she could still feel the moonlight. Anna knew she was going to be all right.

Author

The Gift, which you have just read, is Helen Coutant's second book for children. Her first book was the award-winning *First Snow.* Helen Coutant is an English teacher and translator as well as an author. She and her husband have translated short stories from the Vietnamese language into English.

So Will I

by Charlotte Zolotow

My grandfather remembers long ago
the white Queen Anne's lace that grew wild.
He remembers the buttercups and goldenrod
from when he was a child.

He remembers long ago
the white snow falling falling.
He remembers the bluebird and thrush
at twilight
calling, calling.

He remembers long ago
the new moon in the summer sky.
He remembers the wind in the trees
and its long rising sigh.
And so will I
so will I.

Mary McLeod Bethune

by Eloise Greenfield
Illustrated by J. Brian Pinkney

The sun had just come up when Mary Jane McLeod left the house with her mother and father and her brothers and sisters to go to the fields. Every morning, the whole family had to get up very early to work on the farm. But they didn't mind. The farm belonged to them. It gave them vegetables to eat and cotton to sell.

Mary knelt on the ground and pulled the weeds from around a head of cabbage. She had pulled weeds so many times before that she didn't have to think about it with her whole mind. She used part of her mind to think about her favorite dream. She thought about one day being able to read, and about having her own book and going to school.

Where Mary lived, near Mayesville, South Carolina, there were no schools for black children. She had been born there, not many years after the slaves were freed. No one in her family could read. During slavery, it had been against the law and very dangerous for anyone to teach slaves to read. Some black people had gone to secret hiding places to study and learn, but many had not been able to do that.

Mary's parents, Samuel and Patsy McLeod, had grown up as slaves, each on a different plantation. They had met and fallen in love, but they could not marry until Mr. McLeod saved enough money to buy his bride. He had to work hard all day without pay, and at night he worked to earn money. It took him many months to earn enough.

After the wedding, Mr. and Mrs. McLeod were both slaves on the same plantation. Their first fourteen children were slaves, too. They had to work on other people's farms and clean other people's houses and wash other people's clothes, all without pay. They were not happy. They wanted a place of their own where they could work and live in freedom.

Several years after the law against slavery was passed, Mr. and Mrs. McLeod were able to start their own farm. Mr. McLeod and his sons went into the woods and cut down trees to get logs. They built a four-room log cabin for the family.

Mary was born in the log cabin on July 10, 1875. She was the fifteenth child and two others were born later. Mary loved the farm. When she was very small, her father let her ride on the back of Old Bush, the mule with the bushy tail, as he pulled the plow. When she was a little older, she weeded the vegetables and picked cotton. In the house, she swept the floor and washed and shined the kerosene lamps and helped take care of the younger children.

Every morning and evening the family stood in front of the fireplace and said prayers and sang hymns together. After dinner, the children gathered around their mother as she sat in her favorite chair and told them true stories about Africa and talked about the Bible.

Listening to the stories, Mary wanted even more to be able to read. She talked about reading all the time. She told everybody in her family over and over that she didn't know how but someday she would learn to read.

One day when Mary was eleven years old, Miss Emma Wilson, a black teacher, came with the answer. She told Mary's parents that the Presbyterian Church had sent her to Mayesville to start a one-room school for black children.

Mr. and Mrs. McLeod wanted all of their children to go to school, but there was too much work to be done on the farm. Only one could go. That one, they decided, would be Mary.

On the first day of school, Mary left home early, carrying her lunch in a tin bucket. The school was five miles away, but she was happy to walk each mile. Every step was taking her closer to something that she had wanted for a long, long time.

Miss Wilson was a good teacher and Mary was a good student. She studied hard every day, and soon she could read short words and work arithmetic problems. In the evening, she taught her family what she had learned in school. Sometimes neighbors would ask her to read their mail for them or figure out the money they should get for selling their cotton.

A few years later, Mary was graduated from Miss Wilson's school. Her parents sat with the others who had come to hear their children recite and sing on their last day there. Mary received a scholarship to Scotia Seminary, a school for black girls in Concord, North Carolina. The scholarship meant that she would not have to pay.

Mary was nervous about leaving her family for the first time and taking her first train ride. But she was excited, too. Her mother made a dress for her out of a piece of cloth that was pretty, although it wasn't new. Neighbors knitted stockings and crocheted collars as gifts. They made some of their dresses over to fit Mary.

On going-away day, her family and friends went to the train station to see her off. There was a lot of talking and laughing and kissing. They were sorry to see Mary leave, but their happiness was greater than their sadness. Mary was going off to get an education.

Scotia Seminary was a three-story brick building surrounded by grass and trees and flowers. Mary lived in a small room with two beds and two washstands. She had a roommate, Abbie, who became a very good friend. Later, a second brick building was added. It was named Faith Hall. Mary loved to worship in its little chapel.

Mary had classes in mathematics, languages, history, geography, and the Bible. She learned about people who lived in other countries and about people who had lived many years before. She learned about islands and oceans and mountains.

In speech class, Mary was the best student. Her strong, low voice always sounded sure, and her classmates listened closely to what she was saying. Her voice was also good for singing and the music teacher gave her solos.

All of the students at Scotia helped with the housework. Mary dusted and ironed and brought in coal for the fire. Much of her free time she spent in the library reading about Africa.

On graduation day, no one in her family was in the audience. They could not afford to pay the train fare. But Mary knew that they were proud of her and happy for her. She had received another scholarship, this time to Moody Bible Institute in Chicago, Illinois.

Moody Bible Institute would teach Mary to be a missionary. She believed in the Christian religion and wanted other people to believe in it, too. She wanted to teach Christianity, especially in Africa. People in Africa and other parts of the world have their own religions. But Mary thought that hers was best.

Mary and other students at Moody were sent out to visit prisoners in the jail and people who were sick or without money. The students read the Bible to them and prayed and sang hymns. They also helped other people whenever they could and invited them to come to the school for church services. Mary and five other students traveled to other states to start Sunday schools. They rode in a train coach called "The Gospel Car."

By the time Mary finished her work at Moody, she had grown up. She was a woman now, rather large, with smooth, dark skin. She had learned all that Moody could teach and was ready to be a missionary. But she had a very unpleasant surprise. She could find no openings for a black missionary in Africa.

Mary went home to Mayesville. During the years that she was in school, she had not often been able to return home, and she was glad to see her family. But she was disappointed to have to go back home without the job she had studied so hard for. She helped Miss Wilson in Mayesville School until she got a job as a teacher at Haines Institute in Augusta, Georgia.

Haines had been started by Lucy Laney, who had once been a slave. Miss Laney was still in charge of the school. She never seemed to get tired of helping her students and the teachers who worked for her. She always had new ideas to make Haines better. Watching her, Mary soon forgot her disappointment and put all of herself into being the best teacher that she could be.

Most of what Mary earned she sent home to her family. She helped to pay for the education of her

younger sisters and to buy her parents a new home. Their old one had burned down.

A few years after she began teaching, Mary met Albertus Bethune, also a teacher, who became her husband. The following year, their son, Albert, was born.

When Albert was five years old, Mary Bethune made a big decision. She wanted to start a school of her own. She thought of Miss Laney and Miss Wilson, and she remembered herself as a child longing to learn. There were many black children like her who lived in places without schools. They had questions but no answers. They wanted to learn and she wanted to teach them.

She heard about Daytona Beach, Florida, where a new railroad was being built. The workmen who were putting down the railroad track were not being paid enough. They lived with their families in camps that were too crowded. There were no schools. Mrs. Bethune decided that she would go there.

When Mrs. Bethune arrived in Daytona Beach, she had only one dollar and fifty cents. She stayed with a friend, and every day she went for a walk, looking for a building that she could use as a school. Finally, she found an old two-story cottage. The owner said he would rent it to her for eleven dollars a month. He agreed to wait a few weeks until she could raise the first month's rent.

Mrs. Bethune visited the homes of black families, telling them about her school. Neighbors came to paint the cottage and to fix the broken steps. Children helped with the cleaning.

On an autumn day in 1904, Mrs. Bethune stood in the doorway of the cottage, smiling and ringing a bell. It was time for school to start. Five little girls came in and took

their seats. The school was named the Daytona Normal and Industrial School for Girls. It was an elementary school, and Albert would learn there, too, until he was older.

Mrs. Bethune and the students used wooden boxes as desks and chairs. They burned logs and used the charcoal as pencils. They mashed berries and used the juice as ink.

The children loved the school. Some of them lived there with Mrs. Bethune. All of them wanted to help raise money for the rent and for the books and paper and lamps and beds that they needed.

After classes, they made ice cream and pies to sell. The children peeled and mashed sweet potatoes while Mrs. Bethune rolled the crust. They gave programs at hotels and in churches. The children sang and recited. Mrs. Bethune spoke to the audiences about the school. She bought a secondhand bicycle and rode all over Daytona Beach, knocking on doors and asking people for their help.

Many people gave. Some of them were rich, and some of them did not have much money themselves but were willing to share the little that they had.

When too many children wanted to attend and a larger building was needed, adults in the community again gave their time and work. They took away the trash from the land that Mrs. Bethune bought. Those who were carpenters helped to put the building up. Those who were gardeners planted flowers and trees around it.

Mrs. Bethune named the new building Faith Hall in honor of her favorite building at Scotia Seminary. She had faith in God, in herself, and in black people. Over the door she hung a sign that said "Enter to learn."

Across from Faith Hall, Mrs. Bethune started a small farm. The students planted fruits and vegetables to use and to sell. They grew strawberries, tomatoes, string beans, carrots, and corn. They grew sugar cane to make syrup.

As the years passed, more students came to the school, and more teachers. More buildings were added. Albert went away to school, but Mrs. Bethune was busier than ever. Almost every day a new problem arose that she had to solve.

One day, a student became very ill. Because there was no hospital for blacks for many, many miles, Mrs. Bethune rushed her to the nearest white hospital. The doctors agreed to take care of her, but not inside the hospital. They put the patient on the back porch with a screen around her bed.

Mrs. Bethune was very angry, but there was nothing she could do. The student was too sick to be moved to another hospital. But when the girl was well, Mrs. Bethune decided that someone had to start a hospital for blacks in Daytona Beach, and she would do it. She started a little two-bed hospital which later had twenty beds. She named it McLeod Hospital in memory of her father, who had died. It saved many black lives.

Later that same year, one of Mrs. Bethune's brothers came for his first visit. He walked around the campus with his sister and visited classrooms where young people were being taught to use their minds and their hands. The choir sang for him. He was proud of his sister and of all that he saw and heard, and Mrs. Bethune was proud to show him what had been done.

The school that had started as an elementary school for girls became a high school, then a junior college, and finally a college. It joined with a men's college and was given a new name — Bethune-Cookman College — with Mrs. Bethune as president. It had the only library for black people in that part of Florida.

Mrs. Bethune did not spend all of her time at the school. She joined groups of people who were working for the rights of black men, women, and children. She wrote articles for newspapers and magazines. She traveled across the United States making speeches about the need for public schools, jobs, houses, and food. She became famous for her devotion to black youth. The sureness in her voice and her slow, careful way of speaking became well known.

For many years Mrs. Bethune had suffered with asthma. It sometimes made her very sick. She had to struggle for breath. Doctors had told her that she needed more rest. But she said that she had to work until every black boy and girl had a chance for an education. She remembered their African heritage, and hers. "The drums of Africa still beat in my heart," she said. "They will not let me rest."

In the 1920's and 1930's, the United States was in great trouble. There were millions of people without jobs. Some of them starved. Many young people had to stop going to school.

Mrs. Bethune was asked by President Franklin D. Roosevelt to live in Washington, D.C., and work with the National Youth Administration. She did not want to leave her school, but she knew that she was needed for this special job. She moved to Washington and was in

charge of finding jobs for young blacks all over the country. She visited many states and talked to these young people about their problems.

After eight years, she returned to her home on the campus of Bethune-Cookman. Not many years later, Mrs. Bethune had to stop working. She was sick more often and her heart was weak.

Mary McLeod Bethune had spent her life working for others. She had started the National Council of Negro Women. She had been president of the Association for the Study of Negro Life and History, working with Dr. Carter G. Woodson to make known the true history of black people. She had worked with many groups of blacks and women and teachers and church members. The walls of her study were covered with awards and medals that had been presented to her.

Now her hair was white and she was tired, though she was careful not to show her tiredness and continued to give advice when it was needed. But most of the time she stayed at home, enjoying the visits of her son and grandchildren and great-grandchildren, and of the many other people who came to see her.

Sometimes Mrs. Bethune took her cane and went for a very slow walk. She walked across the campus of her school, looking at the hundreds of students and the buildings and lawns and remembering how it all had started.

In 1955 at the age of seventy-nine, Mary McLeod Bethune died of a heart attack. She was buried on the grounds of the school she loved.

In her will Mrs. Bethune left a message for black people. She said that they must believe in themselves and help each other. She said that it is through learning that children grow up to be strong men and women. She said that children must never stop wanting to build a better world.

On a hot summer day, nineteen years after Mrs. Bethune's death, thousands of people gathered in a park in Washington, D.C. They had come to honor her memory. They watched as the large cloth covering a tall statue was lifted for the first time.

The statue is of Mrs. Bethune. She is handing her will to a girl and a boy. Some of the words from the will are written on the base of the statue. People from all over the world go to Washington to visit the park. Children like to play there. They run close to the statue and walk all the way around it to read the last words of Mary McLeod Bethune: "I leave you faith, I leave you hope, I leave you love."

Author

Eloise Greenfield is a well-known writer of biographies, stories, and poems for children. She was born in North Carolina and grew up in Washington, D.C. As a child, she loved to read what other people wrote, but it wasn't until she was married and had two children that she discovered herself as a writer.

Ms. Greenfield's books have won many awards. Among them are the Carter G. Woodson Award for her biography *Rosa Parks. Mary McLeod Bethune,* the biography you have just read, was a runner-up for the Coretta Scott King Award. Ms. Greenfield has also been honored by the Council on Interracial Books for Children.

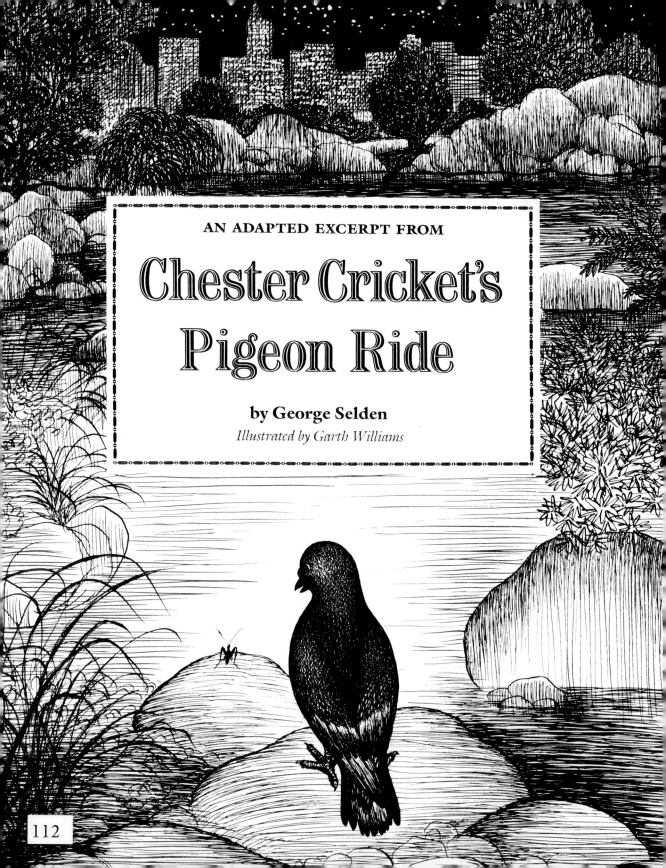

AN ADAPTED EXCERPT FROM

Chester Cricket's
Pigeon Ride

by George Selden

Illustrated by Garth Williams

Chester Cricket had lived a quiet life in the Connecticut countryside. Life became more exciting for Chester when he came to live in New York City, under a sidewalk grating in the Times Square subway station. Things got even more exciting when Chester met a pigeon named Lulu, with whom he shared a thrilling adventure.

Lulu said, "Come on, Chester C., let me show you some of my town" — by which she meant New York.

"Okay," said Chester, and climbed on her claw.

"I want you to see it *all* now!" said Lulu. Her wings were beating strongly, rhythmically. "And the best place for that is the Empire State Building."

They rose higher and higher. And the higher they went, the more scared Chester got. Flying up Fifth Avenue had been fun as well as frightening, but now they were heading straight for the top of one of the tallest buildings in all the world.

Chester looked down — the world swirled beneath him — and felt as if his stomach turned over. Or maybe his brain turned around. But something in him felt queasy and dizzy. "Lulu — " he began anxiously, " — I think — "

"Just hold on tight!" Lulu shouted down. "And trust in your feathered friend!"

What Chester had meant to say was that he was afraid he was suffering from a touch of acrophobia — fear of heights. (And perched on a pigeon's claw, on your way to the top of the Empire State, is not the best place to find that you are afraid of great heights.) But even if Lulu hadn't interrupted, the cricket couldn't have finished his sentence. His words were forced back into his throat. For the wind, which had been just a breeze beside the lake, was turning into a raging gale as they spiraled upward, around the building, floor past floor, and approached their final destination: the television antenna tower on the very top.

And they made it! Lulu gripped the pinnacle of the TV antenna with both her claws, accidentally pinching one of Chester's legs as she did so. The whole of New York glowed and sparkled below them.

Now it is strange, but it is true, that although there are many mountains higher than even the tallest buildings, and airplanes can fly much higher than mountains, *nothing* ever seems quite so high as a big building that's been built by men. It suggests our own height to ourselves, I guess.

Chester felt as if not only a city but the entire world was down there where he could look at it. He almost couldn't see the people. "My gosh!" he thought. "They look just like bugs." And he had to laugh at that: like bugs — perhaps crickets — moving up and down the sidewalks. And the cars, the buses, the yellow taxis, all jittered along like miniatures. He felt that kind of spinning sensation inside his head that had made him dizzy on the way up. But he refused to close his eyes. It was too much of an adventure for that.

"Lulu, my foot," said Chester, "you're stepping on it. Could you please — "

"Ooo, I'm sorry," the pigeon apologized. She lifted her claw.

And just at that moment two bad things happened.

The first was, Chester caught sight of an airplane swooping low to land at LaGuardia Airport across the East River. The dip of it made his dizziness worse. And the second — worse yet — a sudden gust of wind sprang up, as if a hand gave them both a push. Lulu almost fell off the Empire State.

Lulu *almost* fell off — but Chester *did!* In an instant his legs and feelers were torn away from the pigeon's leg, and before he could say, "Old Meadow, farewell!" he was tumbling down through the air. One moment the city appeared above him — that meant that he was upside down; then under him — he was right side up; then everything slid from side to side.

He worked his wings, tried to hold them stiff to steady himself — no use, no use! The gleeful wind was playing with him. It was rolling him, throwing him back and forth, up and down, as a cork is tossed in the surf of a storm. And minute by minute, when he faced that way, the cricket caught glimpses of the floors of the Empire State Building plunging upward as he plunged down.

Despite his panic, his mind took a wink of time off to think: "Well, *this* is something that can't have happened to many crickets before!" (He was right, too — it hadn't. And just at that moment Chester wished that it wasn't happening to *him*.)

He guessed, when New York was in the right place again, that he was almost halfway down. The people were looking more and more like people — he heard the cars' engines — and the street and the sidewalk looked *awfully* hard! Then —

Whump! He landed on something both hard and soft. It was hard inside, all muscles and bones, but soft on the surface — feathers!

"Grab on!" a familiar voice shouted. "Tight! Tighter! That's it."

Chester gladly did as he was told.

"*Whooooey!*" Lulu breathed a sigh of relief. "Thought I'd never find you. Been around this building at least ten times."

Chester wanted to say, "Thank you, Lulu," but he was so thankful he couldn't get one word out till they'd reached a level where the air was friendly and gently buoyed them up.

But before he could even open his mouth, the pigeon — all ready for another adventure — asked eagerly,

"Where now, Chester C.?"

"I guess I better go back to the drainpipe, Lulu. I'm kind of tired."

"Aw, no — !" complained Lulu, who'd been having fun.

"You know, I'm really not all that used to getting blown off the Empire State Building — "

"Oh, all right," said the pigeon. "But first there's one thing you *gotta* see!"

Flying just below the level of turbulent air — good pilot that she was — Lulu headed south, with Chester clinging to the back of her neck. He felt much safer up there, and her wings didn't block out as much of the view as they'd thought. He wanted to ask where they were going, but he sensed from the strength and regularity of her wingbeats that it was to be a rather long flight. And the wind was against them too, which made the flying more difficult. Chester held his peace, and watched the city slip beneath them.

They reached the Battery, which is that part of lower New York where a cluster of skyscrapers rise up like a grove of steel trees. But Lulu didn't stop there.

With a gasp and an even tighter hold on her feathers, Chester realized that they'd flown right over the end of Manhattan. There was dark churning water below them. And this was no tame little lake, like the one in Central Park. It was the great deep wide bay that made New York such a mighty harbor. But Lulu showed no sign whatsoever of slowing. Her wings, like beautiful trustworthy machines, pumped on and on and on and on.

At last, Chester saw where the pigeon was heading. On a little island, off to the right, Chester made out the form of a very big lady. Her right hand was holding something up. Of course it was the Statue of Liberty, but Chester had no way of knowing that. In the Old Meadow in Connecticut he never had gone to school — at least not to a school where the pupils use books. His teacher back there had been Nature herself.

Lulu landed at the base of the statue, puffing and panting to get back her breath. She told him a little bit about the lady — a gift from the country of France, it was, and very precious to America — but she hadn't flown him all that way just to give him a history lesson.

"Hop on again, Chester C.!" she commanded — and up they flew to the torch that the lady was holding. Lulu found a perch on the north side of it, so the wind from the south wouldn't bother them.

"Now, just look around!" said Lulu proudly, as if all of New York belonged to her. "And don't anybody ever tell *this* pigeon that there's a more beautiful sight in the world."

Chester did as he was told. He first peered behind. There was Staten Island. And off to the left, New Jersey. To the right, quite a long way away, was Brooklyn. And back across the black water, with a dome of light glowing over it, the heart of the city — Manhattan.

And bridges! Bridges everywhere — all pricked out with tiny lights on their cables — that joined the island to the lands all round.

"Oh, wow! We're in luck!" exclaimed Lulu. With a flick of her wing, she gestured down. Almost right below them, it seemed, an ocean liner was gliding by, its rigging, like the bridges, strung with hundreds of silver bulbs.

An airplane passed over them. And even *it* had lights on its wings!

Through his eyes, Chester's heart became flooded with wonder. "It's like — it's like a dream of a city, at night."

"You wait till I fly you back," said the pigeon. "You'll see how that dream can turn real."

The wind, which had been a hindrance before, was a help now. Lulu coasted almost all the way back to Manhattan, only lifting a wing now and then to keep them on an even keel. But once or twice, just for the fun of it, she tilted her wings without warning. They zoomed up, fast — then dipped down, faster — a roller coaster in the empty air.

And all the while, the dream city drew nearer. It seemed to Chester like some huge spiderweb. The streets were the strands, all hung with multicolored lights. "Oh, Lulu, it's — I don't know — it's — "

"Hush!" said the pigeon. "Just look and enjoy." They

were flying amid the buildings now. "Enjoy, and remember."

Chester Cricket could not contain himself. He gave a chirp — not a song, just one chirp — but that single chirp said, "I love this! *I love it!*"

Then there was Times Square, erupting with colors. Chester pointed out the grating he'd come through — and Lulu landed next to it.

"How *can* I ever thank you?" said Chester.

"Don't bother, Chester C. Just glad to meet someone who loves New York as much as I do. And come on over to Bryant Park again. I'll be there — one branch or another. Night, Cricket."

"Night, Lulu."

She fluttered away.

Chester bounded through the grate and hopped as fast as he could toward the drainpipe. Tonight he had *really* had an adventure.

Author

George Selden started the adventures of Chester Cricket in *The Cricket in Times Square* when he heard a cricket chirp in a subway station one night. Later he wrote several books about Chester and his friends, including *Tucker's Countryside* and *Chester Cricket's New Home*. Mr. Selden writes for both adults and children and has received many awards and honors for his books. His latest book is *Old Meadow*.

An excerpt from

The Hundred Penny Box

by Sharon Bell Mathis

Illustrated by Higgins Bond

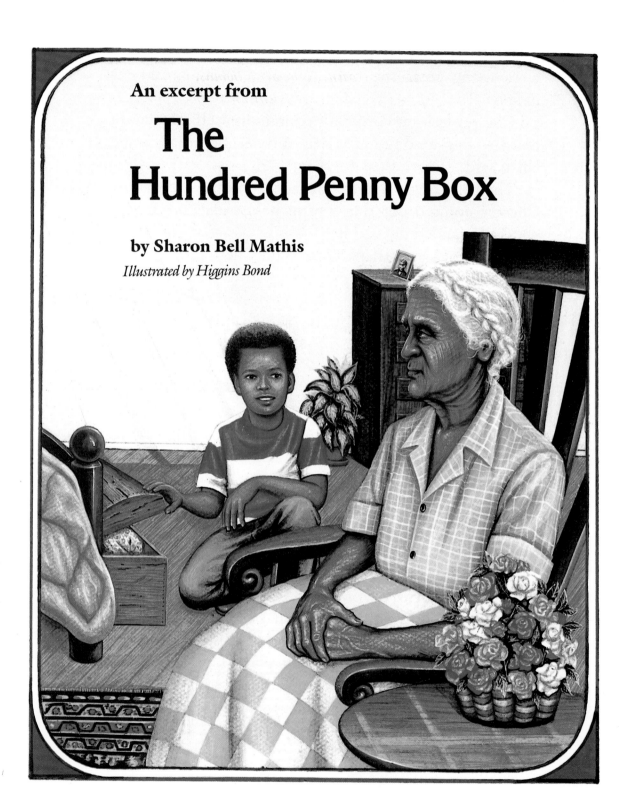

Michael's great-great-aunt, Dewbet Thomas, has come to live with Michael and his parents. "Aunt Dew" has a precious old wooden box — her hundred penny box. The importance of this box is not understood by Michael's mother, but Michael feels that the box is very important. He knows how much it means to Aunt Dew. As this part of the story opens, Michael has just told Aunt Dew that he is going to hide the box to keep it safe.

"No, don't hide my hundred penny box!" Aunt Dew said out loud. "Leave my hundred penny box right alone. Anybody takes my hundred penny box takes me!"

"Just in case," Michael said impatiently and wished his great-great-aunt would sit back down in her chair so he could talk to her. "Just in case Momma puts it in the furnace when you go to sleep like she puts all your stuff in the furnace in the basement."

"What your momma name?"

"Oh, no," Michael said. "You keep *on* forgetting Momma's name!" That was the only thing bad about being a hundred years old like Aunt Dew — you kept *on* forgetting things that were important.

"Hush, John-boy," Aunt Dew said and stopped dancing and humming and sat back down in the chair and put the quilt back over her legs.

"You keep on forgetting."

"I don't."

"You do, you keep on forgetting!"

"Do I forget to play with you when you worry me to death to play?"

Michael didn't answer.

123

"Do I forget to play when you want?"

"No."

"Okay. What your momma name? Who's that in my kitchen?"

"Momma's name is Ruth, but this isn't your house. Your house is in Atlanta. We went to get you and now you live with us."

"Ruth."

Michael saw Aunt Dew staring at him again. Whenever she stared at him like that, he never knew what she'd say next. Sometimes it had nothing to do with what they had been talking about.

"You John's baby," she said, still staring at him. "Look like John just spit you out."

"That's my father."

"My great-nephew," Aunt Dew said. "Only one ever care about me." Aunt Dew rocked hard in her chair then and Michael watched her. He got off the bed and turned off the record player and put the record back into the bottom drawer. Then he sat down on the hundred penny box.

"See that tree out there?" Aunt Dew said and pointed her finger straight toward the window with the large tree pressed up against it. Michael knew exactly what she'd say.

"Didn't have no puny-looking trees like that near my house," she said. "Dewbet Thomas — that's me, and Henry Thomas — that was my late husband, had the biggest, tallest, prettiest trees and the widest yard in all Atlanta. And John, that was your daddy, liked it most because he was city and my five sons, Henry, Jr., and Truke and Latt and the twins — Booker and Jay — well,

it didn't make them no never mind because it was always there. But when my oldest niece Junie and her husband — we called him Big John — brought your daddy down to visit every summer, they couldn't get the suitcase in the house good before he was climbing up and falling out the trees. We almost had to feed him up them trees!"

"Aunt Dew, we have to hide the box."

"Junie and Big John went out on that water and I was feeling funny all day. Didn't know what. Just feeling funny. I told Big John, I said, 'Big John, that boat old. Nothing but a piece a junk.' But he fooled around and said, 'We taking it out.' I looked and saw him and Junie on that water. Then it wasn't nothing. Both gone. And the boat turned over, going downstream. Your daddy, brand-new little britches on, just standing there looking, wasn't saying nothing. No hollering. I try to give him a big hunk of potato pie. But he just looking at me, just looking and standing. Wouldn't eat none of that pie. Then I said, 'Run get Henry Thomas and the boys.' He looked at me and then he looked at that water. He turned around real slow and walked toward the west field. He never run. All you could see was them stiff little britches — red they was — moving through the corn. Bare-waisted, he was. When we found the boat later, he took it clean apart — what was left of it — every plank, and pushed it back in that water. I watched him. Wasn't a piece left of that boat. Not a splinter."

"Aunt Dew, where can we hide the box!"

"What box?"

"The hundred penny box."

"We can't hide the hundred penny box and if she got to take my hundred penny box — she might as well take me!"

"We have to hide it!"

"No — 'we' don't. It's *my* box!"

"It's *my* house. And I said we have to hide it!"

"How you going to hide a house, John?"

"Not the house! Our hundred penny box!"

"It's *my* box!"

Michael was beginning to feel desperate. "Suppose Momma takes it when you go to sleep?"

Aunt Dew stopped rocking and stared at him again. "Like John just spit you out," she said. "Go on count them pennies, boy. Less you worry me in my grave if you don't. Dewbet Thomas's hundred penny box. Dewbet Thomas a hundred years old and I got a penny to prove it — each year!"

Michael got off the hundred penny box and sat on the floor by his great-great-aunt's skinny feet stuck down inside his father's old slippers. He pulled the big wooden box toward him and lifted the lid and reached in and took out the small cloth roseprint sack filled with pennies. He dumped the pennies out into the box.

He was about to pick up one penny and put it in the sack, the way they played, and say "One," when his great-great-aunt spoke.

"Why you want to hide my hundred penny box?"

"To play," Michael said, after he thought for a moment.

"Play now," she said. "Don't hide my hundred penny box. I got to keep looking at my box and when I don't see my box I won't see me neither."

"One!" Michael said and dropped the penny back into the old print sack.

"18 and 74," Aunt Dew said. "Year I was born. Slavery over! Black men in Congress running things. They was in charge. It was the Reconstruction."

Michael counted twenty-seven pennies back into the old print sack before she stopped talking about Reconstruction. "19 and 01," Aunt Dew said. "I was twenty-seven years. Birthed my twin boys. Hattie said, 'Dewbet, you got two babies.' I asked Henry Thomas, I said 'Henry Thomas, what them boys look like?'"

By the time Michael had counted fifty-six pennies, his mother was standing at the door.

"19 and 30," Aunt Dew said. "Depression. Henry Thomas, that was my late husband, died. Died after he put the fifty-six penny in my box. He had the double pneumonia and no decent shoes and he worked too hard. Said he was going to sweat the trouble out his lungs. Couldn't do it. Same year I sewed that fancy dress for Rena Coles. She want a hundred bows all over that dress. Henry the one started that box, you know. Put the first thirty-one pennies in it for me and it was my birthday. After fifty-six, I put them all in myself."

"Aunt Dew, time to go to bed," his mother said, standing at the door.

"Now, I'm not sleepy," Aunt Dew said. "John-boy and me just talking. Why you don't call him John? Look like John just spit him out. Why you got to call that boy something different from his daddy?"

Michael watched his mother walk over and open the window wide. "We'll get some fresh air in here," she said. "And then, Aunt Dew, you can take your nap better and feel good when you wake up." Michael wouldn't let his mother take the sack of pennies out of his hand. He held tight and then she let go.

"I'm not sleepy," Aunt Dew said again. "This child and me just talking."

"I know," his mother said, pointing her finger at him a little. "But we're just going to take our nap anyway."

"I got a long time to sleep and I ain't ready now. Just leave me sit here in this little narrow piece a room. I'm not bothering nobody."

"Nobody said you're bothering anyone but as soon as I start making that meat loaf, you're going to go to sleep in your chair and fall out again and hurt yourself and John'll wonder where I was and say I was on the telephone and that'll be something all over again."

"Well, I'll sit on the floor and if I fall, I'll be there already and it won't be nobody's business but my own."

"Michael," his mother said and took the sack of pennies out of his hand and laid it on the dresser. Then she reached down and closed the lid of the hundred penny box and pushed it against the wall. "Go out the room, honey, and let Momma help Aunt Dew into bed."

"I been putting Dewbet Thomas to bed a long time and I can still do it," Aunt Dew said.

"I'll just help you a little," Michael heard his mother say through the closed door.

As soon as his mother left the room, he'd go in and sneak out the hundred penny box.

But where would he hide it?

Michael went into the bathroom to think, but his mother came in to get Aunt Dew's washcloth. "Why are you looking like that?" she asked. "If you want to play go in my room. Play there, or in the living room. And don't go bothering Aunt Dew. She needs her rest."

Michael went into his father's and his mother's room and lay down on the big king bed and tried to think of a place to hide the box.

He had an idea!

He'd hide it down in the furnace room and sneak Aunt Dew downstairs to see it so she'd know where it was. Then maybe they could sit on the basement steps inside and play with it sometimes. His mother would never know. And his father wouldn't care as long as Aunt Dew was happy. He could even show Aunt Dew the big pipes and the little pipes.

Michael heard his mother close his bedroom door and walk down the hall toward the kitchen.

He'd tell Aunt Dew right now that they had a good place to hide the hundred penny box. The best place of all.

Michael got down from the huge bed and walked quietly back down the hall to his door and knocked on it very lightly. Too lightly for his mother to hear.

Aunt Dew didn't answer.

"Aunt Dew," he whispered after he'd opened the door and tiptoed up to the bed. "It's me. Michael."

Aunt Dew was crying.

Michael looked at his great-great-aunt and tried to say something but she just kept crying. She looked extra small in his bed and the covers were too close about her neck. He moved them down a little and then her face didn't look so small. He waited to see if she'd stop crying but she didn't. He went out of the room and down the hall and stood near his mother. She was chopping up celery. "Aunt Dew's crying," he said.

"That's all right," his mother said. "Aunt Dew's all right."

"She's crying real hard."

"When you live long as Aunt Dew's lived, honey — sometimes you just cry. She'll be all right."

"She's not sleepy. You shouldn't make her go to sleep if she doesn't want to. Daddy never makes her go to sleep."

"You say you're not sleepy either, but you always go to sleep."

"Aunt Dew's bigger than me!"

"She needs her naps."

"Why?"

"Michael, go play please," his mother said. "I'm tired and I'm busy and she'll hear your noise and never go to sleep."

"She doesn't have to if she doesn't want!" Michael yelled and didn't care if he did get smacked. "We were just playing and then you had to come and make her cry!"

"Without a nap, she's irritable and won't eat. She has to eat. She'll get sick if she doesn't eat."

"You made her cry!" Michael yelled.

"Michael John Jefferson," his mother said too quietly. "If you don't get away from me and stop that yelling and stop that screaming and leave me alone — !"

Michael stood there a long time before he walked away.

"Mike," his mother called but he didn't answer. All he did was stop walking.

His mother came down the hall and put her arm about him and hugged him a little and walked him back into the kitchen.

Michael walked very stiffly. He didn't feel like any hugging. He wanted to go back to Aunt Dew.

"Mike," his mother said, leaning against the counter and still holding him.

Michael let his mother hold him but he didn't hold her back. All he did was watch the pile of chopped celery.

"Mike, I'm going to give Aunt Dew that tiny mahogany chest your daddy made in a woodshop class when he was a teen-ager. It's really perfect for that little sack of pennies and when she sees it on that pretty dresser scarf she made — the one I keep on her dresser — she'll like it just as well as that big old clumsy box. She won't even miss that big old ugly thing!"

"The hundred penny box isn't even *bothering* you!"

His mother didn't answer. But Michael heard her sigh. "You don't even care about Aunt Dew's stuff," Michael yelled a little. He even pulled away from his mother. He didn't care at all about her hugging him. Sometimes it seemed to him that grown-ups never cared about anything unless it was theirs and nobody else's. He wasn't going to be like that when he grew up and could work and could do anything he wanted to do.

"Mike," his mother said quietly. "Do you remember that teddy bear you had? The one with the crooked head? We could never sit him up quite right because of the way

134

you kept him bent all the time. You'd bend him up while you slept with him at night and bend him up when you hugged him, played with him. Do you remember that, Mike?"

Why did she have to talk about a dumb old teddy bear!

"You wouldn't let us touch that teddy bear. I mean it was all torn up and losing its stuffing all over the place. And your daddy wanted to get rid of it and I said, 'No. Mike will let us know when he doesn't need that teddy bear anymore.' So you held onto that teddy bear and protected it from all kinds of monsters and people. Then, one day, you didn't play with it anymore. I think it was when little Corky moved next door."

"Corky's not little!"

"I'm sorry. Yes — Corky's big. He's a very big boy. But Corky wasn't around when you and I cleaned up your room a little while back. We got rid of a lot of things so that Aunt Dew could come and be more comfortable. That day, you just tossed that crooked teddy bear on top of the heap and never even thought about it — "

"I *did* think about it," Michael said.

"But you knew you didn't need it anymore," his mother whispered and rubbed his shoulder softly. "But it's not the same with Aunt Dew. She will hold onto everything that is hers — just to hold onto them! She will hold them tighter and tighter and she will not go forward and try to have a new life. This is a new life for her, Mike. You must help her have this new life and not just let her go backward to something she can never go back to. Aunt Dew does *not* need that huge, broken, half-rotten wooden box that you stumble all over the house with — just to hold one tiny little sack of pennies!"

"I don't stumble around with it!"

His mother reached down then and kissed the top of his head. "You're the one that loves that big old box, Mike. I think that's it."

Michael felt the kiss in his hair and he felt her arms about him and he saw the pile of celery. His mother didn't understand. She didn't understand what a hundred penny box meant. She didn't understand that a new life wasn't very good if you had to have everything old taken away from you — just for a dumb little stupid old funny-looking ugly little red box, a shiny ugly nothing box that didn't even look like it was big enough to hold a sack of one hundred pennies!

Mike put his arms around his mother. Maybe he could make her understand. He hugged her hard. That's what she had done — hugged him. "All Aunt Dew wants is her hundred penny box," Michael said. "That's the only thing ——"

"And all you wanted was that teddy bear," his mother answered.

"You can't burn it," Michael said and moved away from his mother. "You can't burn any more of Aunt Dew's stuff. You can't take the hundred penny box. I said you can't take it!"

"Okay," his mother said.

Michael went down the hall and opened the door to his room.

"No, Mike," his mother said and hurried after him. "Don't go in there now."

"I am," Michael said.

His mother snatched him and shut the door and pulled him into the living room and practically threw him into the stuffed velvet chair. "You're as stubborn as your father," she said. "Everything your way or else!" She was really angry. "Just sit there," she said. "And don't move until I tell you!"

As soon as Michael heard his mother chopping celery again, he got up from the chair.

He tiptoed into his room and shut the door without a sound.

Aunt Dew was staring at the ceiling. There was perspiration on her forehead and there was water in the dug-in places around her eyes.

"Aunt Dew?"

"What you want, John-boy?"

"I'm sorry Momma's mean to you."

"Ain't nobody mean to Dewbet Thomas — cause Dewbet Thomas ain't mean to nobody," Aunt Dew said, and reached her hand out from under the cover and patted Michael's face. "Your Momma Ruth. She move around and do what she got to do. First time I see her — I say, 'John, she look frail but she ain't.' He said, 'No, she ain't frail.' I make out like I don't see her all the time," Aunt Dew said, and winked her eye. "But she know I see her. If she think I don't like her that ain't the truth. Dewbet Thomas like everybody. But me and her can't talk like me and John talk — cause she don't know all what me and John know."

"I closed the door," Michael said. "You don't have to sleep if you don't want to."

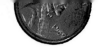

"I been sleep all day, John," Aunt Dew said.

Michael leaned over his bed and looked at his great-great-aunt. "You haven't been sleep all day," he said. "You've been sitting in your chair and talking to me and then you were dancing to your record and then we were counting pennies and we got to fifty-six and then Momma came."

"Where my hundred penny box?"

"I got it," Michael answered.

"Where you got it?"

"Right here by the bed."

"Watch out while I sleep."

He'd tell her about the good hiding place later. "Okay," he said.

Aunt Dew was staring at him. "Look like John just spit you out," she said.

Michael moved away from her. He turned his back and leaned against the bed and stared at the hundred penny box. All of a sudden it looked real *real* old and beat up.

"Turn round. Let me look at you."

Michael turned around slowly and looked at his great-great-aunt.

"John!"

"It's me," Michael said. "Michael."

He went and sat down on the hundred penny box.

"Come here so I can see you," Aunt Dew said.

Michael didn't move.

"Stubborn like your daddy. Don't pay your Aunt Dew no never mind!"

Michael still didn't get up.

"Go on back and do your counting out my pennies.

Start with fifty-seven — where you left off. 19 and 31. Latt married that schoolteacher. We roasted three pigs. Just acting the fool, everybody. Latt give her a pair of yellow shoes for her birthday. Walked off down the road one evening just like you please, she did. Had on them yellow shoes. Rode a freight train clean up to Chicago. Left his food on the table and all his clothes ironed. Six times she come back and stay for a while and then go again. Truke used to say, 'Wouldn't be *my* wife.' But Truke never did marry nobody. Only thing he care about was that car. He would covered it with a raincoat when it rained, if he could."

"First you know me, then you don't," Michael said.

"Michael John Jefferson what your name is," Aunt Dew said. "Should be plain John like your daddy and your daddy's daddy — stead of all this new stuff. Name John and everybody saying 'Michael.'" Aunt Dew was smiling. "Come here, boy," she said. "Come here close. Let me look at you. Got a head full of hair."

Michael got up from the hundred penny box and stood at the foot of the bed.

"Get closer," Aunt Dew said.

Michael did.

"Turn these covers back little more. This little narrow piece a room don't have the air the way my big house did."

"I took a picture of your house," Michael said and turned the covers back some more.

"My house bigger than your picture," Aunt Dew said. "Way bigger."

Michael leaned close to her on his bed and propped his elbows up on the large pillow under her small head.

"Tell me about the barn again," he said.

"Dewbet and Henry Thomas had the biggest, reddest barn in all Atlanta, G-A!"

"And the swing Daddy broke," Michael asked and put his head down on the covers. Her chest was so thin under the thick quilt that he hardly felt it. He reached up and pushed a few wispy strands of her hair away from her closed eyes.

"Did more pulling it down than he did swinging."

"Tell me about the swimming pool," Michael said. He touched Aunt Dew's chin and covered it up with only three fingers.

It was a long time before Aunt Dew answered. "Wasn't no swimming pool," she said. "I done told you was a creek. Plain old creek. And your daddy like to got bit by a cottonmouth."

"Don't go to sleep, Aunt Dew," Michael said. "Let's talk."

"I'm tired, John."

"I can count the pennies all the way to the end if you want me to."

"Go head and count."

"When your hundred and one birthday comes, I'm going to put in the new penny like you said."

"Yes, John."

Michael reached up and touched Aunt Dew's eyes. "I have a good place for the hundred penny box, Aunt Dew," he said quietly.

"Go way. Let me sleep," she said.

"You wish you were back in your own house, Aunt Dew?"

"I'm going back," Aunt Dew said.

"You sad?"

"Hush, boy!"

Michael climbed all the way up on the bed and put his whole self alongside his great-great-aunt. He touched her arms. "Are your arms a hundred years old?" he asked. It was their favorite question game.

"Um-hm," Aunt Dew murmured and turned a little away from him.

Michael touched her face. "Is your face and your eyes and fingers a hundred years old too?"

"John, I'm tired," Aunt Dew said. "Don't talk so."

"How do you get to be a hundred years old?" Michael asked and raised up from the bed on one elbow and waited for his great-great-aunt to answer.

"First you have to have a hundred penny box," his great-great-aunt finally said.

"Where you get it from?" Michael asked.

"Somebody special got to give it to you," Aunt Dew said. "And soon as they give it to you, you got to be careful less it disappear."

Author

The books of Sharon Bell Mathis have won many prizes. Her *Sidewalk Story* received an award from the Council on Interracial Books for Children. *The Hundred Penny Box,* part of which you have just read, was a Boston Globe-Horn Book Honor Book, a Newbery Medal Honor Book, and an American Library Association Notable Book.

Blackberries in the Dark
by Mavis Jukes · pictures by Thomas B. Allen

~ Houghton Mifflin Literature ~

Each of the selections you have just read from *Sharing* offered a different example of what it means to share with others.

Now you are going to read *Blackberries in the Dark* by Mavis Jukes. In this story, Austin visits his grandmother for the first time since the death of his grandfather. Together, they find something special to share that helps them live with their loss.

3

Accepting
Challenges

The Wish at the Top

by Clyde Robert Bulla
illustrated by
Chris Conover

*I*n a far city there once lived a boy named Jan. His father was Anton the blacksmith. The family's home was a little house next door to the blacksmith shop, in the shadow of a great church.

Jan was small and quick and strong. He helped his father shoe the horses that were brought to the shop. He was not afraid when they stamped their feet and blew their breath in his face.

Jan helped his mother, too. He carried firewood and water for the house. Sometimes he went to market to buy something she needed at home.

Often his friend Viktorin went with him. The two boys liked to wander about the city together.

Sometimes they climbed to the top of the city wall. There they could look out over forests and fields to the mountains beyond. Always they shook their fists at the mountains and shouted, "Hah! Laszlo!" This was their way of saying, "Laszlo! We're not afraid of you!"

Laszlo was their enemy. He lived in the mountains. He and his men waited there to rob anyone who went too far outside the city wall.

"Laszlo is a giant," Viktorin told Jan. "He has a black beard that comes down to his belt. He has sharp teeth and big, round eyes. He climbs the highest mountains because he likes the danger. He is a strange and terrible man."

"But we're not afraid of him," said Jan.

"The old governor was once afraid of him," said Viktorin. "This is what I have heard. Laszlo had so much land and such power that he might have ruled all the country if our soldiers hadn't driven him out. He went into the mountains, and the wild mountain men made him their leader."

Jan said, "We're not afraid of him and all his men."

"No," said his friend, "because our soldiers and our city wall will keep us safe."

Viktorin was older than Jan. He knew many things that Jan did not know. If the new governor went by in his carriage, Viktorin told a story about him. If the two boys stopped to drink at a fountain, Viktorin was ready with a story about the fountain.

One day they were playing in the churchyard, and Viktorin began to tell Jan about the church.

"Did you know it took five thousand men five thousand days to cut the stones and bring them here? See how they fit together to make this wall. You couldn't put a knife blade between these stones."

"I know," said Jan.

"But that isn't the most wonderful thing about the church," said Viktorin. "The most wonderful thing is *there*."

He pointed. Jan looked up and up to the golden ball on top of the steeple. Against the blue sky it shone like a small sun.

"You can wish on it," said Viktorin, "and your wish will come true."

"How do you know this?" asked Jan.

"I've heard the old ones tell it to one another," said Viktorin. "The old have secrets from the young. I listen and hear what they say."

"Have you wished on the golden ball?" asked Jan.

149

Viktorin shook his head. "You can make your wish only at the top of the steeple."

Jan was puzzled. "At the *top?*"

"Yes," said Viktorin. "Before you wish, you must rub the ball. You must rub it with your hand."

Jan gazed at the golden ball. It looked as high as the sky. "But — but — " he began.

"Ah, now you understand," said his friend. "No one ever wishes on the golden ball, because who could climb so high?"

"Well, then — " said Jan. "Well, then, it doesn't matter, does it?"

"It is a great wonder, all the same," said Viktorin. "If you could have your wish, what would it be?"

Jan thought. He thought for so long that his friend began to laugh. "I once heard of a man so rich he had nothing left to wish for. Are you like him?"

It was a joke, because Jan was not rich at all. Yet there was truth in the joke. All he really wanted was a horse, and he would have one within a year. His father and mother had promised it to him.

"Yes, I am like that man," he said, and he laughed with Viktorin. "I have nothing left to wish for!"

Then one day his world changed.

His mother had sent him to market to buy some yarn. He was halfway there when he found he had forgotten the money. He ran home and into the house. He came upon his mother with her head bowed over the kitchen table.

She tried to hide her face, but he saw that she was weeping.

"Mother — ," he began.

"It's nothing," she said. But as he stood looking at her, she told him. "It's just — just that today is my mother's birthday."

He waited for her to go on. "Is that all?" he asked.

"Is that *all*?" Suddenly her voice rose, as if she were angry. "Isn't it enough? When I was a girl at home, this was a great day for us all. The family was together, everyone was happy — and now — !" She was weeping again.

He stared at her.

"It is ten years since I have seen my mother and father," she said. "Ten long years! You have *never* seen them, even though they are your own grandmother and grandfather. I may never see them again. In all your life, *you* may never see them!"

"But why?" he asked.

"You know as well as I. Because they live on the other side of the mountains. We are shut inside these city walls as if we were in prison. Here we are, and here we must stay, and all because of Laszlo. Laszlo and his men wait to rob and kill anyone who takes the road through the mountains."

"I never knew you wanted to go — " he said.

"I know," she said. "Because you were happy, you thought everyone else was happy, too." She tried to smile. "I'm all right now. Forget what I said."

But Jan could not forget. He saw what he had never seen before. He saw that his mother's eyes were often sad. He saw his father look at her with eyes that were sad, too.

Many times a day Jan looked up at the church steeple. On clear nights he sat by his window where he could see the golden ball. It began to seem nearer. The steeple did not seem as high as before.

One day he stood in the churchyard. It was the first day of autumn, and he had on his red yarn cap. For a while he looked up at the steeple. Then he went into the church.

No one saw him as he went up the stairs to the loft. He found a small door that led to the roof. He looked out.

He could see the steeple. He was closer to it than he had ever been before.

He saw the stone figures on the steeple. They were figures of saints and angels. From below they looked small, but now he could see that each one was larger than a man. Each figure was inside a frame. The frames were rows of small, square stones.

He had never been close enough to see the stones before. They were set like pegs in the steeple. He thought, I can climb them. I can climb them like a ladder.

He walked out across the roof to the steeple. He put his foot on one of the square stones. He took one step, then another. He was climbing!

Birds flew below him. He heard the brush of their wings, and it pleased him to think that he was higher than the birds. And the climb was not hard. He had only to take care.

Still, he was tired when he came near the top. He could feel his heart pounding. Sometimes one of the stones moved a little under his feet. When this happened, he leaned closer to the steeple, and sweat came out on his forehead.

He climbed to the very top. On an iron rod just above him was the golden ball. It was nearly within reach.

He caught the rod and drew himself up. He touched the ball. It felt smooth and warm. He rubbed it and made his wish. He began to climb down.

But the downward climb was different. When he tried to see where to put his feet, he could not help looking down. He saw the city below. It seemed to be turning slowly, and it was so far . . .

He grew dizzy. His foot slipped, then his hand. He was falling.

Something broke his fall. It was the arm of a stone saint. He was caught between the arm and the side of the steeple.

There he lay, with his face toward the sky. He could move neither up nor down.

Jan's mother had gone to the blacksmith shop. She was asking, "Where is Jan?"

"I thought he was with you," said the blacksmith.

"He must be with Viktorin," said his wife.

"But Viktorin was just here," said the blacksmith. "He was looking for Jan."

They saw a man stop outside. He was looking up into the sunlight. Another man looked up. The two stood together. They began to talk, and they sounded excited.

The blacksmith and his wife went outside. They looked up to where the men were looking.

Near the top of the steeple was a tiny figure. It looked like a doll — a doll in a red cap.

The blacksmith cried out, "It's Jan!"

His wife cried after him, "It's Jan — it's Jan!"

More people gathered. "It's the blacksmith's son!" they said. "He's like a cat up a tree. Now he doesn't know how to get down."

The miller asked, "Why did he climb the steeple?"

Viktorin was there. "I think I know," he said. "He wanted to rub the golden ball and make a wish on it."

"The golden ball doesn't grant wishes," said the miller's wife. "Who told him that?"

"I — I told him," said Viktorin. "I heard people say it was true."

"I don't believe you heard anyone say it," said the woman. "I think you made it up out of your own head. Everybody knows you and the tales you tell. You shall be whipped!"

"No," said Jan's father. "That won't help now."

Bells were ringing. People were crowding into the square.

"What's to be done?" they asked one another.

"I'll climb the steeple," said the blacksmith.

"You could not even begin to climb it. You are too big and too heavy," said the miller. "We need someone small and light, but he must be strong enough to carry the boy down."

A merchant had the idea of bringing many ladders and tying them together. But when the ladders were placed against the church, they broke apart and came tumbling down.

"A scaffold!" said a baker. "Let us build a wooden scaffold as high as the steeple."

"That would take a year," said a weaver.

Jan's mother stood weeping in the square. The

blacksmith stood beside her. "All I own," he said, "to anyone who will save my son!"

And while many people came and many words were spoken, it seemed there was no one who could help.

In the crowd there was a man who wore the ragged robe of a beggar. When evening came, he made his way to the city gate. There he threw off his rags and began to run. In truth, he was no beggar, but a spy for Laszlo.

Late at night he came to Laszlo's camp. "I bring news," he said. "A boy has climbed the church steeple and cannot get down. The people keep watch below. There is hardly a guard left on the city wall. Now is the time for us to attack and take the city."

"No," said Laszlo. "We are too few, and we fight best in mountain passes."

But he began to ask questions. "The son of Anton the blacksmith, you say? Once I knew Anton when we were both very young. His son could be the age of my own son. Why does someone not bring the boy down?"

"The footholds are small — not large enough for a man," answered the spy.

Laszlo was thinking. An idea had come to him.

He was a strange man, but not all the tales told about him were true. He was no giant. He was slim and rather small. His eyes were no bigger than those of any other man, and his teeth were no sharper. He did have a long beard. And it was true that he climbed mountains because he liked the danger.

"How would it be," he said, "if I brought the boy down?"

"No!" said his men.

"There is no mountain peak I cannot climb," he said. "Surely a church steeple is not too much for Laszlo."

"Why should you help the people who took your land and drove you into the mountains?" asked the spy.

"Surely the blacksmith's boy is not my enemy," said Laszlo.

"They will kill you if you go there," said the spy.

"I think they will not know me," said Laszlo.

He cut off his beard. He dressed himself in a goatskin suit. He threw a rope over his arm and rode away on his fastest horse.

By morning he was at the city gate.

A guard called down from the wall, "Who are you?"

"A farmer from the plains," said Laszlo. "I have heard of the boy on the steeple. I have come to help if I can."

"The blacksmith will give all he owns to anyone who can save his son," said the guard.

He led the way to the church. Laszlo looked up at the steeple. He saw the boy there, looking no larger than a doll.

People were still gathered in the square. Most of them had not slept all night. They were warming themselves at small fires.

"But there is no fire to warm the blacksmith's boy," said a woman.

The blacksmith looked at Laszlo with the rope about his shoulders. He asked, "Have you come to help me? Do you know a way?"

"It may be," said Laszlo, and he disappeared into the church.

The people saw him move out across the church roof. They saw him put his hands on the steeple.

He made a noose in the rope and threw it up to the hand of a stone angel. He climbed a little way. He found a foothold and threw the rope again.

The people watched from below. They grew very still.

Jan lay on his back, behind the arm of the stone saint. The night had gone by. He had looked at the stars and thought of his mother and father and home.

By morning he was numb and cold. He could not turn his head far enough to look down. He wondered if his mother and father could see him now, if he could make them hear him.

He tried to shout, but his voice sounded faraway. He could hardly hear himself.

He felt as if he were turning to stone.

A sound came to him. It was like a voice. "Jan," it seemed to say.

He listened.

The sound came again. It was nearer, and it *was* a voice. "Can you hear me?" it said. "If you can hear me, move your foot."

Jan moved his foot.

Something touched his knee. Something pushed him up from behind the stone arm.

"Now," said the voice, "hold out your hands."

He held out his hands. For a moment he looked into a man's face — a face he had never seen before. It was long and dark, more young than old, with straight, black eyebrows. Then he was lying over the man's shoulder.

"Don't move," said the man, "and don't look."

Jan closed his eyes. He felt himself being carried down, now slowly, now quickly.

They were on the roof. They were inside the church. Jan saw his father and mother, and he was caught in their arms.

He forgot the long night on the steeple. He forgot how cold and afraid he had been.

"Listen to me!" he said. "I rubbed the golden ball. I rubbed it and made a wish. I wished the mountain road would be open so we could go to the other side. Now we can see my grandmother and grandfather!"

They were outside the church. Jan's father was shaking the stranger's hand and saying over and over, "Thank you — thank you!"

People were asking, "Who is this man?"

"Only one in the land could climb up the steeple and down," someone said. "It is Laszlo."

Others began to cry, "Laszlo!"

Soldiers were there. They pushed forward. But before they could seize the stranger, the blacksmith blocked their way.

"This man has saved my son," he said. "He risked his life, and you shall not lay a hand on him."

"Whoever this man may be, he has done what none of you could do," said Jan's mother, and she stood beside her husband.

The soldiers stopped. Some of them looked ashamed. While they talked about what should be done, the shout went up, "He is gone!"

Laszlo had slipped through the crowd and back to his horse. There was no one to stop him as he rode off across the plain.

The next day a guard found an arrow fixed to the city gate. Tied to the shaft of the arrow was a letter to "Anton the Blacksmith."

The blacksmith read the letter:

YOU AND YOUR FAMILY ARE FREE TO TRAVEL THE MOUNTAIN ROAD. AS YOU CAME TO MY AID, SO SHALL I HOLD YOU SAFE FROM HARM. LASZLO

He read the words to his wife and son.

"Can this be true?" she said.

"Of course, it is true," said Jan. "This was my wish when I rubbed the golden ball."

Some of the neighbors shook their heads. "It is a trick," they said. "Don't go outside the wall."

But the blacksmith and his family did not listen. One morning they set out on three horses. No one stopped them as they rode through the mountain pass. And on the other side there was a joyful meeting with Jan's grandmother and grandfather.

164

Not once, but many times, the blacksmith and his family took the mountain road. Sometimes they talked with Laszlo and his men. Jan and Laszlo's son met and became friends. Jan took Viktorin with him into the mountains, and the three boys rode their horses together.

One day the new governor asked to meet Laszlo. They met on the plain near the city, and friendship grew out of the meeting.

Laszlo was given a farm on the edge of the forest. In the spring he and his family came to live in their new home. Jan and his father and mother were waiting to welcome them. Others were there from the city, and many of Laszlo's men had come, too. Everyone joined in a celebration, and for a long time afterward there was peace in the land.

Author

Clyde Robert Bulla grew up on a Missouri farm. He went to a one-room school where his sister was the teacher. There he began writing stories and songs. Later, while working on a newspaper, he started to write for children. His first children's book was published in 1946. Since then Mr. Bulla has written more than fifty books and received many awards — for *White Bird, Shoeshine Girl,* and others. Mr. Bulla says, "I write, I travel, I come home to write again."

An excerpt from
STONE FOX

by John Reynolds Gardiner
Illustrated by James Watling

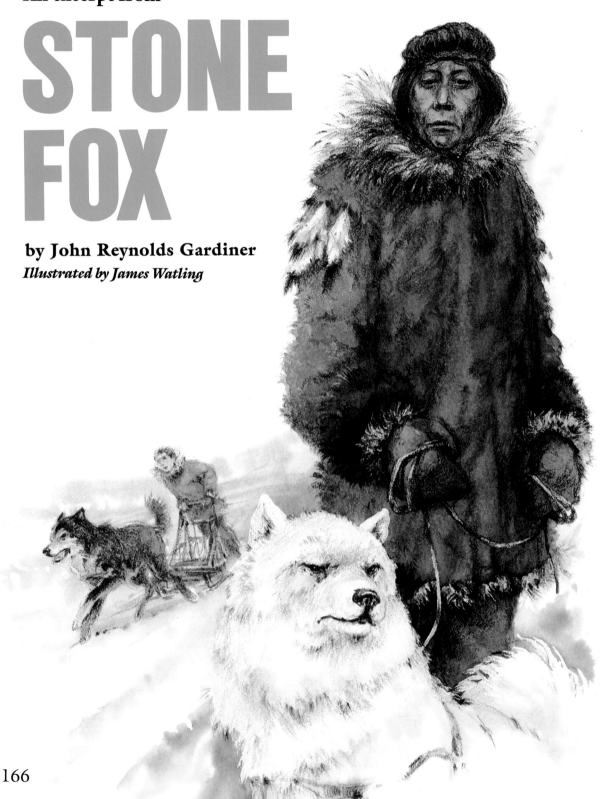

Little Willy needs five hundred dollars to save his grandfather's farm. Five hundred dollars just happens to be the prize in the big dogsled race to be held in his town of Jackson, Wyoming. Little Willy is sure that he and his dog Searchlight can win the race.

Little Willy went to see Mayor Smiley at the city hall building in town to sign up for the race.

The mayor's office was large and smelled like hair tonic. The mayor sat in a bright red chair with his feet on his desk. There was nothing on the desk except the mayor's feet.

"We have a race for you youngsters one hour before." Mayor Smiley mopped sweat from his neck with a silk handkerchief, although little Willy thought it was quite cool in the room.

"I wanna enter the *real* race, Mr. Mayor."

"You must be funning, boy." The mayor laughed twice and blotted his neck. "Anyway, there's an entrance fee."

"How much?"

"Fifty dollars."

Little Willy was stunned. That was a lot of money just to enter a race. But he was determined. He ran across the street to the bank.

"Don't be stupid," Mr. Foster told little Willy. "This is not a race for amateurs. Some of the best dog teams in the Northwest will be entering."

"I have Searchlight! We go fast as lightning. Really, Mr. Foster, we do."

Mr. Foster shook his head. "You don't stand a chance of winning."

"Yes, we do!"

"Willy . . . the money in your savings account is for your college education. You know I can't give it to you."

"You have to."

"I do?"

"It's *my* money!"

Little Willy left the bank with a stack of ten-dollar gold pieces — five of them, to be exact.

He walked into the mayor's office and plopped the coins down on the mayor's desk. "Me and Searchlight are gonna win that five hundred dollars, Mr. Mayor. You'll see. Everybody'll see."

Mayor Smiley counted the money, wiped his neck, and entered little Willy in the race.

When little Willy stepped out of the city hall building, he felt ten feet tall. He looked up and down the snow-covered street. He was grinning from ear to ear. Searchlight walked over and stood in front of the sled, waiting to be hitched up. But little Willy wasn't ready to go yet. He put his thumbs in his belt loops and let the sun warm his face.

He felt great. In his pocket was a map Mayor Smiley had given him showing the ten miles the race covered. Down Main Street, right on North Road — little Willy could hardly hold back his excitement.

Five miles of the race he traveled every day and knew with his eyes closed. The last five miles were back into town along South Road, which was mostly straight and flat. It's speed that would count here, and with the lead he knew he could get in the first five miles, little Willy was sure he could win.

As little Willy hitched Searchlight to the sled, something down at the end of the street — some moving

objects — caught his eye. They were difficult to see because they were all white. There were five of them. And they were beautiful. In fact, they were the most beautiful Samoyeds little Willy had ever seen.

The dogs held their heads up proudly and strutted in unison. They pulled a large but lightly constructed sled. They also pulled a large — but by no means lightly constructed — man. Way down at the end of the street the man looked normal, but as the sled got closer, the man got bigger and bigger.

The man was an Indian — dressed in furs and leather, with moccasins that came all the way up to his knees. His skin was dark, his hair was dark, and he wore a dark-colored headband. His eyes sparkled in the sunlight, but the rest of his face was as hard as stone.

The sled came to a stop right next to little Willy. The boy's mouth hung open as he tilted his head way back to look up at the man. Little Willy had never seen a giant before.

"Gosh," little Willy gasped.

The Indian looked at little Willy. His face was solid granite, but his eyes were alive and cunning.

"Howdy," little Willy blurted out, and he gave a nervous smile.

But the Indian said nothing. His eyes shifted to Searchlight, who let out a soft moan but did not bark.

The Giant walked into the city hall building.

Word that Stone Fox had entered the race spread throughout the town of Jackson within the hour, and throughout the state of Wyoming within the day.

Stories and legends about the awesome mountain man followed shortly. Little Willy heard many of them at Lester's General Store.

Little Willy learned that no white man had ever heard Stone Fox talk. Stone Fox refused to speak with the white man because of the treatment his people had received.

His tribe, the Shoshone, who were peaceful seed gather-ers, had been forced to leave Utah and settle on a reservation in Wyoming with another tribe called the Arapaho.

Stone Fox's dream was for his people to return to their homeland. Stone Fox was using the money he won from racing to simply buy the land back. He had already purchased four farms and over two hundred acres.

That Stone Fox was smart, all right.

In the next week little Willy and Searchlight went over the ten-mile track every day, until they knew every inch of it by heart.

Stone Fox hardly practiced at all. In fact, little Willy only saw Stone Fox do the course once, and then he sure wasn't going very fast.

The race was scheduled for Saturday morning at ten o'clock. Only nine sleds were entered. Mayor Smiley had hoped for more contestants, but after Stone Fox had entered, well . . . you couldn't blame people for wanting to save their money.

It was true Stone Fox had never lost a race. But little Willy wasn't worried. He had made up his mind to win. And nothing was going to stop him. Not even Stone Fox.

It was Friday night, the night before the race, when it happened.

Grandfather was out of medicine. Little Willy went to see Doc Smith.

"Here." Doc Smith handed little Willy a piece of paper with some scribbling on it. "Take this to Lester at the drugstore right away."

"But it's nighttime. The store's closed."

"Just knock on the back door. He'll hear you."

"But . . . are you sure it's all right?"

"Yes. Lester knows I may have to call on him any time — day or night. People don't always get sick just during working hours, now, do they?"

"No, I guess they don't." Little Willy headed for the door. He sure wished he could stay and have some of that cinnamon cake Doc Smith was baking in the oven. It smelled mighty good. But Grandfather needed his medicine. And, anyway, he wouldn't think of staying without being asked.

"One other thing, Willy," Doc Smith said.

"Yes, ma'am?"

"I might as well say this now as later. It's about the race tomorrow."

"Yes, ma'am?"

"First, I want you to know that I think you're a darn fool for using your college money to enter that race."

Little Willy's eyes looked to the floor. "Yes, ma'am."

"But, since it's already been done, I also want you to know that I'll be rooting for you."

Little Willy looked up. "You will?"

"Win, Willy. Win that race tomorrow."

Little Willy beamed. He tried to speak, but couldn't find the words. Embarrassed, he backed over to the door, gave a little wave, then turned quickly to leave.

"And, Willy . . ."

"Yes, ma'am?"

"If you stay a minute, you can have some of that cinnamon cake I've got in the oven."

"Yes, ma'am!"

Later, on his way to town, little Willy sang at the top of his lungs. The sled's runners cut through the snow with a swish. This was a treacherous road at night, but the moon was out and Searchlight could see well. And, anyway, they knew this road by heart. Nothing was going to happen.

Lester gave little Willy a big bottle of what looked like dirty milk.

"How's your grandfather doing?" Lester asked.

"Not so good. But after I win the race tomorrow, he'll get better. Doc Smith thinks so too."

Lester smiled. "I admire you, Willy. You got a heap of courage, going up against the likes of Stone Fox. You know he's never lost, don't you?"

"Yes, I know. Thank you for the medicine."

Little Willy waved good-bye as Searchlight started off down Main Street.

Lester watched the departing sled for a long time before he yelled, "Good luck, son!"

On his way out of town, along North Road, little Willy heard dogs barking. The sounds came from the old deserted barn near the schoolhouse.

Little Willy decided to investigate.

He squeaked open the barn door and peeked in. It was dark inside and he couldn't see anything. He couldn't hear anything either. The dogs had stopped barking.

He went inside the barn.

Little Willy's eyes took a while to get used to the dark, and then he saw them. The five Samoyeds. They were in the corner of the barn on a bed of straw. They were looking at him. They were so beautiful that little Willy couldn't keep from smiling.

Little Willy loved dogs. He had to see the Samoyeds up close. They showed no alarm as he approached, or as he held out his hand to pet them.

And then it happened.

There was a movement through the darkness to little Willy's right. A sweeping motion, fast at first; then it appeared to slow and stop. But it didn't stop. A hand hit little Willy right in the face, sending him over backward.

"I didn't mean any harm, Mr. Stone Fox," little Willy said as he picked himself up off the ground, holding a hand over his eye.

Stone Fox stood tall in the darkness and said nothing. Searchlight barked outside. The Samoyeds barked in return.

Little Willy continued, "I'm going to race against you tomorrow. I know how you wanna win, but . . . I wanna win too. I gotta win. If I don't, they're gonna take away our farm. They have the right. Grandfather says that those that want to bad enough, will. So I will. I'll win. I'm gonna beat you."

Stone Fox remained motionless. And silent.

Little Willy backed over to the barn door, still holding his eye. "I'm sorry we both can't win," he said. Then he pushed open the barn door and left, closing the door behind him.

In the barn, Stone Fox stood unmoving for another moment; then he reached out with one massive hand and gently petted one of the Samoyeds.

That night little Willy couldn't sleep — his eye was killing him. And when little Willy couldn't sleep, Searchlight couldn't sleep. Both tossed and turned for hours,

and whenever little Willy looked over to see if Searchlight was asleep, she'd just be lying there with her eyes wide open, staring back at him.

Little Willy needed his rest. So did Searchlight. Tomorrow was going to be a big day. The biggest day of their lives.

The day of the race arrived.

Little Willy got up early. He couldn't see out of his right eye. It was swollen shut.

As he fed Grandfather his oatmeal, he tried to hide his eye with his hand or by turning away, but he was sure Grandfather saw it just the same.

After adding more wood to the fire, little Willy kissed Grandfather, hitched up Searchlight, and started off for town.

At the edge of their property he stopped the sled for a moment and looked back at the farmhouse. The roof was covered with freshly fallen snow. A trail of smoke escaped from the stone chimney. The jagged peaks of the Teton Mountains shot up in the background toward the clear blue sky overhead. "Yes, sir," he remembered Grandfather saying. "There are some things in this world worth dying for."

Little Willy loved this country. He loved to hike and to fish and to camp out by a lake. But he did not like to hunt. He loved animals too much to be a hunter.

He had killed a bird once with a slingshot. But that had been when he was only six years old. And that had been enough. In fact, to this day, he still remembered the spot where the poor thing was buried.

Lost in his thoughts, little Willy got to town before he knew it. As he turned onto Main Street, he brought the sled to an abrupt halt.

He couldn't believe what he saw.

Main Street was jammed with people, lined up on both sides of the street. There were people on rooftops and people hanging out of windows. Little Willy hadn't expected such a big turnout. They must have all come to see Stone Fox.

Searchlight pulled the sled down Main Street past the crowd. Little Willy saw Miss Williams, his teacher, and Mr. Foster from the bank, and Hank from the post office. And there were Doc Smith and Mayor Smiley. The city slickers were there. And even Clifford Snyder, the tax man, was there. Everybody.

Lester came out of the crowd and walked alongside little Willy for a while. It was one of the few times little Willy had ever seen Lester without his white apron.

"You can do it, Willy. You can beat him," Lester kept saying over and over again.

They had a race for the youngsters first, and the crowd cheered and rooted for their favorites. It was a short race. Just down to the end of Main Street and back. Little Willy didn't see who won. It didn't matter.

And then it was time.

The old church clock showed a few minutes before ten as the contestants positioned themselves directly beneath the long banner that stretched across the street. They stood nine abreast. Stone Fox in the middle. Little Willy right next to him.

Little Willy had read all about the other contestants in the newspaper. They were all well-known mountain men with good racing records and excellent dog teams. But, even so, all bets were on Stone Fox. The odds were as high as a hundred to one that he'd win.

Not one cent had been bet on little Willy and Searchlight.

"What happened to Willy's eye?" Doc Smith asked Lester.

"Bumped it this morning when he got up, he told me. Just nervous. Got a right to be." Lester was chewing on his hand, his eyes glued on Stone Fox. "Big Indian," he whispered to himself.

Although little Willy's eye was black, puffy, and swollen shut, he still felt like a winner. He was smiling.

Searchlight knew the route as well as he did, so it really didn't matter if he could see at all. They were going to win today, and that was final. Both of them knew it.

Stone Fox looked bigger than ever standing next to little Willy. In fact, the top of little Willy's head was dead even with Stone Fox's waist.

"Morning, Mr. Stone Fox," little Willy said, looking practically straight up. "Sure's a nice day for a race."

Stone Fox must have heard little Willy, but he did not look at him. His face was frozen like ice, and his eyes seemed to lack that sparkle little Willy remembered seeing before.

The crowd became silent as Mayor Smiley stepped out into the street.

Miss Williams clenched her hands together until her knuckles turned white. Lester's mouth hung open, his lips wet. Mr. Foster began chewing his cigar. Hank stared

without blinking. Doc Smith held her head up proudly. Clifford Snyder removed a gold watch from his vest pocket and checked the time.

Tension filled the air.

Little Willy's throat became dry. His hands started to sweat. He could feel his heart thumping.

Mayor Smiley raised a pistol to the sky and fired.

The race had begun!

Searchlight sprang forward with such force that little Willy couldn't hang on. If it weren't for a lucky grab, he would have fallen off the sled for sure.

In what seemed only seconds, little Willy and Searchlight had traveled down Main Street, turned onto North Road, and were gone. Far, far ahead of the others. They were winning. At least for the moment.

Stone Fox started off dead last. He went so slowly down Main Street that everyone was sure something must be wrong.

Swish! Little Willy's sled flew by the schoolhouse on the outskirts of town, and then by the old deserted barn.

Swish! Swish! Swish! Other racers followed in hot pursuit.

"Go, Searchlight! Go!" little Willy sang out. The cold wind pressed against his face, causing his good eye to shut almost completely. The snow was well packed. It was going to be a fast race today. The fastest they had ever run.

The road was full of dangerous twists and turns, but little Willy did not have to slow down as the other racers did. With only one dog and a small sled, he was able to take the sharp turns at full speed without risk of sliding off the road or losing control.

Therefore, with each turn, little Willy pulled farther and farther ahead.

Swish! The sled rounded a corner, sending snow flying. Little Willy was smiling. This was fun!

About three miles out of town the road made a half circle around a frozen lake. Instead of following the turn, little Willy took a shortcut right across the lake. This was tricky going, but Searchlight had done it many times before.

Little Willy had asked Mayor Smiley if he was permitted to go across the lake, not wanting to be disqualified. "As long as you leave town heading north and come back on South Road," the mayor had said, "anything goes!"

None of the other racers attempted to cross the lake. Not even Stone Fox. The risk of falling through the ice was just too great.

Little Willy's lead increased.

Stone Fox was still running in last place. But he was picking up speed.

At the end of five miles, little Willy was so far out in front that he couldn't see anybody behind him when he looked back.

He knew, however, that the return five miles, going back into town, would not be this easy. The trail along South Road was practically straight and very smooth, and Stone Fox was sure to close the gap. But by how much? Little Willy didn't know.

Doc Smith's house flew by on the right. The tall trees surrounding her cabin seemed like one solid wall.

Grandfather's farm was coming up next.

When Searchlight saw the farmhouse, she started to pick up speed. "No, girl," little Willy yelled. "Not yet."

As they approached the farmhouse, little Willy thought he saw someone in Grandfather's bedroom window. It was difficult to see with only one good eye. The someone was a man. With a full beard.

It couldn't be. But it was! It was Grandfather!

Grandfather was sitting up in bed. He was looking out the window.

Little Willy was so excited he couldn't think straight. He started to stop the sled, but Grandfather indicated no, waving him on. "Of course," little Willy said to himself. "I must finish the race. I haven't won yet."

"Go, Searchlight!" little Willy shrieked. "Go, girl!"

Grandfather was better. Tears of joy rolled down little Willy's smiling face. Everything was going to be all right.

And then Stone Fox made his move.

One by one he began to pass the other racers. He went from last place to eighth. Then from eighth place to seventh. Then from seventh to sixth. Sixth to fifth.

He passed the others as if they were standing still.

He went from fifth place to fourth. Then to third. Then to second.

Until only little Willy remained.

But little Willy still had a good lead. In fact, it was not until the last two miles of the race that Stone Fox got his first glimpse of little Willy since the race had begun.

The five Samoyeds looked magnificent as they moved effortlessly across the snow. Stone Fox was gaining, and

he was gaining fast. And little Willy wasn't aware of it.

Look back, little Willy! Look back!

But little Willy didn't look back. He was busy thinking about Grandfather. He could hear him laughing . . . and playing his harmonica . . .

Finally little Willy glanced back over his shoulder. He couldn't believe what he saw! Stone Fox was nearly on top of him!

This made little Willy mad. Mad at himself. Why hadn't he looked back more often? What was he doing? He hadn't won yet. Well, no time to think of that now. He had a race to win.

"Go, Searchlight! Go, girl!"

But Stone Fox kept gaining. Silently. Steadily.

"Go, Searchlight! Go!"

The lead Samoyed passed little Willy and pulled up even with Searchlight. Then it was a nose ahead. But that

was all. Searchlight moved forward, inching *her* nose ahead. Then the Samoyed regained the lead. Then Searchlight . . .

When you enter the town of Jackson on South Road, the first buildings come into view about a half a mile away. Whether Searchlight took those buildings to be Grandfather's farmhouse again, no one can be sure, but it was at this time that she poured on the steam.

Little Willy's sled seemed to lift up off the ground and fly. Stone Fox was left behind.

But not that far behind.

The crowd cheered madly when they saw little Willy come into view at the far end of Main Street, and even more madly when they saw that Stone Fox was right on his tail.

"Go, Searchlight! Go!"

Searchlight forged ahead. But Stone Fox was gaining!

"Go, Searchlight! Go!" little Willy cried out.

Searchlight gave it everything she had.

She was a hundred feet from the finish line when her heart burst. She died instantly. There was no suffering.

The sled and little Willy tumbled over her, slid along the snow for a while, then came to a stop about ten feet from the finish line. It had started to snow — white snowflakes landed on Searchlight's dark fur as she lay motionless on the ground.

The crowd became deathly silent.

Lester's eyes looked to the ground. Miss Williams had her hands over her mouth. Mr. Foster's cigar lay on the snow. Doc Smith started to run out to little Willy, but stopped. Mayor Smiley looked shocked and helpless. And so did Hank and so did the city slickers, and so did Clifford Snyder, the tax man.

Stone Fox brought his sled to a stop alongside little Willy. He stood tall in the icy wind and looked down at the young challenger, and at the dog that lay limp in his arms.

"Is she dead, Mr. Stone Fox? Is she dead?" little Willy asked, looking up at Stone Fox with his one good eye.

Stone Fox knelt down and put one massive hand on Searchlight's chest. He felt no heartbeat. He looked at little Willy, and the boy understood.

Little Willy squeezed Searchlight with all his might. "You did real good, girl. Real good. I'm real proud of you. You rest now. Just rest." Little Willy began to brush the snow off Searchlight's back.

Stone Fox stood up slowly.

No one spoke. No one moved. All eyes were on the Indian, the one called Stone Fox, the one who had never lost a race, and who now had another victory within his grasp.

But Stone Fox did nothing.

He just stood there. Like a mountain.

His eyes shifted to his own dogs, then to the finish line, then back to little Willy, holding Searchlight.

With the heel of his moccasin Stone Fox drew a long line in the snow. Then he walked back over to his sled and pulled out his rifle.

Down at the end of Main Street, the other racers began to appear. As they approached, Stone Fox fired his rifle into the air. They came to a stop.

Stone Fox spoke.

"Anyone crosses this line — I shoot."

188

189

And there wasn't anybody who didn't believe him.

Stone Fox nodded to the boy.

The town looked on in silence as little Willy, carrying Searchlight, walked the last ten feet and across the finish line.

A Postscript from the Author

The idea for this story came from a Rocky Mountain legend that was told to me in 1974 by Bob Hudson over a cup of coffee at Hudson's Café in Idaho Falls, Idaho. Although Stone Fox and the other characters are purely fictitious and of my creation, the tragic ending to this story belongs to the legend and is reported to have actually happened.

Author

John Reynolds Gardiner is an engineer who has also written stories for television. *Stone Fox* is his first book.

An excerpt from

Child of the Silent Night

by Edith Fisher Hunter

Illustrated by Sandra Speidel

When Laura Bridgman was two years old, an illness left her deaf, blind, and unable to speak. All that she could learn was what she could feel with her fingers. She was able to help with chores around the house and farm, but she did not have a way to make those around her understand what she wanted.

When Laura was nearly eight years old, a professor at Dartmouth College visited the Bridgmans' farm in Hanover, New Hampshire and wrote an article about Laura. Dr. Samuel Gridley Howe, the director of a school for blind people, read the article with great interest. Although a person who was both blind and deaf had never been educated before, Dr. Howe believed that he could help Laura. When he visited the Bridgmans and saw that Laura was intelligent and eager to learn, he became even more certain. It was decided that Laura would go to Dr. Howe's school in Boston.

It was Columbus Day, October 12, 1837, just a few weeks before her eighth birthday, when Laura Bridgman started out on her great adventure. Seated in a light carriage, called a chaise, between her father and mother, Laura was tense with excitement. Where was she going? No one could tell her.

Why had she helped her mother put the best of her old clothes and many new ones in a large trunk that she knew was in the carriage with them? Why had her treasures been put in a box in among her clothes?

Laura knew that something very unusual was happening. Exactly what it was she did not know, but at least her parents were with her.

Of course she could not see how beautiful Hanover was on this October day. As yet there had been no killing frost and the late autumn flowers, especially the goldenrod and asters, were lovely. The sugar maples were at the peak of their golden glory and the red maples were brilliant to the seeing eye. The woodbine curled like tongues of fire up and around the trees along the road. Laura did not know that she was saying goodbye to all this beauty for a while.

The trip from Hanover to Boston was a long one in those days. The Bridgmans had to change from the chaise to a stagecoach and spend several days along the way.

Never had Laura been on such a long journey; never had she felt herself in the midst of so many strangers. She tried to hide behind her mother's skirts and her father's greatcoat. When would they get to wherever it was they were going?

After what must have seemed to Laura an endlessly long time the coach finally stopped. Mr. and Mrs. Bridgman and Laura were helped out. Laura clung to her mother as they went up a short flight of stairs and into a building. In another moment Laura felt her small hand once again held by the large hand that belonged to the unusually tall man who had visited her once in Mill Village. Was this his home? What was she doing here? No one could explain, of course.

Then Laura felt a woman's soft hand take hers. Laura could not know that this was Miss Jeannette Howe. Laura and her mother took off their coats and bonnets. Following the strange woman they walked along — what was it? A room? A hall? Laura could somehow sense the largeness of the rooms. She was accustomed to small, low-ceilinged rooms at home. She felt very small and lost in so much space. She clung to the strange but friendly woman on one side of her and to her mother on the other.

Now they had entered a smaller room and she was allowed to feel about. There was a bed, a rocking chair, a washstand and a little table. The furnishings here were not unlike those in her own room at the farm. She was encouraged to help her mother take her dresses and other clothes out of the trunk in which they had been placed at home. Were they perhaps going to stay here for a visit? Where was her mother's bag?

There, now they had come to her box of treasures. She felt her mother take it and place it on the table by the bed. Was this going to be her own room? Would her little brothers, Addison and John, be coming too? Would her treasures be safe on the table? No one can know whether questions such as these passed through Laura's mind and no one, of course, could have made her understand the answers to them.

Now they were going back through the long hall to the large room from which they had come. Laura was led over to a low chair near her father and the tall man and given a cup of milk and a cookie. When she had finished eating she sat quietly in her chair.

Then she felt people getting up around her. Her father leaned down and patted her. Laura started to jump up. That pat usually meant that he was going away. His firm hand pushed her back down into the chair again. Now her mother leaned over and patted her.

Laura was terrified. This too was a goodbye pat. Surely her father and mother were not going away! Surely they were not going to leave her in a strange place! Laura struggled to get out of the chair. But now it was the large hand of the friendly man and the gentle hand of the woman that were holding her back.

Laura felt a door close. She was allowed to get out of the chair and she rushed madly in the direction in which she knew the door lay. It was closed. Laura let out a loud unpleasant sound. It sounded almost like a wounded animal. She began crying and pounding on the door with her little fists.

"We must let her tire herself out some with her grief and tears," said Dr. Howe to his sister. "She is already tired from the long journey, and the fear and sorrow of this separation will exhaust her further. In a little while we must take her to her room. Her box of treasures and her clothes at least will be familiar to her."

"Oh, Sam, it is so pathetic to see her frightened and upset," said Miss Jeannette. "If there were only some way to let her know that it is all for her own good that she has come here." Dr. Howe and his sister watched the terrified little girl crying, beating the door, feeling about the room for some familiar object or person. When she came near them they tried to comfort her, but each time she would draw away.

At last, when they felt that Laura would allow it, they led her to her room. They left her there and locked the door. When Miss Jeannette returned in less than half an hour she found Laura sound asleep on her bed.

"We can expect that there will be several more scenes like the one we have just witnessed before Laura will accept the fact that she must stay here," said Dr. Howe to his sister.

"Of course!" said Miss Jeannette. "Can you imagine how she must feel? Suddenly, with no warning — for how could anyone warn her? — she has been taken from the familiar surroundings of the farm, separated from her father, her mother, and her little brothers. Why, it is as if she had been suddenly plunged into an even darker prison than the one she has always lived in: still no light, no sound, almost no smells or tastes and now not even the familiar things and people around her to touch!"

"I had thought of having Mrs. Bridgman remain here at the school for a few days," said Dr. Howe. "But I decided that since Laura is so bright and friendly, she would recover from the shock of separation quickly and I could begin her education sooner if we did not have to wean her gradually from her mother. I hope I am not wrong about this."

"She *is* bright and friendly, Sam," said Miss Jeannette enthusiastically. "I could see that even in the little while before her parents left."

And Dr. Howe was right in thinking that Laura would quickly recover from the first shock of separation. In less than a week Laura began to be her own lively self once more. She began to reach out with her wonderful hands to learn all she could about her new home.

The room that had been given to Laura was in Dr. Howe's own apartment and he and his sister quickly became another father and mother to her. In a very short time she began learning, through her hands of course, to identify every member of the school family. There were more than forty people: blind children and teachers. Laura soon knew every one of them by touch.

At the end of two weeks Laura was so happy in her new surroundings that Dr. Howe felt he could begin the experiment he had planned. The night before he began he discussed his plans aloud with his sister.

"My goal is perfectly clear to me, Jeannette," he said. "I am going to try to bring into Laura's mind the idea that there are twenty-six different signs or letters that everyone uses. This is our alphabet. I want her to know that by combining these letters into words we can share our thoughts with each other."

"But Sam, how in the world are you going to 'tell' Laura that?" asked Miss Jeannette, puzzled. "If she were just blind you could have her feel the raised-up letters with her fingers and tell her their names. Or, if she were just deaf and mute, you could show her letters. But she is blind and deaf and mute, so what can you do?"

"I know just exactly how I am going to try to do it," said Dr. Howe, smiling. "You may attend the first class with Laura tomorrow morning and see for yourself."

The great day dawned. When the first lesson began Laura was seated at a table across from Dr. Howe. Beside her sat Miss Drew, who was to be Laura's own special teacher. Miss Jeannette Howe sat watching nearby.

The doctor had arranged a row of objects on the table in front of him. There were a large key, a spoon, a knife, a fork, a book, a cup and a few other things with which he felt sure Laura would be familiar.

First Dr. Howe put the key into Laura's hand. It was a very large key. He let her handle it and feel it all over. She knew immediately what it was. The key at home with which she locked the cupboard was very much like this one — except for one thing. Her sensitive fingers paused as they felt the long key. There was something *on* this one.

Dr. Howe had fastened a paper label on the key. On the label the word *key* was written in a special kind of raised lettering or embossing that was used at that time in writing for the blind. The Braille system, now so widely used, had not yet been adopted. Dr. Howe guided Laura's fingers over the raised lines of the letters several times. She had no idea, of course, what the letters were.

Then he took the key away from Laura and handed her a spoon. She took it, felt it and immediately recognized it as a spoon much like the ones with which she set the table at home. Again there was one important difference. Along the handle of the spoon Dr. Howe had pasted a label with the letters S-P-O-O-N written in raised type. Dr. Howe guided her fingers carefully over this word several times.

Now the doctor took away the spoon and gave the key back to Laura. He directed her fingers to the label on the key again. Then he gave her back the spoon and directed her fingers to the label on the spoon once more. He wanted Laura to feel that the shape of the lines on the key label and the shape of the lines on the spoon label were just as different from each other as the key and spoon themselves were different from one another.

Now the doctor did something else. He took away the key and the spoon and gave Laura just a piece of paper with some raised letters on it. The letters were K-E-Y again. Taking the key once more, Dr. Howe directed Laura's fingers to the label on it.

An expression on Laura's face made it quite clear that she recognized that the raised letters were the same on both papers, the one on the key and the separate label. Dr. Howe went through the same process with the spoon and a separate label that read S-P-O-O-N.

The rest of that first lesson was spent letting Laura feel the remaining objects — cup, knife, book, and so forth — and the labels for these, both those pasted on the object and those that were separate. From that time on Laura had lessons every morning and afternoon. She seemed to enjoy them thoroughly and to consider them just a game, not work. It was difficult for Dr. Howe and Miss Drew to get her to stop "playing" this game.

By about the third day Dr. Howe and Miss Drew were delighted to see that Laura had grasped the important point that the separate label for *key* somehow went with the key and the label that was separate from the spoon went with the spoon. That she understood this was shown by the fact that she could take a separate label, such as the one spelling *book,* and feel about until she found a book without any label. Then she would place the label on the book.

In a very few days Laura could reverse this process. She could pick up an object, such as a spoon, search through a pile of loose labels on the table, feel them until she found the one that read S-P-O-O-N and then put it on a spoon. She could do this for any object for which she had been taught the feeling of the word.

Dr. Howe was greatly encouraged. He felt sure that he was going to succeed with Laura; his only question was how long it was going to take him. In a report that he once wrote about his work with her he said: "It sometimes occurred to me that she was like a person alone and helpless in a deep, dark, still pit, and that I was letting down a cord and dangling it about, in hopes she might find it, and that finally she would seize it by chance, and, clinging to it, be drawn up by it into the light of day and into human society."

The lessons were going so well that Dr. Howe felt Laura was ready to take another important step forward. He had Miss Drew cut the labels for the words *key, spoon, knife,* and so forth, into separate letters. Up until this time Laura had seen words as wholes. Now he wanted her to learn that they are made up of parts — letters. Laura was allowed to follow closely, with her hands, all that

Miss Drew did. After the words had been cut into separate letters, her hands followed Miss Drew's as she arranged the letters back into words.

In an astonishingly short time Laura had grasped the point of this new "game." If Miss Drew handed her the letters O, S, N, O, P, in a flash Laura could arrange them in the correct order to spell S-P-O-O-N. If Miss Drew gave her Y, K, E, Laura arranged them into the word K-E-Y. O, K, O, B and I, K, E, N, F were equally simple for her. After a few more lessons Laura could do this with all the words in her vocabulary and soon after that she could take from a whole pile of loose letters whatever ones she wanted and spell correctly any word she wished of those she had been taught. This would have been a great accomplishment for any eight-year-old. How much more remarkable it was for a little girl like Laura Bridgman!

Dr. Howe thought it would be easier for Laura to arrange the letters if there were some kind of form into which they could be fitted. Therefore he had metal letters — types, he called them — made for her and a frame with grooves into which the letters could be fitted. He had four complete sets made of the twenty-six letters of the alphabet. Within a short time Laura was using the metal letters to build all the words she knew.

Two months had passed before Dr. Howe felt that Laura was ready to take the final step that he had planned for her. Miss Drew was sent to the home of a Mr. George Loring, who was a deaf-mute, to learn the manual alphabet. She learned it in one afternoon.

The manual alphabet is a way of forming the twenty-six letters of the alphabet with the hands. In the United

States the one-handed manual alphabet is used. There is also a two-handed system used in some countries. In the one-handed system the letter *a*, for example, is formed by folding the four fingers over and keeping the thumb straight. *B* is formed by holding the fingers straight up with the thumb folded in. In only a few cases, as with *c* and *y*, for example, does the hand form a shape that very much resembles the shape of that letter as we write it.

A deaf person who has been "talking" with the manual alphabet for a long time can "say" with his hand as many as 130 words a minute. A deaf person who is skilled at watching another person "speak" with his hands can easily "read" 130 words a minute.

Laura, of course, would not be able to see the letters. Miss Drew would have to form them in Laura's hand so that she could feel them.

But how could she teach Laura that the various positions in which she held her fingers meant the letters of the alphabet that she had already learned with raised letters and metal types? This is how Miss Drew did it. She picked up the key and let Laura feel it. Then she took the letter K from the set of metal types and let Laura feel that. Then she shaped the letter *k* in the manual alphabet into Laura's hand, her first two fingers up and bent forward, the next two fingers folded down, and the thumb up. She made Laura feel the way her fingers were held. Then she let Laura feel the metal letter K again.

The same procedure was followed with the letter *e*. First Laura must feel the metal type of the E, then Miss Drew formed *e* in the manual alphabet, all the fingers folded over and the thumb folded down, and then back to the metal type again. Finally the letter Y was taken from the metal types and Laura allowed to feel it. The manual *y* is formed with thumb up, little finger up and other fingers all folded down. This one almost looks like a *y* as we write it. Now Miss Drew had set the metal types K-E-Y in the form. She let Laura run her hand over the whole word. Then she formed again, in the manual alphabet, the letters *k-e-y* in Laura's hand and she placed the key itself in Laura's other hand. This was done with the spoon, the cup, and the key again.

And then it happened! For two months Laura had been "playing" these games with letters and words almost the way a trained dog performs certain tricks. Now, suddenly, it was different. Dr. Howe always said that he knew almost the exact moment when Laura's face showed that she at last really understood what all this meant.

Suddenly it seemed to become clear to her that every object had a name, that these names could be spelled by letters, either in raised letters, metal types or, most easily of all, by the manual alphabet.

In one of his yearly reports about his work with Laura Bridgman, Dr. Howe wrote:

> . . . Now the truth began to flash upon her, her intellect began to work, she perceived that here was a way by which she could herself make up a sign of anything that was in her own mind, and show it to another mind, and at once her countenance lighted up with a human expression . . . I could almost fix upon the moment when this truth dawned upon her mind and spread its light to her countenance. . . .

Laura had found the rope that Dr. Howe was dangling before her. She had caught hold of it at last and could be drawn up from the dark pit in which she lived into the light of day!

Author

Edith Fisher Hunter was born and grew up in Boston, Massachusetts. She has written many magazine articles and books for adults. While working on one of her books, she learned about Laura Bridgman. This gave her the idea for writing *Child of the Silent Night,* her first book for children.

HOPE

by Langston Hughes

Sometimes when I'm lonely,
Don't know why,
Keep thinkin' I won't be lonely
By and by.

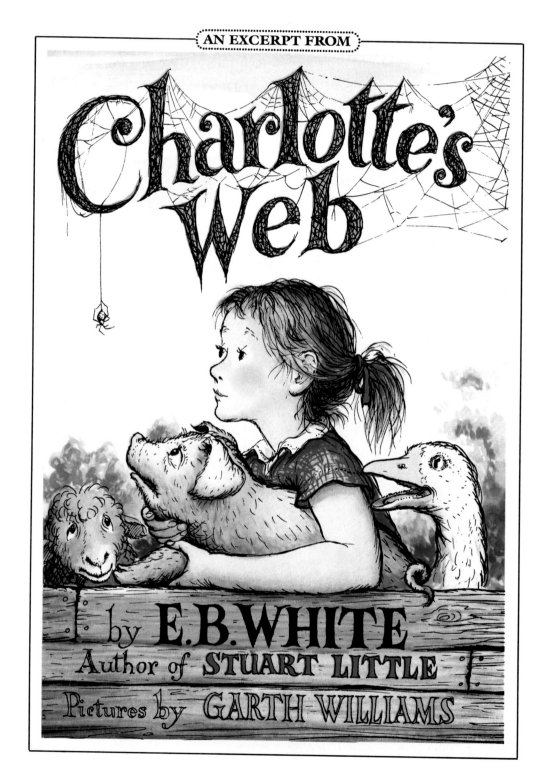

Charlotte's Web

by E. B. WHITE

Author of STUART LITTLE

Pictures by GARTH WILLIAMS

Wilbur's Escape

The barn was very large. It was very old. It smelled of hay and it smelled of manure. It smelled of the perspiration of tired horses and the wonderful sweet breath of patient cows. It often had a sort of peaceful smell — as though nothing bad could happen ever again in the world. It smelled of grain and of harness dressing and of axle grease and of rubber boots and of new rope. And whenever the cat was given a fish-head to eat, the barn would smell of fish. But mostly it smelled of hay, for there was always hay in the great loft up overhead. And there was always hay being pitched down to the cows and the horses and the sheep.

The barn was pleasantly warm in winter when the animals spent most of their time indoors, and it was pleasantly cool in summer when the big doors stood wide open to the breeze. The barn had stalls on the main floor for the work horses, tie-ups on the main floor for the cows, a sheepfold down below for the sheep, a pigpen down below for Wilbur, and it was full of all sorts of things that you find in barns: ladders, grindstones, pitch forks, monkey wrenches, scythes, lawn mowers, snow shovels, ax handles, milk pails, water buckets, empty grain sacks, and rusty rat traps. It was the kind of barn that swallows like to build their nests in. It was the kind of barn that children like to play in. And the whole thing was owned by Fern's uncle, Mr. Homer L. Zuckerman.

Wilbur's new home was in the lower part of the barn, directly underneath the cows. Mr. Zuckerman knew that a manure pile is a good place to keep a young pig. Pigs need warmth, and it was warm and comfortable down there in the barn cellar on the south side.

Fern came almost every day to visit him. She found an old milking stool that had been discarded, and she placed the stool in the sheepfold next to Wilbur's pen. Here she sat quietly during the long afternoons, thinking and listening and watching Wilbur. The sheep soon got to know her and trust her. So did the geese, who lived with the sheep. All the animals trusted her, she was so quiet

and friendly. Mr. Zuckerman did not allow her to take Wilbur out, and he did not allow her to get into the pigpen. But he told Fern that she could sit on the stool and watch Wilbur as long as she wanted to. It made her happy just to be near the pig, and it made Wilbur happy to know that she was sitting there, right outside his pen. But he never had any fun — no walks, no rides, no swims.

One afternoon in June, when Wilbur was almost two months old, he wandered out into his small yard outside the barn. Fern had not arrived for her usual visit. Wilbur stood in the sun feeling lonely and bored.

"There's never anything to do around here," he thought. He walked slowly to his food trough and sniffed to see if anything had been overlooked at lunch. He found a small strip of potato skin and ate it. His back itched, so he leaned against the fence and rubbed against

the boards. When he tired of this, he walked indoors, climbed to the top of the manure pile, and sat down. He didn't feel like going to sleep, he didn't feel like digging, he was tired of standing still, tired of laying down. "I'm less than two months old and I'm tired of living," he said. He walked out to the yard again.

"When I'm out here," he said, "there's no place to go but in. When I'm indoors, there's no place to go but out in the yard."

"That's where you're wrong, my friend, my friend," said a voice.

Wilbur looked through the fence and saw the goose standing there.

"You don't have to stay in that dirty-little dirty-little dirty-little yard," said the goose, who talked rather fast. "One of the boards is loose. Push on it, push-push-push on it, and come on out!"

"What?" said Wilbur. "Say it slower!"

"At-at-at, at the risk of repeating myself," said the goose, "I suggest that you come on out. It's wonderful out here."

"Did you say a board was loose?"

"That I did, that I did," said the goose.

Wilbur walked up to the fence and saw that the goose was right — one board was loose. He put his head down, shut his eyes, and pushed. The board gave way. In a minute he had squeezed through the fence and was standing in the long grass outside his yard. The goose chuckled.

"How does it feel to be free?" she asked.

"I like it," said Wilbur. "That is, I *guess* I like it."

Actually, Wilbur felt queer to be outside his fence, with nothing between him and the big world.

"Where do you think I'd better go?"

"Anywhere you like, anywhere you like," said the goose. "Go down through the orchard, root up the sod! Go down through the garden, dig up the radishes! Root up everything! Eat grass! Look for corn! Look for oats! Run all over! Skip and dance, jump and prance! Go down through the orchard and stroll in the woods! The world is a wonderful place when you're young."

"I can see that," replied Wilbur. He gave a jump in the air, twirled, ran a few steps, stopped, looked all around, sniffed the smells of afternoon, and then set off walking down through the orchard. Pausing in the shade of an apple tree, he put his strong snout into the ground and began pushing, digging, and rooting. He felt very happy. He had plowed up quite a piece of ground before anyone noticed him. Mrs. Zuckerman was the first to see him. She saw him from the kitchen window, and she immediately shouted for the men.

"Ho-*mer!*" she cried. "Pig's out! Lurvy! Pig's out! Homer! Lurvy! Pig's out. He's down there under that apple tree."

"Now the trouble starts," thought Wilbur. "Now I'll catch it."

The goose heard the racket and she, too, started hollering. "Run-run-run downhill, make for the woods, the woods!" she shouted to Wilbur. "They'll never-never-never catch you in the woods."

The cocker spaniel heard the commotion and he ran out from the barn to join the chase. Mr. Zuckerman heard, and he came out of the machine shed where he was mending a tool. Lurvy, the hired man, heard the noise and came up from the asparagus patch where he was pulling weeds. Everybody walked toward Wilbur and Wilbur didn't know what to do. The woods seemed a long way off, and anyway, he had never been down there in the woods and wasn't sure he would like it.

"Get around behind him, Lurvy," said Mr. Zuckerman, "and drive him toward the barn! And take it easy — don't rush him! I'll go and get a bucket of slops."

The news of Wilbur's escape spread rapidly among the animals on the place. Whenever any creature broke loose on Zuckerman's farm, the event was of great interest to the others. The goose shouted to the nearest cow that Wilbur was free, and soon all the cows knew. Then one of the cows told one of the sheep, and soon all the sheep knew. The lambs learned about it from their mothers. The horses, in their stalls in the barn, pricked up their ears when they heard the goose hollering; and soon the horses had caught on to what was happening. "Wilbur's out," they said. Every animal stirred and lifted its head and became excited to know that one of his friends had got free and was no longer penned up or tied fast.

Wilbur didn't know what to do or which way to run. It seemed as though everybody was after him. "If this is what it's like to be free," he thought, "I believe I'd rather be penned up in my own yard."

The cocker spaniel was sneaking up on him from one side, Lurvy the hired man was sneaking up on him from the other side. Mrs. Zuckerman stood ready to head him off if he started for the garden, and now Mr. Zuckerman was coming down toward him carrying a pail. "This is really awful," thought Wilbur. "Why doesn't Fern come?" He began to cry.

The goose took command and began to give orders.

"Don't just stand there, Wilbur! Dodge about, dodge about!" cried the goose. "Skip around, run toward me, slip in and out, in and out, in and out! Make for the woods! Twist and turn!"

The cocker spaniel sprang for Wilbur's hind leg. Wilbur jumped and ran. Lurvy reached out and grabbed. Mrs. Zuckerman screamed at Lurvy. The goose cheered for Wilbur. Wilbur dodged between Lurvy's legs. Lurvy missed Wilbur and grabbed the spaniel instead. "Nicely done, nicely done!" cried the goose. "Try it again, try it again!"

"Run downhill!" suggested the cows.

"Run toward me!" yelled the gander.

"Run uphill!" cried the sheep.

"Turn and twist!" honked the goose.

"Jump and dance!" said the rooster.

"Look out for Lurvy!" called the cows.

"Look out for Zuckerman!" yelled the gander.

"Watch out for the dog!" cried the sheep.

"Listen to me, listen to me!" screamed the goose.

Poor Wilbur was dazed and frightened by this hullabaloo. He didn't like being the center of all this fuss. He tried to follow the instructions his friends were giving him, but he couldn't run downhill and uphill at the same time, and he couldn't turn and twist when he was jumping and dancing, and he was crying so hard he could barely see anything that was happening. After all, Wilbur was a very young pig — not much more than a baby, really. He wished Fern were there to take him in her arms and comfort him. When he looked up and saw Mr. Zuckerman standing quite close to him, holding a pail of warm slops, he felt relieved. He lifted his nose and sniffed. The smell was delicious — warm milk, potato skins, wheat middlings, corn flakes, and a popover left from the Zuckermans' breakfast.

"Come, pig!" said Mr. Zuckerman, tapping the pail. "Come pig!"

Wilbur took a step toward the pail.

"No-no-no!" said the goose. "It's the old pail trick, Wilbur. Don't fall for it, don't fall for it! He's trying to lure you back into captivity-ivity. He's appealing to your stomach."

Wilbur didn't care. The food smelled appetizing. He took another step toward the pail.

"Pig, pig!" said Mr. Zuckerman in a kind voice, and began walking slowly toward the barnyard, looking all about him innocently, as if he didn't know that a little white pig was following along behind him.

"You'll be sorry-sorry-sorry," called the goose.

Wilbur didn't care. He kept walking toward the pail of slops.

"You'll miss your freedom," honked the goose. "An hour of freedom is worth a barrel of slops."

Wilbur didn't care.

When Mr. Zuckerman reached the pigpen, he climbed over the fence and poured the slops into the trough. Then he pulled the loose board away from the fence, so that there was a wide hole for Wilbur to walk through.

"Reconsider, reconsider!" cried the goose.

Wilbur paid no attention. He stepped through the fence into his yard. He walked to the trough and took a long drink of slops, sucking in the milk hungrily and chewing the popover. It was good to be home again.

While Wilbur ate, Lurvy fetched a hammer and some 8-penny nails and nailed the board in place. Then he and Mr. Zuckerman leaned lazily on the fence and Mr. Zuckerman scratched Wilbur's back with a stick.

"He's quite a pig," said Lurvy.

"Yes, he'll make a good pig," said Mr. Zuckerman.

Wilbur heard the words of praise. He felt the warm milk inside his stomach. He felt the pleasant rubbing of the stick along his itchy back. He felt peaceful and happy and sleepy. This had been a tiring afternoon. It was still only about four o'clock but Wilbur was ready for bed.

"I'm really too young to go out into the world alone," he thought as he lay down.

Author

E. B. White, the author of many books, was an editor and writer for *The New Yorker*. *Charlotte's Web,* from which "Wilbur's Escape" was taken, is the best-known of his three stories for children. Mr. White lived on a farm in Maine. He once said, "My barn was always a pleasant place to be, and I tried to bring it to life in a story for young people." *Charlotte's Web* was a Newbery Honor Book and won a Lewis Carroll Shelf Award.

BABE
The Gallant Pig
Dick King-Smith

Houghton Mifflin Literature

In each of the selections you have just read from *Accepting Challenges,* a character faced a difficult challenge with courage and determination.

Now you are going to read *Babe the Gallant Pig* by Dick King-Smith. Like Wilbur, Babe is a young pig who is scared and lonely in a new home. In this story, you will find out how Babe combines good manners and bravery to earn himself an honored place on the Hoggetts' farm.

4

Making Dreams Come True

Bicycle Rider

From the book by Mary Scioscia

Illustrated by J. Brian Pinkney

"Out of the way! Here I come! I'm winning!" shouted Marshall, pedaling his bicycle as fast as he could.

Walter laughed. "But I just won, Shorty. That line back there in the sidewalk is the finish line."

"I almost won," said Marshall, pulling up beside his big brother.

As they entered the kitchen, Mama said, "I'm glad you're home, boys. Walter, we need more wood for the stove. Marshall, please get me a bucket of water from the well. Supper is nearly ready."

Big sister Pearl stirred a huge pot of stew on the iron cookstove. Geneva popped a pan of biscuits into the oven. Carlton carried the eighth chair to the table. Ruth cuddled the baby in her arms as they went back and forth in the rocking chair. Papa stood in the hallway, brushing his red coachman's jacket. Walter set down an armload of wood beside the stove. Marshall brought Mama a bucket of water.

"Supper is ready," said Mama.

The Taylor family sat down together. They all bowed their heads; Papa said grace. Gaslights flickered above the table, making dancing shadows on everyone's face.

"Papa, I almost beat Walter today when we raced home from his job," said Marshall.

"It's true," Walter said as he passed the biscuits. "I'm glad I gave him my old bike."

"I declare," said Mama, "if that boy isn't faster than any horse and carriage in Indiana."

"I'm going to be just like you, Marshall, when I get big," whispered Carlton.

"Papa," said Marshall. "I want a job."

"You're too little to have a job," said Ruth. "You're one of the younger children."

"I'm the oldest of the younger children," said Marshall. "I can't be a carpenter yet, like Walter, or a coachman, like Papa, but I have my bike, and I'm a fast rider. I can deliver packages for a store."

"Maybe," said Papa.

"Can I try this Saturday?"

Papa looked at Mama. "What do you think?" he asked.

Mama nodded. "He's short," she said, "but he's a good bicycle rider, and dependable."

"Yes. You may try to find a job, son," said Papa.

"Not this Saturday," said Carlton. "You promised to take me to the bicycle store, Marshall, and to teach me the bicycle tricks you made up."

"Those tricks? They don't amount to a hill of beans, Carlton."

"Marshall, you promised," complained Carlton.

"All right. We'll go to the bicycle store *after* I look for a job. And I'll teach you the bicycle tricks, too."

On Saturday morning Marshall biked downtown. Mercer's dry goods store was the biggest store on Main Street. Rolls of brown wool and pink and yellow flowered calico were arranged behind gleaming scissors and brightly colored spools of thread in the store window. Inside the store, Mrs. Mercer stood behind the counter.

"Can I help you?" she asked Marshall.

"Yes, ma'am. I want a job. I have my own bicycle. Do you need someone to deliver packages?"

"Dear me, no," she said briskly. "We do everything ourselves. My husband delivers packages on his way home every night."

Next Marshall tried Caldwell's grocery store.

"Mr. Caldwell, sir," said Marshall. "I want a job as an errand boy. I have a bicycle. I'm a fast rider and I can deliver groceries."

Mr. Caldwell was arranging a pyramid of oranges. Slowly, he placed each orange in the design. When he put the last orange carefully at the top of the pyramid he stepped back to admire the arrangement. He patted his stomach.

"Well, young fellow," he finally drawled. "Caldwell's has its own delivery wagon drawn by two fine brown horses. Grocery orders are too big to go out on a bicycle. Come back another year, when you're bigger. We might be able to use you somewhere else in the business."

"Thank you, sir," said Marshall.

Grocery orders might be too big to go on a bicycle but medicines were always in small boxes. Marshall went to Smith's drugstore. Mr. Smith was making a chocolate soda for a woman and her little girl. Marshall stood waiting politely till he finished.

"What would you like?" asked Mr. Smith after he had served the woman and girl.

"I want a job, sir. Could I deliver medicines for you? I have my own bicycle, and I ride fast."

"Right now a high school boy named Roger does that for me. Come back next year, when Roger goes to college," said Mr. Smith.

At home for his midday meal, Marshall was downcast. "Shucks. Job hunting is hard. Everyone thinks I'm too small."

"Don't worry. Next year, when you're bigger, you'll get a job," Mama answered him.

In the afternoon, Carlton got up on the bicycle behind Marshall. They rode down Main Street to Hay and Willit's bicycle store.

"That's my favorite," said Marshall, pointing at a shiny red racing bicycle in the center of the window.

Carlton liked the funny one beside it with a big front wheel and a tiny back wheel. They both admired the sparkling gold medal pinned to a black velvet stand.

"Read me that sign," Carlton said.

"Hay and Willit's bicycle store. Best in Indianapolis. This gold medal will go to the winner of the ten-mile race. May 10, 1892," Marshall read.

"I bet you could win that race," said Carlton.

"Not me," said Marshall. "I'm not that fast. Even though I am almost as fast as Walter. Hey, Carlton. Look how wide the sidewalk is here in front of the store. Want me to show you some of the bike tricks now?"

Carlton clapped his hands. "Yes. Show me, Marshall."

Marshall lay on the bicycle seat and pushed the pedals with his hands. He helped Carlton do the same trick. People walking past the store stopped to look.

Marshall squatted on the bicycle seat and juggled three pennies. Carlton tried squatting on the seat, too. He couldn't do it. Marshall did the trick again.

More people stopped to watch.

A tall thin boy said, "That's a stupid trick. I bet you fall on your head."

A small girl said, "George Pepper, mind your manners."

More people stopped to watch. A coachman pulled his carriage over to the curb to see Marshall's tricks.

Marshall did a headstand on his bicycle seat. Then he rode his bicycle backward. Suddenly, the bicycle shop door opened and Mr. Hay stood in the doorway.

"Now you're in for it," jeered George Pepper. "You're in real trouble now!"

"Young man," called Mr. Hay. "I want to speak to you."

Marshall walked the bicycle over to Mr. Hay.

"Yes, sir?" said Marshall.

"Where did you learn those tricks?" asked Mr. Hay.

"I made them up, sir. I was just showing my little brother. He likes to see them."

"I don't wonder," said Mr. Hay.

"I'm sorry, sir, if we disturbed you."

"Disturbed us! Not at all! Those are the best bicycle tricks I've ever seen. My partner and I could use a boy like you. How would you like a job? We need someone to dust and sweep the store every day and to put coal in the potbellied stove. You could come here after school and on Saturdays to do these jobs. And if there is time, you could do your bicycle tricks in front of our store. It will make people want to come to this bicycle shop."

"Yes, sir!" cried Marshall.

"Start Monday after school," said Mr. Hay.

"I'll be here!" said Marshall.

Carlton climbed up behind Marshall on his bicycle.

As Marshall pedaled home, Carlton said, "It's funny. When you looked for a job, you didn't get one. When you didn't look for a job, you got one!"

Marshall liked his job. He didn't even mind the dusting. Every day he took the medal out and polished it

carefully. Once, when he was alone in the store, Marshall
unpinned the gold medal and stuck it onto his shirt. He
looked at his reflection in the glass case. He turned a little
so the light glinted on the gold.

It was fun to pretend that Mr. Hay had given him the
medal because he could ride faster than anybody else.

"But what if Mr. Hay sees me wearing this medal?"
Marshall thought. "He might get angry."

Marshall put the medal back into the case.

One Saturday Mr. Hay said, "Today you and I are
going to spend the day at the bicycle race track. I need
your help taking bicycles, extra wheels, and riding clothes
out to the track. We usually sell quite a few items on
racing days. Mr. Willit and I thought you'd enjoy working there with me. And you'll be able to see the big
ten-mile race, too."

Hundreds of people were in the grandstand. Children stood by the fence at the edge of the track and looked through the metal crisscrosses. Mr. Hay gave his tickets to the gateman, and he and Marshall walked inside to a booth near the edge of the track. They set out the wheels and shirts and shorts on the counter. Mr. Hay leaned the bicycles against the side of the booth.

More than a hundred racers in bright jersey tops and black shorts stood near the starting line. Beside every racer there was someone holding the bicycle.

"Each rider needs someone to push him off," said Mr. Hay.

"Can't they push off with one of their own feet?" Marshall asked.

Mr. Hay shook his head. "Racers' feet have to be clipped to the pedals. And they have a fixed gear."

At the judges' stand, a man stood up and shouted through a huge megaphone, "Attention, everyone! All those entering the one-mile race, line up at the starting line."

"One-mile race?" said Marshall. "Isn't it ten miles?"

"There will be several short races before the main event," said Mr. Hay.

"I see a lot of our customers lining up to be in the race," said Marshall.

"Land's sakes, Marshall! You just gave me an idea. You should ride in one of the short races. It would remind people of our store."

"Would they let me?"

"I'll ask the judges," said Mr. Hay.

When Mr. Hay came back, he said, "You can ride in the next one-mile race. Come with me to the dressing

room and put on these shorts and this yellow shirt. Choose any one of the bikes we brought."

At the starting line, Mr. Hay said, "Each time around the track is one lap. Five laps make a mile. Don't worry if you forget how many laps you've gone. When you hear the bell ring, you will know it is the bell lap. That means one left to go."

Marshall got on the bicycle. Mr. Hay held it steady while Marshall clipped his feet onto the pedals. A tall thin boy in a red shirt got in line next to Marshall.

"George Pepper!" thought Marshall, wishing George weren't right next to him.

"What are you doing in this race, runt?" said George. "You won't last one lap."

"Come on, George, leave him alone," said another racer. "That's the boy who does those good tricks at the bicycle shop."

"You mean those stupid tricks," said George.

The man in charge blew a whistle. All the racers leaned over their handlebars. Their helpers held the bicycles steady. The man raised his pistol in the air.

"One! Two! Three!" the starter shouted.

Bang! went the pistol.

Mr. Hay gave Marshall a strong push. He shot ahead of George Pepper. A tall boy got ahead of Marshall. Four more people got ahead. Marshall rode past one of them. George came up even with Marshall.

"I'm warning you, runt. You better stay behind me."

Marshall pushed his legs as hard as he could. But George got ahead.

Around and around the racers went. Now there were seven people ahead of Marshall.

Ding, ding, ding, the bell rang.

One more lap to go for the mile. Marshall speeded up.

A racer crossed the finish line. Two more. Another. Next was George Pepper in the red shirt. Right after George came the tall boy.

Then Marshall crossed the line. Mr. Hay hurried over to help Marshall stop.

"You came in number seven. That's great!" said Mr. Hay.

"It wasn't very good," said Marshall. "Six people beat me."

"But you beat over forty people. And you've never even been in a race before. You're good enough to try the ten-mile race."

"Oh, no," said Marshall. "I could never win that."

"No," agreed Mr. Hay. "You couldn't win. But I think you could finish. Try it, Marshall. If you get too tired, you just stop. Many racers will drop out before the fifty laps are done."

During the next race, Mr. Hay spoke to the judges again. Marshall rested with the other riders in the grassy center of the track.

"Good news," said Mr. Hay, joining Marshall. "You can try the ten-mile race."

Marshall wheeled his bicycle over to the starting line.

"Don't try to go too fast at first," said Mr. Hay. "Just keep up with the others, if you can. Save your energy for the sprints."

"What is a sprint?" asked Marshall.

"A sprint means going extra fast for one lap. Whoever passes the finish line first gets points toward winning."

"How will I know when it's time to sprint?"

"The bell rings at the start of the fifth lap. Each mile there will be a sprint race on the fifth lap."

Marshall looked at the riders lining up. "Whew!" he said. "It looks as if all the racers entered this race."

Mr. Hay nodded. "A hundred and seventeen bike racers are in the ten-mile race."

Marshall's bicycle wobbled a little as Marshall bent down to clip his feet onto the pedals. Mr. Hay steadied it.

Marshall could feel his heart thumping hard. His hands felt slippery on the bicycle handles.

"Here," said Mr. Hay. "Use my handkerchief to dry your hands."

The whistle blew. Marshall's legs felt shaky.

"One!" shouted the man. "Two! Three!"

Bang!

Mr. Hay shoved Marshall's bicycle so hard, Marshall could smell the dust that flew up. Marshall pushed his legs down. Around and around went the wheels.

The riders rode in a close pack. Two bicycles bumped and one fell. Marshall swerved around the fallen bicycle and rider. He almost hit another bicycle. Marshall swerved again. It was George Pepper's bicycle.

"Hey, runt," shouted George. "Out of my way."

Ding, ding, ding! The bell lap!

Marshall pulled ahead of the pack for the sprint. George Pepper passed him. Three more riders passed him. Then two more. Marshall pushed his legs hard. He passed one rider, then another. He crossed the finish line.

The first sprint was over. He could hear the crowd cheering. Nine more miles to go! Marshall wondered who had won that sprint. It was hard to know who was ahead, because the riders kept going around and around the track. When Marshall passed someone, he wondered if that person had already done more laps than he had.

Around and around they all went. Marshall's legs ached. His chest felt tight.

"I hope I can finish the first half of the race," he said to himself.

Ding, ding, ding! Another bell lap. Everyone pushed harder. Marshall shot forward. He passed George Pepper.

George caught up with Marshall and passed him. George crossed the finish line just ahead of Marshall, but it was impossible for Marshall to know who had won the sprint. The racers were no longer riding in a close pack. They were strung out along the whole track. A few riders had dropped out.

Around and around. Around and around.

When the bell rang, Marshall couldn't remember which sprint it was. His breath came in noisy puffs. More riders dropped out of the race.

Marshall's throat felt dry. His mouth tasted dusty. His legs hurt.

"I want to drop out," Marshall thought. "I can't make the halfway mark."

Someone shouted, "Hurray, Marshall Taylor!"

It made Marshall feel glad. He felt stronger. "Maybe I can finish a few more laps," he thought.

His bicycle went faster. Around the track. Around and around. There were more bell laps and more sprints. Marshall lost count. Around and around. His damp shirt stuck to his back. His legs ached. His back was sore from being bent over the handlebars.

The people in the grandstand stamped their feet and cheered. He heard Mr. Hay, standing at the edge of the track, shout, "Last lap coming up next!"

Ding, ding, ding!

Marshall pushed with all his strength. The wheels seemed to say, "Got to finish. Got to finish."

Scrunch.

He heard the sound of clashing metal and felt his rear wheel being pushed.

"Out of my way," shouted George, trying to knock him down.

A man at the edge of the track blew his whistle.

"Foul!" he shouted. "George Pepper. Over to the side!"

George pretended he didn't hear. He tried to get ahead of Marshall. The man blew his whistle again. Marshall rode past George. Several riders seemed to be riding exactly even with one another. Marshall speeded over the finish line. Everyone was so close, he couldn't tell who was ahead or behind. His bicycle was going so fast he couldn't stop. He went around another lap to slow down.

Marshall heard the crowd shout something that sounded like "Marshall Taylor! Marshall Taylor!" Hats and programs flew into the air.

Mr. Hay hurried over to Marshall to hold his bicycle. He hugged him.

"You won, Marshall. You won!"

"Who? Me!" said Marshall.

The judges held up their hands to quiet the crowd. Then a man with a megaphone shouted, "Marshall Taylor, the winner by sixteen seconds! Marshall Taylor has won the annual Indianapolis ten-mile bicycle race!"

The crowd cheered and clapped and stamped their feet.

Mr. Hay and Marshall walked to the judges' platform. A judge gave Marshall the gold medal.

A thunder of applause came from the audience.

Marshall felt as if he were in the middle of a dream.

At supper that night, Marshall's legs ached so much it hurt to sit on his chair.

"What's the matter with you?" Carlton asked. "You're sitting in a funny way."

Marshall shrugged and gave no answer. He waited until the whole family was seated for supper and had finished saying grace. Then he held up the gold medal.

"What's that, son?" asked Papa.

"It's the gold medal for the ten-mile race," said Marshall.

"Did Mr. Hay say you could take it out of the store window?" asked Carlton.

"Out of the store window!" cried Mama. "Son, what have you done?"

Everybody stopped eating. Papa frowned.

"Marshall Taylor! Have you brought home something that does not belong to you?"

Marshall grinned. "I won it," he said.

Mama sucked in her breath. "Marshall, are you telling a story?"

"No. Honest, Mama. I won it."

Papa said sternly, "Explain what you mean, Marshall Taylor."

"I rode in the bicycle race today. Mr. Hay took me to help sell bicycle equipment at the track. Then he said, why didn't I enter, too. He said I could drop out if I got tired."

"Are you talking about the *big* ten-mile race? Fifty times around the track?" asked Walter.

Marshall nodded.

"You've never raced before. How could you go fifty laps without stopping?" Pearl asked.

"It was Mr. Hay's idea," Marshall explained. "I didn't think I could even finish the race. Over a hundred started. Lots dropped out before the end. But I kept going. And I won!"

Carlton touched the bright medal. "Can you keep it always?"

Marshall grinned and nodded. "I can keep it forever."

Mama jumped up and ran to hug Marshall. "Son, you are really something."

Everyone else jumped up, too. Walter shook his hand. Pearl and Ruth hugged him. Papa clapped him on the back.

"Congratulations, son!"

"I knew you wouldn't lie," said Carlton. "And I knew all along that you were the best bicycle rider in Indiana."

Epilogue

Marshall Taylor became the fastest bicycle rider in the world. Nicknamed Major Taylor because he stood so straight, he was the first black person to participate in national bicycle races that were integrated. His first professional race in 1896 was at Madison Square Garden in New York City. During the years from 1896 to 1910 he raced in the U.S.A., Europe, and Australia. Several times he won American and World Championships.

Bicycle racing was a major sport in the late 1800's and early 1900's. Huge crowds would go to see any race Major Taylor rode in. All the newspapers would cover the event.

Taylor was especially loved by his fans for his remarkable riding skills and for his fairness and good sportsmanship.

Author

Bicycle Rider is Mary Scioscia's first book for children. Mrs. Scioscia was born in Canada and has lived in California, where her sons were in amateur bicycle races. Because of their racing, she became interested in Marshall Taylor and his exciting achievements.

Maria's House

**From the book
by Jean Merrill**

*Illustrated by
Eileen McKeating*

"Maria, Maria!"

Mama looked in the door of Maria's room.

"Today is Saturday," Mama said. "Wake up. You will be late for the art class."

Maria lay in bed staring at a crack in the ceiling. She did not want to go to her art class today.

Could she tell Mama that she was sick?

No. Mama would know.

Usually, Maria could not wait for Saturday morning. She loved her art class at the museum. And she loved Miss Lindstrom, her beautiful art teacher.

Usually, Maria was so excited on Saturday morning that she woke up even before the Sanitation Department started banging down the garbage cans outside her window. She would be up and dressed before Mama had set the table for breakfast.

She would brush and braid her hair. Then it would take a long time to decide which of her three smocks she would wear.

Mama had made her three smocks for the art class — a blue one, a yellow one, and a tan one. "Art coats" Mama called them. They were exactly like the smocks Maria's art teacher wore. Except that all Miss Lindstrom's smocks were blue.

When Maria came into the kitchen on Saturday morning, Mama would look up to see which smock she was wearing.

"Ah, pretty," Mama would say. "Pretty color on you."

Mama always said "pretty" — no matter which of the three smocks Maria chose.

Maria knew that Mama looked forward to Saturday as

much as she did. Mama always looked very pleased with herself as she brought out the old brown teapot in which she kept the money she earned from ironing shirts for the Overnite Laundry.

Every Saturday morning it was the same. Mama would count out three quarters from the teapot — two for Maria's bus fare to the museum, and an extra one "just in case of something."

Mama would hand the quarters to Maria. Then she would stand at the kitchen door, holding Maria's portfolio, while Maria put on her coat.

"Art bag" Mama called the portfolio. Mama had bought the portfolio at an uptown art store for Maria's birthday.

"Special art bag, so pictures should not be damaged on the way to art class," Mama had explained.

Only two other girls in the class had portfolios. Two other girls and Miss Lindstrom. Maria was very proud of her portfolio.

Everything about Saturday morning made it seem a special day — the clean smock, the three quarters in her coat pocket, Mama's handing her the portfolio. Maria always felt taller than usual as she walked down to the corner of Market Street to get the bus to the museum.

Her friends, in their Saturday clothes, would be playing on the street as Maria, scrubbed and neat, hurried past, carrying her portfolio. Her friends would stare curiously at her.

Most of them did not understand why anyone would want to go to a class on Saturday. But they were not artists.

Maria even liked the long bus ride across town to the

museum. She liked watching the city change from block to block.

First there were the streets near the river. Busy and noisy. People sitting on steps. Boys playing stickball in the street.

Then there were the clean, modern buildings with wide glass windows in the uptown shopping district. And finally the bus would turn up a quiet tree-lined avenue of old houses that were set far back from the street. This was the part of town where the museum was.

Watching the city flow past her was like being at a movie. The pictures Maria saw framed in the bus window kept changing.

Yes, everything about Saturday was wonderful. And knowing that Saturday was coming made the rest of the week wonderful, too.

All week Maria could dream that the next Saturday might be the day that Miss Lindstrom would stop at her easel and admire the drawing there. Might even choose her drawing to go on the bulletin board that ran around two sides of the large room in which the art class was held.

That hadn't happened yet. Maybe it wouldn't for a long time.

Miss Lindstrom was always kind and encouraging. But she praised you only when your work was very, very good. If one small detail in a drawing pleased Miss Lindstrom, it was enough to make Maria happy all week.

Once Maria had drawn purely for the fun of it, filling notebook after notebook with pictures. Decorating the margins of her school books, and making birthday cards for her friends.

But since Mama had been sending her to the classes at the museum, Maria had begun to draw with one purpose — to make a painting or drawing that Miss Lindstrom would find beautiful.

That was why she could not make herself get out of bed this Saturday. Maria did not want to show Miss Lindstrom the picture that she had finished last night.

The Saturday before, Miss Lindstrom had given the class an assignment to do at home. Usually, Maria was very happy when Miss Lindstrom suggested assignments to be done outside of class.

Such assignments gave Maria a whole week to plan the beautiful picture she would draw for Miss Lindstrom. Drawing or painting in class, Maria never felt she had enough time to make a picture as perfect as she would have liked. She often had a better idea on the bus going home.

Then, too, when there were outside assignments, Miss Lindstrom would come around to her easel at least twice during class. Once to look at the work she'd done at home. Then again to see what she was doing in class.

So Maria had been pleased last week when Miss Lindstrom gave them a special assignment. It wasn't until she got off the bus at Market Street that she realized that she could not do it.

Miss Lindstrom had asked the class to make paintings or drawings of the houses where they lived. As Maria walked down Market Street after class, she saw suddenly that she could not take Miss Lindstrom a picture of the building in which her family and fourteen other families lived.

Miss Lindstrom had said to draw a house. Maria did not think of the building in which she lived as a "house."

It was just an ugly, old building. Squeezed into the middle of a block of ugly buildings, each one as tired and worn-out looking as the next. How could she make a beautiful picture of 79 Market Street?

Inside the building, the apartment where Maria lived looked bright and fresh. Mama and Papa scrubbed the kitchen floor every day and put new paint on the walls every year.

"Can't put up beautiful pictures on dirty walls," Mama said. Mama had Maria's best paintings and drawings pinned up in every one of the apartment's three rooms.

The apartment looked nice enough. But from outside, the building looked terrible.

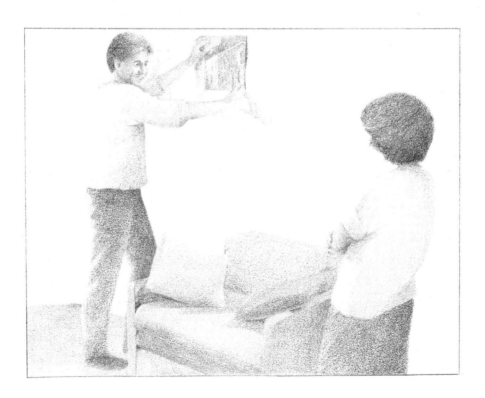

Maria was sure that when Miss Lindstrom said to draw a house, that she was thinking of a house where one family lived, a neat, freshly painted building set apart from other houses by grass, gardens, and shade trees. The kind of house that would have a front yard and a backyard with flowering bushes planted here and there. A house with a private driveway, and even a private sidewalk leading from the city sidewalk up to the front door.

The other children in the art class probably all lived in such houses. Out on the edge of the city, just before you came to the country.

Why, of course. That was why the parents of many of them drove them to the museum on Saturday morning.

Maria had been thinking that their parents brought them to the museum because they did not trust them, as Mama trusted her, to take the bus by themselves.

That wasn't it at all. It was that they lived so far from the center of the city. The city buses didn't run out there.

Of course. They all lived miles and miles from the noisy, dirty streets of the city. In beautiful houses. On streets that looked like parks.

None of them lived in buildings like those on Market Street. Nobody on Market Street sent their children to art classes at the museum. Except Mama.

Miss Lindstrom probably thought Maria lived in the same sort of house as the rest of the class. When Maria walked into the museum on Saturday, she was always neatly dressed, and she had her beautiful portfolio. How would Miss Lindstrom know that she lived on Market Street?

Maria had worried all week about the assignment. How could she do it? There was no way of making a rundown tenement building look beautiful, if you drew it the way it was.

Could she make a little watercolor painting of the inside of the apartment? Perhaps of the sunny corner of the kitchen where Mama had her spice shelf and the pots of basil and parsley growing?

But she would have to explain to Miss Lindstrom why she had drawn the inside of a house, instead of the whole house.

Maria had put off doing the assignment all week. Then last night, Friday night, she had opened her drawing pad on the kitchen table.

She had a new set of colored markers that Mama had bought her. She wanted to do a drawing with the markers.

She tried all the colors on the cover of the pad. Then she sat for a long time, staring at a clean sheet of drawing paper. Finally, she started to draw.

She drew a large white house with picture windows. The windows looked out over a wide lawn that sloped down to a pond.

Maria sketched in a winding driveway with birch trees on either side. To one side of the house, she drew a stone terrace and colored in some chairs, covered in a gay, striped cloth.

She wondered if she should put a car in the driveway. Or a station wagon.

No, she decided. Miss Lindstrom might have seen her getting off the Eastside bus in front of the museum.

At the far end of the driveway, Maria drew a figure of a girl on a bicycle.

Mama, who was ironing one of Maria's smocks, looked over at the drawing.

"Pretty," Mama nodded. "Like a picture in the magazines. But what are you drawing for the art class?"

"This is for class," Maria said.

"A *magazine* picture?" Mama said.

Mama had learned a lot about art, and she knew by now that art was not like a picture in a magazine. So when she asked about the house, Maria could not lie to her.

"We have to draw a house this week," she said.

"Just a house," Mama said. "Any house? Just a plain house?"

Maria did not answer for a minute. Then she told Mama, "It's supposed to be a picture of the house where we live."

"Oh," Mama said. She looked at Maria's picture again.

"Our house?" she said.

"No," Maria said. "I can't draw our house."

"Can't *draw* it?" Mama said. "Before you ever went to art class, you could draw a whole block of houses burning down and five fire engines and ten cops and a hundred people in the picture. Now you can't draw one house?"

"That's not what I mean," Maria said.

Maria tried to explain to Mama that a three-room apartment on Market Street wasn't the same as a house. And so to do the assignment, she would have to imagine a house.

"But a three-room apartment is *in* a house," Mama said. "So it's a big house. Apartment house. Your teacher means draw where you live."

Maria jabbed a pencil into the kitchen table.

"Oh, Mama!" she said. "This house is no good to draw. How can I make a beautiful picture of this house? I was trying to make a beautiful picture."

Mama looked down at the house Maria had drawn and shook her head.

"It's nice art should be beautiful," Mama said. "But it should also be true. Your teacher asks you to draw what you know."

Maria did not say anything. What was wrong with using her imagination? An artist should be able to imagine things, too.

But the picture did look like a magazine picture. Mama was right about that.

Maria tore the picture from her drawing pad and slipped it into her portfolio. She started another drawing.

She sketched in the outline of the house she lived in. With angry slashes of a marker, she drew the rusted fire escape zigzagging down the front of the building. She drew the sagging window frames and the crumbling cement steps leading up to the front door.

There were the broken windows in Mrs. Sedita's apartment on the ground floor. The landlord had refused to fix them, and Mrs. Sedita had had cardboard tacked over the missing panes for a year.

On the windowsill outside the Durkins' apartment, Maria drew three milk cartons. The power company kept turning off the Durkins' electricity, and Mrs. Durkin had to put her milk on the windowsill to keep it cool.

Maria drew Mrs. Katz leaning out of a third-floor window, screaming at a bum slumped on the steps below.

Then she took a marker and lettered on the front of the building the words some kids had painted there in a nasty green color a long time ago.

She was drawing very fast. Putting in all the things that made the building look so sad, old, tired, dirty, and ugly. Mama would see that she could not take a picture like this to Miss Lindstrom.

Maria paused and looked at her drawing.

It was 79 Market Street all right. And she hadn't had to go out and look at the building. She knew exactly how it looked.

Except that she had forgotten to put in the carved stone heads. They were the only thing she really liked about the building.

Between the first and second floors, just above the first-floor windows, were four carved stone heads. When

the building was built, eighty or ninety years ago, the four stone heads had been set into the brickwork to decorate the building.

Under the heads were four names carved into the stone bases: BACH,[1] MOZART,[2] BEETHOVEN,[3] and WAGNER.[4] Mr. Bocci, the super, had told Maria that they were the names of four famous musicians.

"This was probably some fancy building when it was built," Mr. Bocci said.

If the man who built it could see it now, Maria thought as she chose a gray marker and carefully drew in the stone heads.

She knew the exact expression on each musician's face, and how each musician's hair was carved. She was just finishing Bach's funny little sausage curls when Mama came over to look.

Mama studied the picture for a long time.

"It's true," she said finally. "It's Market Street."

Mama sighed. "You take to art class?"

"Mama! I can't."

It *was* true. It *was* Market Street. And Maria was afraid she was going to cry.

She ripped the picture off the pad and stuffed it into her portfolio. She put away her markers and pencils, washed, and went to bed.

Maria heard Mama come into her room much later to hang a freshly ironed smock in her closet. Mama stood at

---

[1]**Bach** (bäKH)

[2]**Mozart** (**mōt′** särt′)

[3]**Beethoven** (bā′ tō vən)

[4]**Wagner** (**väg′** nər)

the foot of her bed for a minute, as if she wanted to say something. But Maria pretended to be asleep.

What difference would it make which drawing she showed Miss Lindstrom? Miss Lindstrom would not know that the first drawing was an imaginary house. Only Mama knew.

Only Mama. Mama, who never complained about the hours she spent ironing for the Overnite Laundry. Working sometimes until long after Papa and Maria were asleep.

But last night Maria had not been able to sleep. Even so, morning had come too fast. And now she lay in bed listening to the Sanitation Department throwing the garbage cans down on the sidewalk, and could not make herself get up.

Maria heard Mama calling her for the second time.

No, she could not tell Mama she was sick.

Maria dressed, braided her hair, and put on her yellow smock.

When Mama said, "Pretty," as Maria came into the kitchen, Maria could not look Mama in the eye.

Mama did not say much at breakfast. And when she took down the brown teapot and fished out the three quarters, Maria wanted to say, "Please, Mama, try to understand."

But she couldn't say it. And when Mama went to wake up Papa, Maria knew what she had to do.

She opened up her portfolio and took out the drawing of the white house with the picture windows. She looked at the drawing for a minute. Then she tore it up and put it in the garbage can.

Mama must have known. She nodded her head in a proud stern way as Maria went out the door.

Maria felt better as she walked to the bus stop. But once on the bus, she began to think about Miss Lindstrom again, and wished she had stayed home.

She hunched down in her seat and stared out the window. It wasn't like watching a movie this morning. The city streets flashed by in the crazy way they do in a dream that is going too fast and is going to end in a terrible way. And suddenly the bus was at the museum.

Maria walked quickly through the big entrance room. Usually, she walked very slowly through this room. She loved its high ceilings and the sunlight slanting down through windows placed high on the outside walls. The sound of her footsteps echoing from the stone walls and the serious faces of the six lions who guarded the hallway that led to the art class made Maria feel as if she were a distinguished person arriving at a great palace for an important occasion.

But this morning Maria hurried past the lions without a glance.

Most of the kids in the class were already at their easels when Maria came in, and were pinning up the drawings they had done during the week.

If only she'd come a few minutes earlier, Maria thought, she might have gone up and explained quietly to Miss Lindstrom that she'd forgotten to bring her drawing. Had forgotten to do the assignment even.

Coming in late, though, Maria felt as if everyone was watching her. Quickly, she opened up her portfolio and took out her drawing.

Her hands were clumsy as she tacked the drawing to her easel, afraid someone might laugh. But no one did.

Glancing over her shoulder, Maria saw that the other students were looking at their own work, some of them adding a few lines to their pictures. Or trying to smudge out bits they didn't like.

Miss Lindstrom was already walking around, looking at what everyone had done. At one easel, she would nod and smile. At another, she would ask a question. Now and then she would call the whole class to look at something unusual in someone's drawing.

Maria trailed behind the others, hardly hearing what the silvery voice was saying.

Most of the drawings on the easels were of houses with yards and trees as Maria had expected. But many of the houses pictured were less grand than she'd imagined.

None as grand as the one she'd wanted to draw for Miss Lindstrom.

And there was one picture that surprised Maria because the house in it looked quite old and shabby. The house was set in a big yard and had a funny tower on one side, which perhaps had made it look very handsome at one time. But the house looked now as if it needed painting, and there was one very messy-looking corner of the yard with a lot of boards and boxes scattered around.

A redheaded boy named Jasper had painted the picture. Jasper pointed to the house in the painting.

"This is where I live," he told Miss Lindstrom. "But over here is where I'm *going* to live." He pointed to the boards and boxes.

"That's the most important part of the picture," he explained. "I'm building my own house out here. I'm

designing it myself, and it's going to be really beautiful."

Miss Lindstrom laughed. "Is it going to have a tower?" she asked.

"Certainly not," Jasper said. "It's going to be a very modern house. With see-through walls that you can walk through to get outdoors."

The whole class laughed, and then Miss Lindstrom talked a little about how it was clear from the way Jasper had placed the house off to one side in the picture that the messy pile of boards *was* the most important part of the picture.

There was always something funny in Jasper's paintings, a kind of crazy way of looking at things. But Miss Lindstrom seemed to like Jasper's work.

Maria was puzzling over this when Miss Lindstrom moved over to her easel. Maria's hands felt cold. Her mouth felt dry. She wanted to run down the hall to the washroom and hide. But she just stood there by Jasper's easel, watching Miss Lindstrom.

Maria caught the brief look of surprise on Miss Lindstrom's face and wished she could sink through the floor.

Miss Lindstrom did not say anything for a minute. Then she looked around for Maria.

"Maria," she called. "Come." She put an arm around Maria's shoulder.

"Everyone come here," she called.

The rest of the class crowded around Maria's easel.

"Maria didn't quite understand the assignment," Miss Lindstrom was saying. "But it doesn't matter. Look what she's done."

Miss Lindstrom stepped back so that everyone could see.

"I'd meant for you to draw your own house," Miss Lindstrom said to Maria. "But what you've done is very interesting."

Miss Lindstrom asked the class whether any of them had ever driven through Carpenter Street, Market Street, or Water Street — the old part of town down near the river.

"I have," Jasper said. "My uncle goes there to buy fish."

"If any of you have," Miss Lindstrom said, "you will see how perfectly Maria has caught the feeling of the crowded tenements in that part of town.

"Look." Miss Lindstrom bent over Maria's drawing. "See here," she said, " — and here — and here — " The art teacher's beautiful hands touched the paper lightly.

"So many beautiful things," she said.

Miss Lindstrom pointed to Mrs. Katz's laundry strung across the fire escape on the third floor. To the cats fighting over a spilled garbage can in front of the house. To a tired figure leaning on a windowsill. To the milk cartons on another sill.

"I can almost hear the kids yelling in the street," Miss Lindstrom said. "I can hear people yelling, laughing, and crying inside the apartments. I can smell spaghetti cooking. And chicken soup."

"Not me," Jasper said. "I smell fish."

Miss Lindstrom laughed. "You're right, Jasper. I can smell that, too. There's so much going on in this house."

"And these heads," she said. "Look at these. When this building was built years ago, someone lovingly carved

262

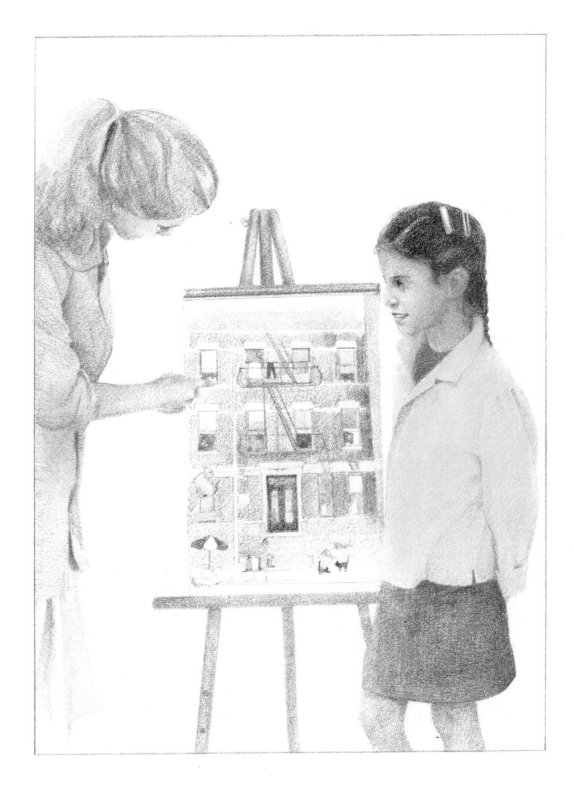

those heads, and Maria has drawn them so lovingly that you can feel the care the stonecutter took in carving them."

"Hey, that's Beethoven!" Jasper said, pointing to one of the heads.

"How did you know?" Maria asked in surprise. Because she had not put the musicians' names under the heads.

"I saw his picture in a book once," Jasper said.

Miss Lindstrom asked the class if they knew that there was an exhibition of carved stone heads, like those in Maria's drawing, on the top floor of the museum. They were taken from old buildings in the city, before the buildings were torn down, she said.

Maria looked at her drawing. Would Bach, Mozart, Beethoven, and Wagner be in the museum someday? She tried to imagine their faces looking down on museum visitors instead of her friends on Market Street.

Miss Lindstrom was talking to the class again.

"Does everyone see what is so good about Maria's drawing?" she asked.

"All those little details," one girl said. "The heads, the cats, the milk cartons, and the writing on the front of the building."

"No," another girl said. "All those bits are nice. Maria can draw anything. But what's really good is that her picture isn't just a picture of a building. You feel as if you know the people who live in it."

"Yes," Miss Lindstrom said. "That's it. It's a beautiful drawing, Maria. Full of life and feeling. The nicest thing you've done this year." She gave Maria a hug and moved on to another easel.

Maria stood staring at her picture.

Miss Lindstrom had hugged her and told her that her picture was beautiful. But it wasn't Miss Lindstrom with her spun-gold hair that Maria was seeing as she stared at her picture.

She was seeing Mama. Mama standing dark and stern over the ironing board. Mama saying stubbornly, "Art must be true." Mama standing and nodding gravely as Maria would tell her what Miss Lindstrom had said about her drawing today. . . .

Then Maria heard Miss Lindstrom say her name again.

"Maria's picture gave me an idea for next week's assignment," Miss Lindstrom was saying.

"Next week," she said, "I want each of you to visit a part of the city where you have never been before and to draw a picture of the houses there — or the stores — or the street.

"Except Maria," said Miss Lindstrom.

"Since you have already done that, Maria," she said, "maybe you would like to draw your own house next week."

Maria felt as if Mama's grave eyes were on her as she looked up at her art teacher and said in a clear, sure voice, "But that *is* my house in the picture."

Author

Jean Merrill worked as an editor in New York City. The description of Maria's apartment house comes from the author's knowledge of a big city. The popular *Toothpaste Millionaire* is another of Jean Merrill's books.

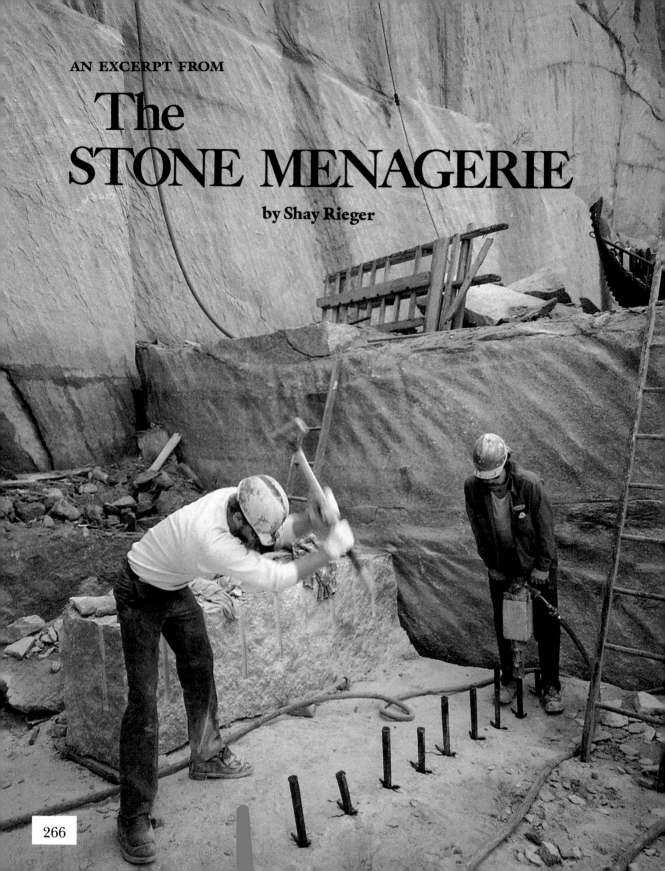

AN EXCERPT FROM

The STONE MENAGERIE

by Shay Rieger

CARVING IN STONE

As a sculptor I have worked with clay, plaster, wood, bronze, and stone. For me, carving in stone — because stone is so very hard — is the most exciting. When a block of marble is carved into a figure that is alive with form and feeling, I feel good.

Finding and Choosing Stones

Stones can be found everywhere. I have found them in the country, in city lots, and even in torn-down buildings. But most of the carving stones come from quarries. A quarry is a huge open hole in the earth from which stones are dug. The stones are then cut into different sizes and shipped to where they are needed. As a rule, I work with a stone I can handle. If a stone is very heavy, however, a pulley can be used for lifting and moving it.

Each stone has its own beauty. When choosing the right stone for my subject, I note the color and graining as well as the feel and shape of a stone. Sometimes the shape of a stone tells me what I should make. A piece of limestone that I found in a city lot was already formed like a snail. I carved it just a little, set it on a base, and had a finished piece. Most of the time, though, I pick a stone that looks nothing at all like what I want to make. I may just feel that the stone is beautiful or different.

Once the stones have been made into fish, insects, and other animals, they are sent to the art gallery. I believe that stone sculptures should be pleasant to the touch as well as to the eye. For this reason, there are no signs near my pieces that say "Do not touch."

Using Different Stones

The stones I use most often are marble, limestone, alabaster,[1] and granite.[2]

Granite is the hardest of all stone. It comes from deep inside the earth where it is so hot that the granite is a liquid. Over millions of years, the liquid rises to the surface of the earth. There it cools and becomes very hard. The colors of granite range from shades of pink and red to white and gray.

Limestone is a soft stone. It is the result of plants and the shells of sea animals having settled on the ocean floor and hardened. Limestone may be buff[3] or white or gray.

[1]**alabaster** (ăl′ ə băs′ tər)
[2]**granite** (grăn′ ĭt)

[3]**buff:** A yellowish tan color.

Above: Granite.
Left: Limestone.

Marble was once limestone. It was changed over the ages by heat from deep under the sea and by the weight of rocks and water bearing down on it. Marble comes in many beautiful colors. There are oranges, purples, and reds. Some marble is as white as snow, and some is as black as coal. One kind of marble, called serpentine,[4] is green and takes a high polish. It can be made as smooth as glass.

Alabaster is softer than most marble. Some alabaster stones are clear. Some are solid. Some have colorful patterns. The colors range from white, brown, and gold to soft pink with a shading of deep red.

---

[4]**serpentine** (**sûr′** pən tēn′)

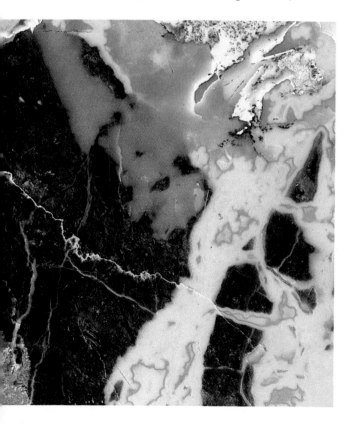

Left: Serpentine marble.
Right: Alabaster.

A praying mantis, like this one, was the model for a stone sculpture by Shay Rieger.

Planning a Sculpture

Let me describe how I carve a sculpture from the beginning. Let's take the praying mantis, for example. This is a pale green insect that folds its front legs as if in prayer when it is resting. I saw one in the country and made drawings of it.

As I begin to think about carving, I look at the drawings I made in the country. I note the mantis's long, narrow body and bulgy eyes and the front legs that look like hands.

I choose a serpentine stone because the shape and the jade green color seem right for the insect. Also, there is a hint of brown graining in the stone that reminds me of the earth.

Carving the Mantis

At the studio, everything is ready for work. These are the tools used for carving the stones. Hammers and chisels do most of the chopping. The files and electric sander are for shaping and smoothing. A sculptor must always wear goggles for protection against the flying chips of stone. A sculptor must also wear a mask to keep from breathing in the stone dust.

I now begin to carve the stone. In my left hand I hold the chisel. I aim it at the part of the stone I want to chop away. With my right hand, I hold the hammer and hit the top of the chisel. The chips start flying.

I chip away freely to rough out the shape of the mantis. At this stage, I pay little attention to detail.

I have cut away much of the stone. It is as though I were freeing the mantis that lay hidden within the rock.

Below: A stone carver's tools.
Right: A sculptor uses a special hammer to shape the stone she is carving.

The body of the insect has become quite clear now. I make tool marks to separate the base from the sculpture itself.

After much filing, rubbing, and sanding, the stone takes on a high polish.

I place two wires in the mantis's head. These are its antennae. Then I wipe away the stone dust with some clear oil.

After five weeks of work, the praying mantis is finished. It is set on a rosewood base. Then it is sent to the art gallery.

Author

While still a child, Shay Rieger began working with clay. Since then she has had all kinds of sculpture exhibited at galleries, libraries, schools, and museums. At one of her exhibits, she asked viewers to write down how they felt about her art. The questions children asked made Miss Rieger decide to write about how she forms her sculptures. That is how *The Stone Menagerie,* part of which you have just read, came to be written. Her books *Animals in Clay, Animals in Wood,* and *The Bronze Zoo* show the different materials with which she has worked.

An excerpt from

The Wright Brothers
Pioneers of American Aviation

by Quentin Reynolds

Illustrated by John Holder

Susan Wright wasn't like other mothers.

She was younger and prettier than most other mothers, and she liked to laugh and she liked to play games with her three youngest children; Wilbur, who was eleven; Orville, who was seven; and Katharine, who was four.

The other mothers would shake their heads and say, "Susan Wright spoils those children; lets 'em do anything they want. No good will come of it."

But Susan Wright only laughed. In the summer she'd pack a picnic lunch and she, the two boys and little Kate (no one ever called her Katharine) would go and spend a day in the woods. Mrs. Wright knew the name of every bird and she could tell a bird by his song. Wilbur and Orville learned to tell birds too.

One day they sat on the banks of a river near Dayton, where they lived. Wilbur and Orville were fishing. Everyone called Wilbur "Will," and of course Orville was "Orv." The fish weren't biting very well. Suddenly a big bird swooped down, stuck his long bill into the river, came out with a tiny fish, and then swooped right up into the sky again.

"What makes a bird fly, Mother?" Wilbur asked.

"Their wings, Will," she said. "You notice they move their wings and that makes them go faster."

"But Mother," Will said, not quite satisfied, "that bird that just swooped down didn't even move his wings. He swooped down, grabbed a fish, and then went right up again. He never moved his wings at all."

"The wind doesn't just blow *toward* you or *away* from you," she said. "It blows *up* and *down,* too. When a current of air blows up, it takes the bird up. His wings support him in the air."

"If we had wings, then we could fly too, couldn't we, Mother?" Wilbur asked.

"But God didn't give us wings." She laughed.

"Maybe we could make wings," Wilbur insisted.

"Maybe," his mother said thoughtfully. "But I don't know. No one ever did make wings that would allow a boy to fly."

"I will some day," Wilbur said, and Orville nodded and said, "I will, too."

"Well, when you're a little older maybe you can try," their mother said.

That was another thing about Susan Wright. Most other mothers would have said, "Oh, don't be silly, who ever heard of such nonsense!" But not Susan Wright. She knew that even an eleven-year-old boy can have ideas of his own, and just because they happened to come from an eleven-year-old head — well, that didn't make them foolish. She never treated her children as if they were babies, and perhaps that's why they liked to go fishing with her or on picnics with her. And that's why they kept asking her questions. She always gave them sensible answers.

They asked their father questions too, but he was a traveling minister and he was away a lot.

"It's getting chilly," Mrs. Wright said suddenly. "Look at those gray clouds, Will."

Wilbur looked up. "It's going to snow, I bet," he said happily.

"No more picnics until next Spring," his mother said.

"Yes, it looks like snow. We'd better be getting home."

As they reached home, the first big white snowflakes started to fall. They kept falling all that night and all the next day. It was the first real snowstorm of the year.

In the morning the wind was blowing so fiercely that Wilbur found it hard to walk to the barn where the wood was stored. The wind was so strong it almost knocked him down. He burst through the kitchen door with an armful of wood for the stove, and he told his mother about the wind.

"The thing to do is to lean forward into the wind," she said. "Bend over, and that way you get closer to the ground and you get under the wind."

That night, when Wilbur had to make the trip for more wood, he tried his mother's idea. To his surprise it worked! When he was bent over, the wind didn't seem nearly so strong.

After a few days the wind stopped, and now the whole countryside was covered with snow. Wilbur and Orville, with little Kate trailing behind, hurried to the Big Hill not far from the house.

Orville's schoolmates were all there with their sleds. It was a good hill to coast down because no roads came anywhere near it, and even if they had, it wouldn't have mattered. This was 1878 and there were no automobiles. Horse-drawn sleighs traveled the roads in winter. The horses had bells fastened to their collars, and as they jogged along the bells rang and you could hear them a mile away.

Most of the boys had their own sleds; not the flexible fliers boys have now, but old-fashioned sleds with two wooden runners. No one ever thought of owning a "bought" sled. In those days a boy's father made a sled for him.

The boys who had sleds of their own let Wilbur and Orville ride down the hill with them. Ed Sines and Chauncey Smith and Johnny Morrow and Al Johnston all owned sleds, but they liked to race one another down the long hill. When this happened Wilbur and Orville just had to stand there and watch. Late that afternoon the boys came home, with little Kate trailing behind, and their mother noticed that they were very quiet. She was wise as well as very pretty, and she soon found out why they were unhappy.

"Why doesn't Father build us a sled?" Wilbur blurted out.

"But Father is away, Will," his mother said gently. "And you know how busy he is when he is at home. He has to write stories for the church paper and he has to write sermons. Now suppose we build a sled together."

Wilbur laughed. "Whoever heard of anyone's mother building a sled?"

"You just wait," his mother said. "We'll build a better sled than Ed Sines has. Now get me a pencil and a piece of paper."

"You goin' to build a sled out of paper?" Orville asked in amazement.

"Just wait," she repeated.

Will and Orv brought their mother a pencil and paper, and she went to the minister's desk and found a ruler. Then she sat down at the kitchen table. "First we'll draw a picture of the sled," she said.

"What good is a picture of a sled?" Orville asked.

"Now Orville, watch Mother." She picked up the ruler in one hand and the pencil in the other.

"We want one like Ed Sines has," Orville said.

"When you go coasting, how many boys will Ed Sines's sled hold?" she asked.

"Two," Wilbur said.

"We'll make this one big enough to hold three," she said. "Maybe you can take Kate along sometimes." The outline of a sled began to appear on the paper. As she drew it she talked. "You see, Ed's sled is about four feet long. I've seen it often enough. We'll make this one five feet long. Now, Ed's sled is about a foot off the ground, isn't it?"

Orville nodded, his eyes never leaving the drawing that was taking shape. It was beginning to look like a sled now, but not like the sleds the other boys had.

"You've made it too low," Will said.

"You want a sled that's faster than Ed's sled, don't you?" His mother smiled. "Well, Ed's sled is at least a foot high. Our sled will be lower — closer to the ground. It won't meet so much wind resistance."

"Wind resistance?" It was the first time Wilbur had ever heard the expression. He looked blankly at his mother.

"Remember the blizzard last week?" she asked. "Remember when you went out to the woodshed and the wind was so strong you could hardly walk to the shed? I told you to lean over, and on the next trip to the woodshed you did. When you came back with an armful of wood you laughed and said, 'Mother, I leaned 'way forward and got under the wind.' You were closer to the ground and you were able to lessen the wind resistance. Now, the closer to the ground our sled is the less wind resistance there will be, and the faster it will go."

"Wind resistance . . . wind resistance," Wilbur repeated, and maybe the airplane was born in that moment. Certainly neither Will nor Orville Wright ever forgot that first lesson in speed.

"How do you know about these things, Mother?" Wilbur asked.

"You'd be surprised how much mothers know, Will." She laughed. She didn't tell the boys that when she was a

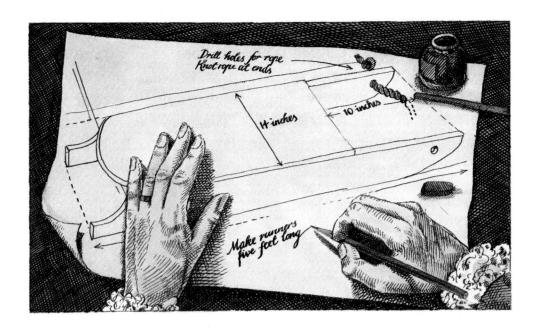

little girl at school her best subject had been arithmetic. It just came naturally to her. It was the same when she went to high school. And when she went to college, algebra and geometry were her best subjects. That was why she knew all about things like "wind resistance."

Finally she finished the drawing. The boys leaned over the table to look at it. This sled was going to be longer than Ed's sled and much narrower. Ed's sled was about three feet wide. This one looked as if it would be only half that wide.

"You made it narrow," Wilbur said shrewdly, "to make it faster. The narrower it is, the less wind resistance."

"That's right." His mother nodded. "Now let's put down the exact length of the runners and the exact width of the sled."

"But that's only a paper sled," Orville protested.

"If you get it right on paper," she said calmly, "it'll be right when you build it. Always remember that."

"'If you get it right on paper, it'll be right when you build it,'" Wilbur repeated, and his mother looked at him sharply. Sometimes Will seemed older than his eleven years. Little Orville was quick to give you an answer to anything, but as often as not he'd forget the answer right away. When Will learned something he never forgot it.

"Mother, you make all your clothes," Wilbur said thoughtfully. "You always make a drawing first."

"We call that the pattern," his mother said. "I draw and then cut out a pattern that's exactly the size of the dress I am going to make. And . . ."

"If the pattern is right, it'll be right when you make the dress," he finished. She nodded.

"Now you two boys get started on your sled." She smiled. "There are plenty of planks out in the barn. Find the very lightest ones. Don't use planks with knots in them. You saw the planks to the right size, Will — don't let Orville touch the saw."

"May we use Father's tools?" Wilbur asked breathlessly.

His mother nodded. "I don't think your father will mind. I know you'll be careful with them. Just follow the drawing exactly," she warned once more.

The two boys, followed by little Kate, hurried out to the barn. Both realized that this was an important occasion. Wilbur always chopped the wood for the stove when his father was away, but he had never been allowed to use the gleaming tools that lay in his father's tool chest.

Three days later their sled was finished. They pulled it out of the barn and asked their mother to inspect it. She had her tape measure with her and she measured it. The

runners were exactly the length she had put down in her drawing. In fact, the boys had followed every direction she had given them. The runners gleamed. Orville had polished them with sandpaper until they were as smooth as silk.

"We thought of one other thing, Mother," Will said. "We found some old candles in the woodshed. We rubbed the runners with the candles. See how smooth they are?"

Mrs. Wright nodded. She had forgotten to tell the boys that, but they'd thought it out for themselves. "Now try your sled," she told them.

Followed by Kate, the boys dragged their new sled to the hill only a half a mile away, where their pals were coasting. They looked at the new sled in amazement. It was long and very narrow. It looked as though it wouldn't hold anyone. The runners were thin compared to those on their own sleds.

"Who made that for you?" Ed Sines asked.

"Mother showed us how," Wilbur said proudly. Some of the boys laughed. Whoever heard of a boy's mother knowing how to make a sled?

"It looks as if it would fall apart if you sat on it," Al Johnston said, and he laughed too.

"Come on, we'll race you down the hill," another cried out.

"All right, two on each sled," Wilbur said. He wasn't a bit afraid. He was sure the drawing had been right, and because he and Orv had followed the drawing, he knew that the sled was right.

They lined the four sleds up. Will and Orv sat on their sled, but it didn't "fall apart." Suddenly Wilbur got an idea.

"Get up, Orv," he said. "Now lie down on the sled . . . that's it . . . spread your legs a bit." Will then flopped down on top of his brother. "Less wind resistance this way," he whispered.

"Give us all a push," Ed Sines yelled.

And then they were off. It was an even start. The four sleds gathered speed, for at the top the slope was steep. Will looked to the right. Then to the left. He brushed the stinging snow out of his eyes but he couldn't see the other sleds. He looked behind. They were straggling along, twenty and now thirty feet in back of him. The new sled skimmed along, the runners singing happily. Both Will and Orv felt a strange thrill of excitement. They approached the bottom of the long hill. The other sleds were far, far behind now.

Usually when the sleds reached the bottom of the hill they slowed down abruptly and stopped. But not this sled. It kept on; its momentum carried it on and on a hundred yards farther than any of the other sleds had ever reached. Finally it stopped.

Shaking with excitement, Will and Orv stood up. "We flew down the hill, Orv," Will said breathlessly.

"We flew," Orv repeated.

Now Ed and Al and Johnnie ran up, excited at what had happened. No sled had gone so far or so fast as the one Will and Orv had built.

"You *flew* down the hill," Ed Sines gasped. "Let me try it?"

Wilbur looked at Orv, and some secret message seemed to pass between them. They had built this sled together, and it was the best sled there was. They'd always work together building things.

"Orv," Will said, "I've got an idea. This sled can do everything but steer. Maybe we can make a rudder for it. Then we can make it go to the right or to the left."

"We'll get Mother to draw one," Orv said.

"We'll draw one, you and I," Wilbur said. "We can't run to Mother every time we want to make something."

By now little Kate had come running down the hill.

"You promised," she panted. "You said you'd take me for a ride."

"Come on, Kate." Will laughed. "The three of us will coast down once. And then you can try it, Ed."

They trudged up the hill, pulling the sled. Two words kept singing in Wilbur's ears. "We flew . . . we flew . . . we flew. . . ."

All through their lives Orville and Wilbur Wright planned and worked together. In the Wright Cycle Shop they made over and improved bicycles. They built a printing press on which they printed a newspaper. Together they planned and built a glider in which they flew at Kitty Hawk, North Carolina. Later they improved it and added an engine. For the first time, on December 17, 1903, a glider flew under its own power. That glider, which Wilbur and Orville had built, was the first airplane to fly with a man on board. Soon the Wright brothers were famous all over the world.

These men remembered well the lesson they had learned from their mother. They always worked by a plan. "Get it right on paper, and it'll be right when you build it," Susan Wright had said. That is exactly what they did.

Author

Quentin Reynolds, a well-known reporter, wrote many books for adults and children about his experiences as a war correspondent during World War II. He also wrote a book for children about the FBI. Because Mr. Reynolds loved planes, he wrote *The Wright Brothers: Pioneers of American Aviation*. The selection you have just read was taken from this book.

The Ants at the Olympics

by Richard Digance

At last year's Jungle Olympics,
the Ants were completely outclassed.
In fact, from an entry of sixty-two teams,
the Ants came their usual last.

They didn't win a single medal.
Not that that's a surprise.
The reason was not lack of trying,
but more their unfortunate size.

While the cheetahs won most of the sprinting
and the hippos won putting the shot,
the Ants tried sprinting but couldn't,
and tried to put but could not.

It was sad for the Ants 'cause they're sloggers.
They turn out for every event.
With their shorts and their bright orange tee shirts,
their athletes are proud they are sent.

They came last at the high jump and hurdles,
which they say they'd have won, but they fell.
They came last in the four hundred meters
and last in the swimming as well.

Illustrated by Lorinda Cauley

They came last in the long-distance running,
though they say they might have come first.
And they might if the other sixty-one teams
hadn't put in a finishing burst.

But each year they turn up regardless.
They're popular in the parade.
The other teams whistle and cheer them,
aware of the journey they've made.

For the Jungle Olympics in August,
they have to set off New Year's Day.
They didn't arrive the year before last.
They set off but went the wrong way.

So long as they try there's a reason.
After all, it's only a sport.
They'll be back next year to bring up the rear,
and that's an encouraging thought.

289

Ernie and the Mile-Long Muffler

by Marjorie Lewis
Illustrated by Dee de Rosa

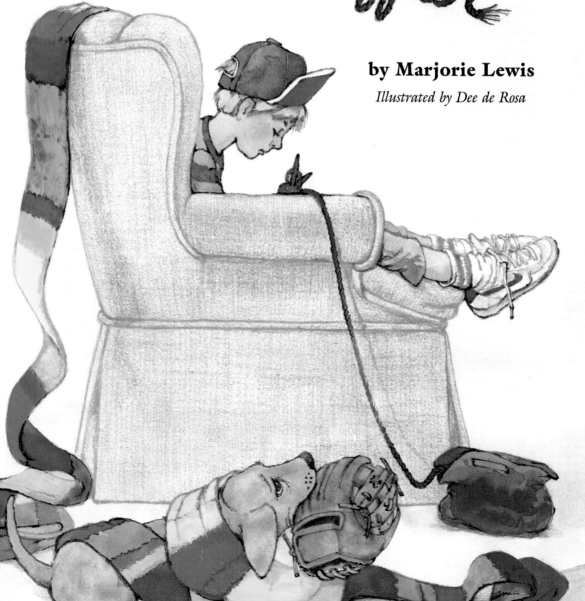

Ernie learned to knit one October afternoon when he was home waiting for the scabs from his chicken pox spots to fall off. Even though nobody could catch the chicken pox from him anymore, he looked pretty awful. Now that he didn't itch and feel terrible, he was bored. Ernie was so bored he couldn't wait to get back to school. He wondered what exciting things his friends in the fourth grade and Mrs. Crownfeld, his teacher, were doing while he spent his time waiting for scabs to fall off. When the doorbell suddenly rang, Ernie was glad. Even answering the door was something to do.

When Ernie looked through the peephole in the door to find out who was there before opening it, he saw it was his Uncle Simon, his mother's brother, who was a sailor. Ernie and his mother hadn't seen Uncle Simon in two years because he had been away at sea. Ernie had thought of Uncle Simon often during those two years and had imagined Uncle Simon climbing the rigging, doing things with the mizzen mast, swabbing the deck, and standing watch with a spy glass — all the things that sailors did in the stories Ernie read.

Ernie and Uncle Simon sat and talked with each other and drank soda and ate pretzels while Ernie's mother made dinner. Uncle Simon showed Ernie pictures of the places he had been and of the ship he'd sailed on.

Then Uncle Simon asked Ernie what he liked best to eat. Ernie told him his best thing was a hamburger with red onion circles, lots of ketchup on the top part, lots of

mayonnaise on the bottom part, and a roll with seeds to hold it all together. Ernie told Uncle Simon his worst thing to eat was anything shaky. Uncle Simon said he didn't like shaky things either, especially tapioca pudding because the tapioca beads look like fish eyes. Uncle Simon told Ernie all about the weird foods he had eaten in his travels: rattlesnake, turtle soup, candied grasshoppers, rabbit stew, cows' eyes, calves' brains, chocolate-covered ants. Ernie began to feel sick.

Uncle Simon changed the subject and asked Ernie what kinds of things he liked to do. Ernie told him about reading comics and cereal boxes, trading baseball cards, making cookies, and shooting baskets.

Uncle Simon told Ernie he liked most to read mystery stories; next, to bake bread; and third, to knit. He told Ernie that on his ship, when he wasn't working, he had lots of time to do all three. Ernie said that he didn't know that men knitted. Uncle Simon said that men have knitted for centuries, especially men in armies and navies who spend a lot of time waiting for things to happen. Uncle Simon opened his seabag and took out a sweater that looked like a rainbow and let Ernie try it on. Ernie thought it was the most terrific sweater he had ever seen. Then Uncle Simon took some knitting needles out of his bag and a big ball of yellow yarn. By the time Ernie's mother called them for dinner, Uncle Simon had taught Ernie to knit.

The next few days, while Ernie waited for the scabs to fall off and his spots to fade, he knitted a sweater for his dog Buster, socks for his father's golf clubs, a Christmas stocking for the canary, and a muffler for his mother for her birthday. The muffler was so beautiful and fit his

mother's neck so well that Ernie decided to make mufflers for everyone he knew. Then he had a better idea. The idea came to him one morning while he was eating breakfast and reading his world-record book for the hundred-millionth time. Ernie decided that he would knit the world's longest muffler. He would make it a mile long! Ernie wrote a letter to Uncle Simon, who was back at sea, and told him about his plan.

He asked his mother to get all the record books she could find in the library. Ernie looked through all of them and found that none of them mentioned a record for muffler-knitting. Ernie pictured himself holding the victorious knitting needles crossed in front of him with foot after foot of muffler looping around the throne he would be sitting on when they took his picture for the record book.

Ernie told his mother about his idea. She told him that there were 5,280 feet in a mile. Then Ernie and his mother figured out that there were 63,360 inches in a mile. Ernie's mother said that it would sure be a lot of muffler to knit!

Ernie asked his mother to ask her friends to give him all the extra yarn they had. By the time Ernie was well

enough to go back to school, he had finished about two feet of muffler. Ernie thought that the two feet had been done so quickly that it wouldn't be hard at all to do a mile of knitting.

His first day back at school, Ernie packed his gym bag with his gym shorts, his T-shirt, and his knitting. He kept his knitting with him all morning. When he was sitting and waiting for late-comers to be present for morning attendance, or for the assembly program to begin, or for the fire drill to be over, Ernie knitted. Mrs. Crownfeld said she thought it was wonderful to be able to knit and asked Ernie if, after recess, he would demonstrate to the class how to knit. Ernie said he would.

At recess, the class went outside. Ernie sat down on the bench to wait for his turn to shoot baskets. He took out his knitting.

"I can't believe you're doing that," said Frankie.

"I mean my *mother* does that!" said Alfred.

"So what," said Ernie. "Your mother bakes cookies, Alfred, and so do you. And so do I."

"It's different," Alfred said. "Knitting is different."

Alfred watched while Ernie's fingers made the needles form stitches. When Edward came over, Frankie and Alfred moved away. Edward leaned over and watched Ernie.

"No boy I ever saw did that," Edward said. "Boys don't do that." Edward reached out and grabbed the ball of yarn tearing it off from the knitting. Ernie watched silently while Edward, Frankie, and Alfred played basketball with the yarn ball. Then they dropped it into a puddle. They fished it out and tossed it to Ernie.

Ernie looked at the ball of yarn with glops of mud and leaves tangled in it. Then he put his needles and the two feet of muffler on the bench and threw it away into the bushes.

The three boys, Frankie, Alfred, and Edward, formed a circle around Ernie. They began to run around like crazies with their thumbs in their ears and their fingers flapping yelling: "Nyah, nyah, Ernie knits!" Over and over again. Then the three boys called Ernie a nitwit (or was it a knitwit? thought Ernie miserably). The other children in the class came over to watch. Some of them joined the group around Ernie.

"Maybe Ernie has nits," said Howard. Howard walked over to Ernie and pretended to search Ernie's head for bugs.

"Hey Ernie," called Richard. Raising his voice to a screech that he thought sounded like a girl's voice, Richard said: "Oh, Ernie. Would you make me a pink sweater?"

By the time the bell rang for the end of recess, Ernie felt terrible. When Mrs. Crownfeld asked him to show the class how to knit, everyone began to giggle. Ernie walked up to the front of the classroom. In his hands, he held the needles and the two-foot piece of the record-making mile-long muffler. He took a deep breath and waited until the class quieted down.

He told them all about his Uncle Simon's being a sailor. He told them about the things Uncle Simon had eaten in his travels and the places Uncle Simon had been. He told them about Uncle Simon's terrific sweater. He told them that Uncle Simon liked best to read mysteries; next, to bake bread; and third, to knit. He told them what Uncle Simon had said about armies and navies having lots of time while they waited for things to happen, so soldiers and sailors for hundreds of years knitted to keep from being bored.

Finally, Ernie told the class that he was going to knit the longest muffler in the world, a mile long, and get his name and his picture in the record books. The class was absolutely quiet.

Mrs. Crownfeld said that she would be very proud to have one of her fourth-grade students be a record-maker. Then Mrs. Crownfeld asked Ernie to demonstrate how to knit. Ernie said that he couldn't because he had lost his ball of yarn during recess. Ernie promised to show Mrs. Crownfeld and the class how to knit the next day during homeroom period.

At the end of the day, Ernie was walking home by himself with his knitting in his gym bag.

"Ernie, Ernie," called Frankie. "Wait up!"

Frankie walked along with Ernie. "Thanks for not telling the teacher what happened to your yarn," he said. "I think it's neat how you're going to win the muffler-knitting record."

Ernie and Frankie went to Ernie's house and ate some cookies that Ernie had baked when he was sick. Ernie showed Frankie all the stuff he had knitted when he had been home with the chicken pox. Frankie admired the dog's sweater most of all. Ernie next showed Frankie the bags of different-colored yarns that his mother's friends had given him for his muffler project.

"Say, Ernie," said Frankie. "I bet my mother's got some yarn left over from the sweater she knitted for my sister. I'll ask her if I can give it to you."

"That would be great, Frankie," said Ernie. "I'm going to need all the yarn I can get!"

The next day in school, Ernie showed the class how the needle went in front of the stitch to make a knit stitch and how it went in back to make a purl stitch. He showed them how the two kinds of stitches together made the bumpy ridges that kept the sleeves tight at the wrists. He showed the class how to make the pieces get bigger and smaller to fit next to each other so that they could be sewn together to make a swell outfit. He offered to teach anyone in class who wanted to learn. Mrs. Crownfeld was the first to ask Ernie for lessons.

Gradually, everyone in fourth grade learned to knit. Mrs. Crownfeld made a deal with them: the class could knit during homeroom, firedrills (while they were outside waiting to go back in), or rainy-day recess, plus a special knitting time right after lunch each day when the class could knit while Mrs. Crownfeld put her knitting aside and read them a story from the library.

In return for all the knitting lessons from Ernie, the class brought in all the yarn they could get from anyone who would give it to them. Ernie kept the yarn in a big plastic garbage bag in the corner of the classroom. Each day, a knitting monitor measured Ernie's muffler and wrote the measurement in a diary book Mrs. Crownfeld had given the class as a present.

By Thanksgiving, Ernie's muffler was sixteen feet long and Ernie was looking pale. He never went outside to play anymore. He didn't do anything at all but go to school, do his homework, eat his meals, and knit. Cynthia, who was very good in math, subtracted the sixteen feet Ernie had finished from the 5,280 feet in a mile. That left 5,264 feet to go before the end of school. Since school would be over and summer vacation begin in twenty-eight weeks, Ernie would have to knit over 188 feet of muffler *every week,* or about 27 feet *every day* (including Saturday and Sunday) to finish the muffler by the end of fourth grade.

Ernie listened to Cynthia very carefully. He remembered the picture he had dreamed of: sitting on a throne, his knitting needles crossed in front of him, foot after foot of muffler looping around him. His name and photograph in the record books. The pride in the faces of his mother and his teacher. The admiration of all his friends. Then Ernie thought of how long it had been since he played with his friends or baked cookies or read a book — or even a cereal box.

Ernie decided to take it easy. It wasn't important when the muffler got finished. He could finish it anytime. So maybe it wouldn't be the longest muffler in the world. Mrs. Crownfeld would be disappointed not to have a fourth-grade record-breaker, but Ernie figured if he ever did finish it — in fifth grade maybe, or sixth — he would publicly thank her for her encouragement when he became famous.

Ernie told his mother, Mrs. Crownfeld, and his friends what he had decided. Now he could go out and shoot baskets during recess. He began to read his cereal boxes again. Sometimes, while he was watching television or waiting for the dentist to see him, or riding in the car for a long time, he would knit. He even had time to write to Uncle Simon and tell him everything that had happened since he learned to knit.

Ernie's class continued to bring in yarn for him. Ernie decided to contribute the yarn to the class because now that they all could knit, they could have a Christmas fair or something to raise money to buy games and books for children in the town hospital. All the things sold at the fair were knitted by the fourth grade. Frankie was good at mittens and so was Edward. Frankie knitted all the right-hand ones and Edward all the left-hand ones. Between them, they made five pairs of mittens for the fair. Alfred made some bean bags. Cynthia made pot holders. Other people made mufflers (the regular length). Mrs. Crownfeld made some cat and dog sweaters. Someone else made pincushions. Everyone in the fourth grade made something. The fair was a huge success. They sold $173.42 worth of stuff including six pairs of slipper socks in bright colors that Ernie made and delicious cookies that Frankie, Alfred, and Ernie baked and sold.

By the time spring came, the fourth grade was famous. Everyone in town knew about their knitting and Ernie's muffler, which was getting very long even if it wasn't anywhere near a mile. When the local paper did a story about the class and took a picture to go with it, on the front page right in the middle of the photograph there was Ernie sitting on a chair holding his knitting needles crossed in front of him. Ernie's muffler was looped around each member of the class and Mrs. Crownfeld with several feet to spare. It made Ernie as

happy as if he had finished his mile of muffler. Suddenly, Ernie decided the time had come. Even though people were always saying you should finish everything you start, Ernie knew better. Three hundred fourteen feet was long enough. Long enough, Ernie thought, is long enough.

He asked Mrs. Crownfeld who was an expert fringe maker to put fringe at each end of the muffler. When the muffler was done, it was exhibited all over school — in the fourth-grade room, down the hall, in the principal's office, in the library. People came to see it and admire the way Ernie made all the colors of fuzzy and thin yarns come together into a multicolored muffler. People who had contributed yarn could recognize their bits and were very pleased to see them used in Ernie's muffler.

When summer vacation came, Ernie's mother took the muffler home. Ernie helped her wrap it and put it away in a box. Then he went out to ride bikes with Frankie, Alfred, and Edward.

Author

Marjorie Lewis says, "I believe in stories — in giving children delight. I believe in the power of words to create music, laughter, and tears." Mrs. Lewis, a school librarian, has written several books for young readers. Like Ernie, she enjoys knitting projects that don't take too long to finish.

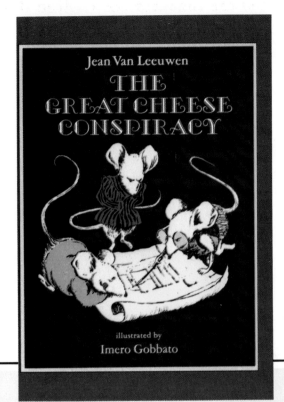

~ *Houghton Mifflin Literature* ~

In the selections you have just read from *Making Dreams Come True,* the importance of having a goal or a dream was shown in a number of different ways.

In *The Great Cheese Conspiracy* by Jean Van Leeuwen you will read about a gang of mice who live in a movie theater. One day their leader, Marvin the Magnificent, gets a "big idea" and leads the rest of the gang in working toward his unusual goal.

5

Facing
the Truth

Why Mosquitoes Buzz

A West African tale retold by Verna Aardema

Illustrated by Leo and Diane Dillon

in People's Ears

One morning a mosquito saw an iguana drinking at a waterhole. The mosquito said, "Iguana, you will never believe what I saw yesterday."

"Try me," said the iguana.

The mosquito said, "I saw a farmer digging yams that were almost as big as I am."

"What's a mosquito compared to a yam?" snapped the iguana grumpily. "I would rather be deaf than listen to such nonsense!" Then he stuck two sticks in his ears and went off, mek, mek, mek, mek, through the reeds.

The iguana was still grumbling to himself when he happened to pass by a python.

The big snake raised his head and said, "Good morning, Iguana."

The iguana did not answer but lumbered on, bobbing his head, badamin, badamin.

"Now, why won't he speak to me?" said the python to himself. "Iguana must be angry about something. I'm afraid he is plotting some mischief against me!" He began looking for somewhere to hide. The first likely place he found was a rabbit hole, and in it he went, wasawusu, wasawusu, wasawusu.

When the rabbit saw the big snake coming into her burrow, she was terrified. She scurried out through her back way and bounded, krik, krik, krik, across a clearing.

A crow saw the rabbit running for her life. He flew into the forest crying kaa, kaa, kaa! It was his duty to spread the alarm in case of danger.

A monkey heard the crow. He was sure that some dangerous beast was prowling near. He began screeching and leaping kili wili through the trees to help warn the other animals.

As the monkey was crashing through the treetops, he happened to land on a dead limb. It broke and fell on an owl's nest, killing one of the owlets.

Mother Owl was not at home. For though she usually hunted only in the night, this morning she was still out searching for one more tidbit to satisfy her hungry babies. When she returned to the nest, she found one of them dead. Her other children told her that the monkey had killed it. All that day and all that night, she sat in her tree — so sad, so sad, so sad!

Now it was Mother Owl who woke the sun each day so that the dawn could come. But this time, when she should have hooted for the sun, she did not do it.

The night grew longer and longer. The animals of the forest knew it was lasting much too long. They feared that the sun would never come back.

At last King Lion called a meeting of the animals. They came and sat down, pem, pem, pem, around a council fire. Mother Owl did not come, so the antelope was sent to fetch her.

When she arrived, King Lion asked, "Mother Owl, why have you not called the sun? The night has lasted long, long, long, and everyone is worried."

Mother Owl said, "Monkey killed one of my owlets. Because of that, I cannot bear to wake the sun."

The king said to the gathered animals:

"Did you hear?
It was the monkey
who killed the owlet —
and now Mother Owl won't wake the sun
so that the day can come."

Then King Lion called the monkey. He came before him nervously glancing from side to side, rim, rim, rim, rim.

"Monkey," said the king, "why did you kill one of Mother Owl's babies?"

"Oh, King," said the monkey, "it was the crow's fault. He was calling and calling to warn us of danger. And I went leaping through the trees to help. A limb broke under me, and it fell taaa on the owl's nest."

The king said to the council:

"So, it was the crow
who alarmed the monkey,
who killed the owlet —
and now Mother Owl won't wake the sun
so that the day can come."

Then the king called for the crow. That big bird came flapping up. He said, "King Lion, it was the rabbit's fault! I saw her running for her life in the daytime. Wasn't that reason enough to spread the alarm?"

The king nodded his head and said to the council:

"So, it was the rabbit
who startled the crow,
who alarmed the monkey,
who killed the owlet —
and now Mother Owl won't wake the sun
so that the day can come."

Then King Lion called the rabbit. The timid little creature stood before him, one trembling paw drawn up uncertainly.

"Rabbit," cried the king, "why did you break a law of nature and go running, running, running, in the daytime?"

"Oh, King," said the rabbit, "it was the python's fault. I was in my house minding my own business when that big snake came in and chased me out."

The king said to the council:

"So, it was the python
who scared the rabbit,
who startled the crow,
who alarmed the monkey,
who killed the owlet —
and now Mother Owl won't wake the sun
so that the day can come."

King Lion called the python, who came slithering, wasawusu, wasawusu, past the other animals. "But, King," he cried, "it was the iguana's fault! He wouldn't speak to me. And I thought he was plotting some mischief against me. When I crawled into the rabbit's hole, I was only trying to hide."

The king said to the council:

"So, it was the iguana
 who frightened the python,
 who scared the rabbit,
 who startled the crow,
 who alarmed the monkey,
 who killed the owlet —
 and now Mother Owl won't wake the sun
 so that the day can come."

Now the iguana was not at the meeting. For he had not heard the summons.

The antelope was sent to fetch him.

All the animals laughed when they saw the iguana coming, badamin, badamin, with the sticks still stuck in his ears!

King Lion pulled out the sticks, purup, purup. Then he asked, "Iguana, what evil have you been plotting against the python?"

"None! None at all!" cried the iguana. "Python is my friend!"

"Then why wouldn't you say good morning to me?" demanded the snake.

"I didn't hear you, or even see you!" said the iguana. "Mosquito told me such a big lie, I couldn't bear to listen to it. So I put sticks in my ears."

"Nge, nge, nge," laughed the lion. "So that's why you had sticks in your ears!"

"Yes," said the iguana. "It was the mosquito's fault."

King Lion said to the council:

"So, it was the mosquito
  who annoyed the iguana,
  who frightened the python,
  who scared the rabbit,
  who startled the crow,
  who alarmed the monkey,
  who killed the owlet —
  and now Mother Owl won't wake the sun
  so that the day can come."

"Punish the mosquito! Punish the mosquito!" cried all the animals.

When Mother Owl heard that, she was satisfied. She turned her head toward the east and hooted: "Hoo! Hooooo! Hooooooo!"

And the sun came up.

Meanwhile the mosquito had listened to it all from a nearby bush. She crept under a curly leaf, semm, and was never found and brought before the council.

But because of this the mosquito has a guilty conscience. To this day she goes about whining in people's ears: "Zeee! Is everyone still angry at me?"

When she does that, she gets an honest answer.

KPAO!

Author

Verna Aardema was born in New Era, Michigan. She decided at the age of eleven to become a writer, and she won several writing contests while a student at Michigan State College. Ms. Aardema worked as a teacher and a journalist before retiring to become a full-time writer and storyteller. *Why Mosquitoes Buzz in People's Ears* won the Caldecott Award in 1976.

The Once-A-Year Day

by Eve Bunting

Illustrated by Mai Vo-Dinh

The bucket was almost filled with the wrinkled purple berries. Annie knew her mother would be pleased. She straightened her back, looking once again across the dark waters of the bay. Something moved in the immense stillness, but it was only a skein of ducks flying south, and as she listened she heard their honking clear in the empty air.

The short Alaskan summer was almost over. Already the tufts of grass beneath her feet were hardening and the tender summer moss was gone. Soon snow would fall and the sea would freeze over, closing them in. Annie sighed. She touched the coins in her pocket, counting them one by one. They were there, waiting. Summer was not yet gone, not with the barges still to come. The radio had told them last week that the big ship was steaming north from Hooper Bay. Soon, soon the barges would come.

It was at that instant that she saw them, gliding like surfaced whales across the dark bay. There were two of them, flat-nosed, low in the water. Annie picked up her bucket and began to run. The barges had come! This was the day . . . the wonderful, wonderful once-a-year day!

She was almost halfway down the hill when she remembered. Anger rose in her, sudden and hot.

"Emma!" she called. "Where are you, Emma?" There was no answer. That silly Emma! Annie scrambled back up the hill. "Emma! Emma!"

She saw a swatch of red against the brown of the grass. Emma sat motionless, her eyes closed, her face upturned to the pale coolness of the midday sun. Her berry bucket was beside her, a scattering of berries on the bottom, not even a handful.

"Emma!" Annie heard the righteous wrath in her own voice. What had Emma been doing all this time? No berries to speak of, and now, because of her, Annie was missing the barges.

Emma's eyes opened. Her face wore the sulky look that Annie knew so well. She rose slowly, without a word, and picked up the almost empty bucket.

"Is that all you've got?" Annie knew the answer, but the question helped to ease some of the frustration she felt.

Emma nodded. She was twelve years old, one year younger than Annie, but she was much smaller. Her black braids trailed wisps, fine as feathers. Her sweater was buttoned wrong so that one end hung down. Emma was Annie's cousin, and an orphan, and now that she had come to live at Annie's house she was going to be the sister that Annie had never had. That was what Annie's mother had said.

"Well, hurry up." Annie emptied half of her berries into Emma's bucket. "You can at least help me carry them."

Emma shrugged, moving her thin shoulders. Her mouth drooped at the corners.

Annie began slipping and sliding back down the hill. "The barges have come," she said, and waited for Emma's question. But behind her there was only silence.

The village below was moving with excitement. People were running from their houses to the edge of the bay. Annie could see the crowd already gathered on the muddy banks. The first barge was almost in, its straight nose churning the water, nudging the shore.

Emma's feet were slow and uncaring behind her. Annie wished she could run on by herself and leave her cousin, but that would make her mother angry. "Come on, come on, come on!" she urged, grabbing Emma's bucket and carrying it with her own. "Can't you hurry?" She felt like crying with impatience. To think, she had probably been the first person in the village to see the barges and she would probably be the last to reach them. It wasn't fair. Nothing was fair since Emma had come. Annie had to share her bed, her clothes, her father and brothers, and, worst of all, her mother.

"I couldn't let my own sister's child go all the way to the city, to the orphanage," her mother had said. "How could I, Annie? What we have we will share with her. And you will have a sister to go egging with. She will be company for you on the goose drive. It will be good."

It hadn't been good. Emma *had* gone egging with them, yes. But her egg basket had been as empty at the end of that day as her berry bucket today. Annie's father and her brothers, Daniel and Thomas, had climbed the steep cliffs with the other men from the village. High on the ledges the big blue crowbill eggs lay, ripe for the taking. The women and girls had stood in a cluster below, admiring and anxious. All but Emma. Emma sat alone among the tussocks of grass, pulling the golden heads from the Arctic poppies, her face blank and empty. Even when an angry crowbill swooped, almost knocking Daniel from his perch, Emma had sat unmoving, staring into space. She had walked home with them afterwards, seldom stopping as the others did to gather the pale eggs of the eider ducks. Lazy Emma, Annie thought. Thoughtless Emma. She wasn't a sister to Annie. She didn't belong in the Koonooka family.

And the goose drive was worse. Emma had lagged behind, and when two of the geese escaped the net she had let them run right past her. Didn't she know that geese were food and food was life? The smallest child in the village knew that. Annie couldn't understand her mother. Whatever Emma did, Annie's mother excused it with a gentle word. It was almost more than Annie could bear.

Emma's own mother had died the year before on the mail plane on the way to the hospital. Her father had been lost last winter when an off-shore wind blew the pack ice on which he stood away from the floe. He had never been found. It was summer before Emma could be brought to them. Bad enough, Annie thought, to suffer through the short summer with sulky old Emma who didn't want to play and didn't want to talk. How would it be in the winter when they would be together inside the small house for days and weeks at a time?

"It will be all right," her mother said. "Emma is strange now. She doesn't care about anything. But as time passes, she will."

Sulky old Emma. Annie didn't believe she'd ever change. I won't think about it now, Annie decided. Not on the once-a-year day. I won't spoil it.

They were down the hill now and running along the short stubble of grass in front of the houses. There was no one in sight. Even the dogs had gone down to the shore to share in the excitement. The buckets banged against Annie's legs. She could feel their edges through her sealskin boots. From the bay came a drift of voices and the dull putt-putt of an outboard motor.

Annie opened the door of her house and thumped the two buckets inside — just inside — and then she was running again toward the dark water line and the voices and the laughter. Her hand closed tightly on the coins in her pocket and she counted again. The one with the crinkled edge was the dime, the bigger one was the nickel, the other fifteen were the pennies. They were all there, safe, ready.

"Don't you even want to know about the barges?" she called to Emma over her shoulder.

Emma didn't answer.

"Once a year the big ship brings supplies from Seattle." Annie's fast-moving legs kept a rhythm with the words she flung back to Emma. "The ship can't come in here because the water's too shallow. The barges bring the goods from the ship to us. We have to be quick. All the best things sell first."

Only the wind of her running answered her. Sulky old Emma doesn't understand, Annie thought. I don't know why I bother to tell her.

Mr. Odark, the storekeeper, had an old army truck and it was waiting at the edge of the bay. Gordon Okukchuk's big caterpillar was there too, the drag sled

behind it, hitched and ready to haul the supplies from the beach to the village.

Annie saw her mother standing with the other women. Her two brothers were kneedeep in the water, pulling on the first barge, helping to wedge it in the mud. The front gate was down; the slide from the deck to the dry ground already in position. Annie could see that this barge carried only the big drums of fuel for heating the school and the houses of those who had oil stoves. Fuel for the snowmobiles and to run the boats next summer.

The second barge was coming in and Mr. Odark stepped forward with his list. Annie felt a faint quivering, deep inside. Would it be on this one? No. These were the

wooden crates filled with fishnets, harpoons, dog harnesses. There were bags of nails and lamps, carefully packed, and big bright boxes of washing soap. Here were the cartons of shells and the cartridges for the hunting rifles.

Everything was piled on the shore and the smaller children ran to peer between the slats in the packing cases. Not yet, not yet. With one part of her mind Annie sensed Emma, motionless beside her, but there was no time to think about Emma now.

The second barge moved out. There would be a while to wait before the first one came back, reloaded, from the big ship.

Daniel and Thomas and some of the other boys began rolling the heavy oil drums up the hill toward the store. The men hefted the big crates up onto the truck, piling them untidily, lashing them down with ropes so they wouldn't slide off. Mr. Odark scurried around, giving instructions, telling them to be careful of this and to be careful of that, but everyone was so excited they paid him little attention.

At last Chip, Mr. Odark's assistant, jumped behind the wheel and the old engine grumbled and rumbled and whined, coughed once, and stopped. Chip shook his head. He turned the key and the growling began again. Everyone held their breaths, and then with a roar the engine caught and the truck began to move. There were shouts of triumph and some of the men ran along behind, and some of the women too, pushing the poor old beast as it wheezed up the hill, everyone laughing and happy, the men trying to hide their feelings, the women twittering like birds. Oh yes, Annie thought, it's the once-a-year day, the wonderful, magical once-a-year day!

When she looked again she saw that the first barge was gliding back across the bay, humped high with the rest of the supplies. She felt a sudden rush of saliva to her mouth and a faintness inside of her. This must be it! She wanted to plunge into the water and tow the barge behind her like a lead dog pulling a sled. Hurry, hurry, she begged silently. And then it was there, nosing in, jamming itself on the shore.

Here were the sacks of flour, sugar, coffee, salt. Dried peas and beans, baking soda, powdered milk. It was hard for Mr. Odark to check with the people crowding around. Suddenly Annie saw it — the big slatted crate with the one word stamped in black on its side. It came bumping and slithering down the slide. Annie breathed deeply. It was here. No need to worry now. There was only the waiting till Mr. Odark got everything up to his store. The barge was empty. The second barge would stay out with the big ship. There was nothing else to bring ashore.

"Anyone for a ride?" one of the bargemen yelled, and he stood back as the children swarmed and crawled all over the boat.

"Come on, Emma," Annie called, running forward. But Emma stood still, unmoving. Let sulky old Emma stay! From the back of the barge Annie saw her mother speak to Emma and Emma shake her head. Then they were moving, sliding through the dark, clear bay, with the people on the shore getting smaller and smaller and the village itself disappearing from sight. This was the once-a-year ride on the once-a-year day. It didn't last long. When they got back they watched as the barge disappeared behind the line of sea and sky, and for an instant everyone was very, very quiet. Goodbye, Annie thought. Goodbye barges, goodbye big ship. Don't forget to come back next year.

The drag sled was filled, the truck back for another load. Annie searched and found the crate with bold black letters on the front of the sled. Not long now, not long.

The caterpillar ground its way up the hill and Annie raced along beside it. She didn't see Emma, and she was glad. Nobody knew about the thirty cents. Ten cents for minding Mrs. Ungatt's baby while she went to a meeting in the church. Five cents from Mrs. Quavuk for carrying buckets of fresh water from the stream. The rest saved, penny by penny. Not even her mother knew. This I will not share, she thought. This is going to be all mine!

Mr. Odark's store was crowded. Women stood, fingering smooth bolts of cotton. Men and boys examined guns and ammunition and the long knives for the butchering at whaling season. Annie saw her father, bent over someone else's outboard motor, the same hungry look on his face that she saw on other faces around the room.

Jim Tulimak and his wife whispered together. They had gone to work in the commercial fishery when the salmon were running and they had money when they came back. Now they waited for the plywood and the glass they had ordered. This winter they would have a new floor and good windows.

Mr. Odark was sorting and checking.

"Mr. Odark," Annie whispered, coming to stand beside him. The wooden crate lay unopened on the floor.

The bands of metal that bound it gleamed in the last light from the window.

"Don't bother me now, Annie." Mr. Odark chewed the end of his pencil and frowned.

Annie pulled at his arm and pointed to the crate. "Will you open this one next?"

He paid no attention, crossing off words on the list he held. Then he sighed and smiled. "All right, Annie. We'll open it now."

"Can I have the first one?" Annie took the dime and the nickel and the pennies from her pocket. They were hot and sticky from her clenched fist.

Mr. Odark held out his big hand and Annie poured the money into it, a shining ribbon polished by the rubbing.

"Chip," Mr. Odark called, but Chip was on the beach with the truck. Mr. Odark scratched his head. "I forgot. It's a good thing this day comes only once a year." He got down on his knees beside the crate and snipped first one metal band, then another. With a piece of flat iron he pried up the lid.

It seemed to Annie that everyone in the room gasped at the sight. Big golden oranges lay, row on row, fat and gleaming in their own rich skins, trapping the light, holding it without reflection.

Ruby Bird stretched a hand into the box.

"Uh-uh!" Mr. Odark said. "Annie Koonooka has paid for one already. Take your pick, Annie."

Annie knelt by the crate and took out one of the oranges. It was stamped with the same magic word that had been on the slatted wood — CALIFORNIA.

She carried it outside into the early coldness. The air was filled with the groans of the truck, laboring up the hill with another load. Boys called to one another, their voices high and sharp as the bark of a fox in the night. Annie cradled the orange in her hands. She walked slowly behind the store and sat facing the bay. Then she closed her eyes, lifted the orange to her nose and breathed of it. CALIFORNIA. In her hands she held the sunshine, the warmth, the groves of orange trees, the blue of the ocean, the wonder of the land she had learned of in school but would never see.

The day was shimmering to an end, the special day. She bit into the peel, tasting the first bitter oil, feeling it

wrinkle her tongue. She remembered last year. Ruth Ormuk had eaten the skin and thrown away the inside as one throws away the guts of a fish. Annie smiled. Ruth had thought the outside was all there was! She nibbled at the white beneath the peel and then placed the piece of skin carefully in her pocket. Later, she could take it out, smell and remember. Little by little she undressed the orange till its pale, tender roundness lay free in her hand. She pulled off one section and sank her teeth in. Oh, it was good. It was good beyond believing! Dribbles stung her chin, stickied her fingers. It was like eating summer.

She ate another piece and another, cramming it in her mouth, greedy as a tomcod for the bait on the line. It was half gone. She stopped, considering. Last year she had

had four pieces, one fruit shared with her brothers. The memory had sharpened with the days between. She was going too quickly. Too soon it would be over.

That was when she heard the noise. It was a snuffling noise, a gaspy, raspy noise. Annie sat up and listened. Someone was coming around the side of the store. It was Emma. Annie heard a great gulping sob, and then, as Emma turned, she saw her face. Never in all of Annie's life had she seen such misery. The eyes were screwed up like Mrs. Ungatt's baby's. The mouth was open, moving, saying words without sound.

"Emma," Annie whispered.

Emma saw Annie. In an instant, every expression was gone from her face. She looked blankly at her cousin. She was sulky old Emma again.

Annie got up. Had she really seen Emma's face like that or had she imagined it? I saw it, she thought. That I could never have imagined.

The night wind was coming up. She could hear it moving between them. The orange was sticky in her hand. She looked down — and all at once she knew. Emma's sulky face was what she showed to the world. It was like the orange skin, protecting, hiding everything underneath. I didn't know, Annie thought. Like Ruth Ormuk, I threw it away.

"Emma," she said softly. "I didn't know you felt so bad."

Emma stood looking over the bay. Her hair still feathered from its braids. Her sweater was still buttoned wrong. Her face still wore its sulky look.

Annie held out the half orange. "Here," she said.

"What is it?" Emma took the orange and sniffed it suspiciously.

"It's an orange. I had one last year. Eat it." She watched as Emma took a small bite. "Isn't it good?"

Emma nodded.

A warmth crept around Annie, comforting as rabbit fur. This, she thought, is the first thing I have shared willingly with Emma since she came.

"Please, you have some too," Emma said. Her voice was shy. She broke off a piece of the orange and gave it back to Annie.

Annie put the orange in her mouth, keeping her teeth from it, storing the memory that she would have to hold in her mind for a whole year, till the next time the barges came. This piece tasted best of all. This little bit, shared. Annie smiled. Maybe this was how it was, and how it would be from now on, with Emma.

Author

Eve Bunting, who has written more than one hundred thirty books for young people, says, "Creating stories is the thing I enjoy most in the whole world." When Mrs. Bunting's children were almost grown, she took a course in writing for publication which started her on her career as an author. Since then she has taught courses for other would-be authors. One of her many award-winning books, *The Empty Window,* was chosen as an Outstanding Science Book for Children.

Sea-Sand and Sorrow
by Christina Rossetti

What are heavy? Sea-sand and sorrow:
What are brief? To-day and to-morrow:
What are frail? Spring blossoms and youth:
What are deep? The ocean and truth.

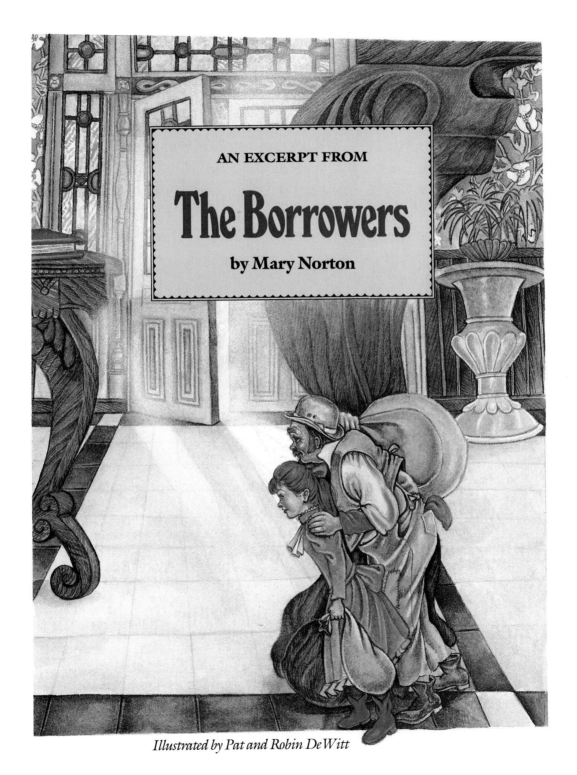

AN EXCERPT FROM

The Borrowers

by Mary Norton

Illustrated by Pat and Robin DeWitt

Have you ever wondered what happens to buttons, safety pins, postage stamps, and all the other little things that "disappear" from around your home? Meet the Borrowers — tiny people who live by "borrowing" things like these from "human beans." The Clock family — Pod, Homily, and their daughter Arrietty — are Borrowers who live in a comfortable apartment under the floor of an English country house. Thirteen-year-old Arrietty, who has never before left the apartment, is finally being allowed to go borrowing with her father. She knows that she must be very careful, because the worst thing that can happen to a Borrower is to be "seen" by a "human bean."

The step was warm but very steep. "If I got down on to the path," Arrietty thought, "I might not get up again," so for some moments she sat quietly. After a while she noticed the shoe-scraper.

"Arrietty," called Pod softly, "where have you got to?"

"I just climbed down the shoe-scraper," she called back.

He came along and looked down at her from the top of the step. "That's all right," he said after a moment's stare, "but never climb down anything that isn't fixed like. Supposing one of them came along and moved the shoe-scraper — where would you be then? How would you get up again?"

"It's heavy to move," said Arrietty.

"Maybe," said Pod, "but it's movable. See what I mean? There's rules, my lass, and you got to learn."

"This path," Arrietty said, "goes round the house. And the bank does too."

"Well," said Pod, "what of it?"

Arrietty rubbed one red kid shoe on a rounded stone. "It's my grating," she explained. "I was thinking that my grating must be just round the corner. My grating looks out on to this bank."

"Your grating!" exclaimed Pod. "Since when has it been your grating?"

"I was thinking," Arrietty went on. "Suppose I just went round the corner and called through the grating to Mother?"

"No," said Pod, "we're not going to have none of that. Not going round corners."

"Then," went on Arrietty, "she'd see I was all right like."

"Well," said Pod, and then he half smiled, "go quickly then and call. I'll watch for you here. Not loud mind!"

Arrietty ran. The stones in the path were firmly bedded and her light, soft shoes hardly seemed to touch them. How glorious it was to run — you could never run under the floor: you walked, you stooped, you crawled — but you never ran. Arrietty nearly ran past the grating. She saw it just in time after she turned the corner. Yes, there it was quite close to the ground, embedded deeply in the old wall of the house; there was moss below it in a spreading, greenish stain.

Arrietty ran up to it. "Mother!" she called, her nose against the iron grille. "Mother!" She waited quietly and, after a moment, she called again.

At the third call Homily came. Her hair was coming down and she carried, as though it were heavy, the screw lid of a pickle jar, filled with soapy water. "Oh," she said in an annoyed voice, "you didn't half give me a turn! What do you think you're up to? Where's your father?"

Arrietty jerked her head sideways. "Just there — by the front door!" She was so full of happiness that, out of Homily's sight, her toes danced on the green moss. Here she was on the other side of the grating — here she was at last, on the outside — looking in!

"Yes," said Homily, "they open that door like that — the first day of spring. Well," she went on briskly, "you run back to your father. And tell him, if the morning-room door happens to be open that I wouldn't say no to a bit of red blotting paper. Mind, out of my way now — while I throw the water!"

"That's what grows the moss," thought Arrietty as she sped back to her father, "all the water we empty through the grating. . . ."

Pod looked relieved when he saw her but frowned at the message. "How's she expect me to climb that desk without me pin? Blotting paper's a curtain-and-chair job and she should know it. Come on now! Up with you!"

"Let me stay down," pleaded Arrietty, "just a bit longer. Just till you finish. They're all out. Except Her. Mother said so."

"She'd say anything," grumbled Pod, "when she wants something quick. How does she know She won't take it into her head to get out of that bed of Hers and come downstairs with a stick? How does she know Mrs. Driver ain't stayed at home today — with a headache? How does she know that boy ain't still here?"

"What boy?" asked Arrietty.

Pod looked embarrassed. "What boy?" he repeated vaguely and then went on: "Or may be Crampfurl —"

"Crampfurl isn't a boy," said Arrietty.

"No, he isn't," said Pod, "not in a manner of speaking. No," he went on as though thinking this out, "no, you wouldn't call Crampfurl a boy. Not, as you might say, a boy — exactly. Well," he said, beginning to move away, "stay down a bit if you like. But stay close!"

Arrietty watched him move away from the step and then she looked about her. Oh, glory! Oh, joy! Oh, freedom! The sunlight, the grasses, the soft, moving air and halfway up the bank, where it curved round the corner, a flowering cherry tree! Below it on the path lay a stain of pinkish petals and, at the tree's foot, pale as butter, a nest of primroses.

Arrietty threw a cautious glance toward the front doorstep and then, light and dancey, in her soft red shoes, she ran toward the petals. They were curved like shells and rocked as she touched them. She gathered several up and laid them one inside the other . . . up and up . . . like a card castle. And then she spilled them. Pod came again to the top of the step and looked along the path. "Don't you go far," he said after a moment. Seeing his lips move, she smiled back at him: she was too far already to hear the words.

A greenish beetle, shining in the sunlight, came toward her across the stones. She laid her fingers lightly on its shell and it stood still, waiting and watchful, and when she moved her hand the beetle went swiftly on. An ant came hurrying in a busy zigzag. She danced in front of it to tease it and put out her foot. It stared at her, nonplused, waving its antennae; then pettishly, as though put out, it swerved away. Two birds came down, quarreling shrilly, into the grass below the tree. One flew away but Arrietty could see the other among the moving grass stems above her on the slope. Cautiously she moved toward the bank and climbed a little nervously in amongst the green blades. As she parted them gently with her bare hands, drops of water plopped on her skirt and she felt the red shoes become damp. But on she went, pulling herself up now and again by rooty stems into this jungle of moss and wood-violet and creeping leaves of clover. The sharp-seeming grass blades, waist high, were tender to the touch and sprang back lightly behind her as she passed. When at last she reached the foot of the tree, the bird took fright and flew away and she sat down suddenly on a gnarled leaf of primrose. The air was filled with scent. "But nothing will play with you," she thought and saw the cracks and furrows of the primrose leaves held crystal beads of dew. If she pressed the leaf these rolled like marbles. The bank was warm, almost too warm here within the shelter of the tall grass, and the sandy earth smelled dry. Standing up, she picked a primrose. The pink stalk felt tender and living in her hands and was covered with silvery hairs, and when she held the flower, like a parasol, between her eyes and the sky, she saw the sun's pale light through the veined petals. On a piece of bark she found a wood louse and she struck it lightly with her swaying flower. It curled immediately and became a ball, bumping softly away downhill in amongst the grass roots. But she knew about wood lice. There were plenty of them at home under the floor. Homily always scolded her if she played with them because, she said, they smelled of old knives. She lay back among the stalks of the primroses and they made a coolness between her and the sun, and then, sighing, she turned her head and looked sideways up the bank among the grass stems. Startled, she caught her breath. Something had moved above her on the bank. Something had glittered. Arrietty stared.

It was an eye. Or it looked like an eye. Clear and bright like the color of the sky. An eye like her own but enormous. A glaring eye. Breathless with fear, she sat up. And the eye blinked. A great fringe of lashes came curving down and flew up again out of sight. Cautiously, Arrietty moved her legs: she would slide noiselessly in among the grass stems and slither away down the bank.

"Don't move!" said a voice, and the voice, like the eye, was enormous but, somehow, hushed — and hoarse like a surge of wind through the grating on a stormy night in March.

Arrietty froze. "So this is it," she thought, "the worst and most terrible thing of all: I have been 'seen'!"

There was a pause and Arrietty, her heart pounding in her ears, heard the breath again drawn swiftly into the vast lungs. "Or," said the voice, whispering still, "I shall hit you with my ash stick."

Suddenly Arrietty became calm. "Why?" she asked.

How strange her own voice sounded! Crystal thin and harebell clear, it tinkled on the air.

"In case," came the surprised whisper at last, "you ran toward me, quickly, through the grass . . . in case," it went on, trembling a little, "you came and scrabbled at me with your nasty little hands."

Arrietty stared at the eye; she held herself quite still. "Why?" she asked again, and again the word tinkled — icy cold it sounded this time, and needle sharp.

"Things do," said the voice. "I've seen them. In India."

Arrietty thought of her Gazetteer[1] of the World. "You're not in India now," she pointed out.

"Did you come out of the house?"

"Yes," said Arrietty.

"From whereabouts in the house?"

Arrietty stared at the eye. "I'm not going to tell you," she said at last bravely.

"Then I'll hit you with my ash stick!"

"All right," said Arrietty, "hit me!"

"I'll pick you up and break you in half!"

Arrietty stood up. "All right," she said and took two paces forward.

There was a sharp gasp and an earthquake in the grass: he spun away from her and sat up, a great mountain in a green jersey. He had fair, straight hair and golden eyelashes. "Stay where you are!" he cried.

Arrietty stared up at him. So this was "the boy"! Breathless, she felt, and light with fear. "I guessed you were about nine," she gasped after a moment.

---

[1]**Gazetteer** (găz′ ĭ tîr′): A geographical dictionary, which lists names of places and gives the pronunciation and a short description of each.

He flushed. "Well, you're wrong, I'm ten." He looked down at her, breathing deeply. "How old are you?"

"Fourteen," said Arrietty. "Next June," she added, watching him.

There was silence while Arrietty waited, trembling a little. "Can you read?" the boy said at last.

"Of course," said Arrietty. "Can't you?"

"No," he stammered. "I mean — yes. I mean I've just come from India."

"What's that got to do with it?" asked Arrietty.

"Well, if you're born in India, you're bilingual. And if you're bilingual, you can't read. Not so well."

Arrietty stared up at him: what a monster, she thought, dark against the sky.

"Do you grow out of it?" she asked.

He moved a little and she felt the cold flick of his shadow.

"Oh yes," he said, "it wears off. My sisters were bilingual; now they aren't a bit. They could read any of those books upstairs in the schoolroom."

"So could I," said Arrietty quickly, "if someone could hold them, and turn the pages. I'm not a bit bilingual. I can read anything."

"Could you read out loud?"

"Of course," said Arrietty.

"Would you wait here while I run upstairs and get a book now?"

"Well," said Arrietty; she was longing to show off; then a startled look came into her eyes. "Oh — " she faltered.

"What's the matter?" The boy was standing up now. He towered above her.

"How many doors are there to this house?" She squinted up at him against the bright sunlight. He dropped on one knee.

"Doors?" he said. "Outside doors?"

"Yes."

"Well, there's the front door, the back door, the gun room door, the kitchen door, the scullery door . . . and the french windows in the drawing room."

"Well, you see," said Arrietty, "my father's in the hall, by the front door, working. He . . . he wouldn't want to be disturbed."

"Working?" said the boy. "What at?"

"Getting material," said Arrietty, "for a scrubbing brush."

"Then I'll go in the side door"; he began to move away but turned suddenly and came back to her. He stood a moment, as though embarrassed, and then he said: "Can you fly?"

"No," said Arrietty, surprised; "can you?"

His face became even redder. "Of course not," he said angrily; "I'm not a fairy!"

"Well, nor am I," said Arrietty, "nor is anybody. I don't believe in them."

He looked at her strangely. "You don't believe in them?"

"No," said Arrietty; "do you?"

"Of course not!"

Really, she thought, he is a very angry kind of boy. "My mother believes in them," she said, trying to appease him. "She thinks she saw one once. It was when she was a girl and lived with her parents behind the sand pile in the potting shed."

He squatted down on his heels and she felt his breath on her face. "What was it like?" he asked.

"About the size of a glowworm with wings like a butterfly. And it had a tiny little face, she said, all alight and moving like sparks and tiny moving hands. Its face was changing all the time, she said, smiling and sort of shimmering. It seemed to be talking, she said, very quickly — but you couldn't hear a word. . . ."

"Oh," said the boy, interested. After a moment he asked: "Where did it go?"

"It just went," said Arrietty. "When my mother saw it, it seemed to be caught in a cobweb. It was dark at the time. About five o'clock on a winter's evening. After tea."

"Oh," he said again and picked up two petals of cherry blossom which he folded together like a sandwich and ate slowly. "Supposing," he said, staring past her at the wall of the house, "you saw a little man, about as tall as a pencil, with a blue patch in his trousers, halfway up a window curtain, carrying a doll's tea cup — would you say it was a fairy?"

"No," said Arrietty, "I'd say it was my father."

"Oh," said the boy, thinking this out, "does your father have a blue patch on his trousers?"

"Not on his best trousers. He does on his borrowing ones."

"Oh," said the boy again. He seemed to find it a safe sound, as lawyers do. "Are there many people like you?"

"No," said Arrietty. "None. We're all different."

"I mean as small as you?"

Arrietty laughed. "Oh, don't be silly!" she said. "Surely you don't think there are many people in the world your size?"

"There are more my size than yours," he retorted.

"Honestly — " began Arrietty helplessly and laughed again. "Do you really think — I mean, whatever sort of a world would it be? Those great chairs . . . I've seen them. Fancy if you had to make chairs that size for everyone? And the stuff for their clothes . . . miles and miles of it . . . tents of it . . . and the sewing! And their great houses, reaching up so you can hardly see the ceilings . . . their great beds . . . the *food* they eat . . . great, smoking mountains of it, huge bogs of stew and soup and stuff."

"Don't you eat soup?" asked the boy.

"Of course we do," laughed Arrietty. "My father had an uncle who had a little boat which he rowed round in the stock-pot picking up flotsam and jetsam. He did bottom-fishing too for bits of marrow until the cook got suspicious through finding bent pins in the soup. Once he was nearly shipwrecked on a chunk of submerged shinbone. He lost his oars and the boat sprang a leak but he flung a line over the pot handle and pulled himself alongside the rim. But all that stock — fathoms of it! And the size of the stockpot! I mean, there wouldn't be enough stuff in the world to go round after a bit! That's why my father says it's a good thing they're dying out . . . just a few, my father says, that's all we need — to keep us. Otherwise, he says, the whole thing gets" — Arrietty hesitated, trying to remember the word — "exaggerated, he says — "

"What do you mean," asked the boy, "to keep us?"

So Arrietty told him about borrowing — how difficult it was and how dangerous. She told him about the storerooms under the floor; about Pod's early exploits, the skill he had shown and the courage; she described

those far-off days, before her birth, when Pod and Homily had been rich; she described the musical snuffbox of gold filigree, and the little bird which flew out of it made of kingfisher feathers, how it flapped its wings and sang its song; she described the doll's wardrobe and the tiny green glasses; the little silver teapot out of the drawing-room case; the satin bedcovers and embroidered sheets . . . "those we have still," she told him, "they're Her handkerchiefs. . . ." "She," the boy realized gradually, was his Great-Aunt Sophy upstairs, bedridden since a hunting accident some twenty years before; he heard how Pod would borrow from Her room, picking his way — in the firelight — among the trinkets on Her dressing table, even climbing Her bedcurtains and walking on Her quilt.

"She gives me dictation and teaches me to write," said the boy. "I only see her in the mornings when she's cross. She sends for me and looks behind my ears and asks Mrs. D. if I've learned my words."

"What does Mrs. D. look like?" asked Arrietty. (How delicious it was to say "Mrs. D." like that . . . how careless and daring!)

"She's fat and has a mustache and gives me my bath and hurts my bruise and my sore elbow and says she'll take a slipper to me one of these days. . . ." The boy pulled up a tuft of grass and stared at it angrily and Arrietty saw his lip tremble. "My mother's very nice," he said. "She lives in India. Why did you lose all your worldly riches?"

"Well," said Arrietty, "the kitchen boiler burst and hot water came pouring through the floor into our house and everything was washed away and piled up in front of the grating. My father worked night and day. First hot, then cold. Trying to salvage things. And there's a dreadful draught[2] in March through that grating. He got ill, you see, and couldn't go borrowing. So my Uncle Hendreary had to do it and one or two others and my mother gave them things, bit by bit, for all their trouble. But the kingfisher bird was spoilt by the water; all its feathers fell off and a great twirly spring came jumping out of its side. My father used the spring to keep the door shut against draughts from the grating and my mother put the feathers in a little moleskin hat. After a while I got born and my father went borrowing again. But he gets tired now and doesn't like curtains, not when any of the bobbles are off. . . ."

"I helped him a bit," said the boy, "with the tea cup. He was shivering all over. I suppose he was frightened."

"My father frightened!" exclaimed Arrietty angrily. "Frightened of you!" she added.

"Perhaps he doesn't like heights," said the boy.

"He loves heights," said Arrietty. "The thing he doesn't like is curtains. I've told you. Curtains make him tired."

The boy sat thoughtfully on his haunches, chewing a blade of grass. "Borrowing," he said after a while. "Is that what you call it?"

"What else could you call it?" asked Arrietty.

"I'd call it stealing."

Arrietty laughed. She really laughed. "But we *are* Borrowers," she explained, "like you're a — a human bean or whatever it's called. We're part of the house. You

---

[2]**draught** (drăft): British spelling of *draft*, a current of moving air.

might as well say that the fire grate steals the coal from the coal scuttle."

"Then what is stealing?"

Arrietty looked grave. "Don't you know?" she asked. "Stealing is — well, supposing my Uncle Hendreary borrowed an emerald watch from Her dressing-table and my father took it and hung it up on our wall. That's stealing."

"An emerald watch!" exclaimed the boy.

"Well, I just said that because we have one on the wall at home, but my father borrowed it himself. It needn't be a watch. It could be anything. A lump of sugar even. But Borrowers don't steal."

"Except from human beings," said the boy.

Arrietty burst out laughing; she laughed so much that she had to hide her face in the primrose. "Oh dear," she gasped with tears in her eyes, "you are funny!" She stared upward at his puzzled face. "Human beans are *for* Borrowers — like bread's for butter!"

The boy was silent awhile. A sigh of wind rustled the cherry tree and shivered among the blossoms.

"Well, I don't believe it," he said at last, watching the falling petals. "I don't believe that's what we're for at all and I don't believe we're dying out!"

"Oh, goodness!" exclaimed Arrietty impatiently, staring up at his chin. "Just use your common sense: you're the only real human bean I ever saw (although I do just know of three more — Crampfurl, Her, and Mrs. Driver). But I know lots and lots of Borrowers: the Overmantels and the Harpsichords and the Rain-Barrels and the Linen-Presses and the Boot-Racks and the Hon. John Studdingtons and — "

He looked down. "John Studdington? But he was our grand-uncle — "

"Well, this family lived behind a picture," went on Arrietty, hardly listening, "and there were the Stove-Pipes and the Bell-Pulls and the — "

"Yes," he interrupted, "but did you see them?"

"I saw the Harpsichords. And my mother was a Bell-Pull. The others were before I was born. . . ."

He leaned closer. "Then where are they now? Tell me that."

"My Uncle Hendreary has a house in the country," said Arrietty coldly, edging away from his great lowering face; it was misted over, she noticed, with hairs of palest gold. "And four children, Harpsichords and Clocks."

"But where are the others?"

"Oh," said Arrietty, "they're somewhere." But where? she wondered. And she shivered slightly in the boy's cold shadow which lay about her, slant-wise, on the grass.

He drew back again, his fair head blocking out a great piece of sky. "Well," he said deliberately after a moment, and his eyes were cold, "I've only seen two Borrowers but I've seen hundreds and hundreds and hundreds and hundreds and hundreds — "

"Oh no — " whispered Arrietty.

"Of human beings." And he sat back.

Arrietty stood very still. She did not look at him. After a while she said: "I don't believe you."

"All right," he said, "then I'll tell you — "

"I still won't believe you," murmured Arrietty.

"Listen!" he said. And he told her about railway stations and football matches and racecourses and royal processions and Albert Hall concerts. He told her about

India and China and North America and the British Commonwealth. He told her about the July sales. "Not hundreds," he said, "but thousands and millions and billions and trillions of great, big, enormous people. Now do you believe me?"

Arrietty stared up at him with frightened eyes: it gave her a crick in the neck. "I don't know," she whispered.

"As for you," he went on, leaning closer again, "I don't believe that there are any more Borrowers anywhere in the world. I believe you're the last three," he said.

Arrietty dropped her face into the primrose. "We're not. There's Aunt Lupy and Uncle Hendreary and all the cousins."

"I bet they're dead," said the boy. "And what's more," he went on, "no one will ever believe I've seen *you*. And you'll be the very last because you're the youngest. One day," he told her, smiling triumphantly, "you'll be the only Borrower left in the world!"

He sat still, waiting, but she did not look up. "Now you're crying," he remarked after a moment.

"They're not dead," said Arrietty in a muffled voice; she was feeling in her little pocket for a handkerchief. "They live in a badger's set[3] two fields away, beyond the spinney.[4] We don't see them because it's too far. There are weasels and things and cows and foxes . . . and crows. . . ."

"Which spinney?" he asked.

"I don't KNOW!" Arrietty almost shouted. "It's along

---

[3]**badger's set:** *Chiefly British.* The underground home of a badger (a burrowing animal related to the weasel.)
[4]**spinney** (**spĭn′** ē): *Chiefly British.* A small grove of trees or shrubs.

by the gas-pipe — a field called Parkin's Beck." She blew her nose. "I'm going home," she said.

"Don't go," he said, "not yet."

"Yes, I'm going," said Arrietty.

His face turned pink. "Let me just get the book," he pleaded.

"I'm not going to read to you now," said Arrietty.

"Why not?"

She looked at him with angry eyes. "Because — "

"Listen," he said, "I'll go to that field. I'll go and find Uncle Hendreary. And the cousins. And Aunt Whatever-she-is. And, if they're alive, I'll tell you. What about that? You could write them a letter and I'd put it down the hole — "

Arrietty gazed up at him. "Would you?" she breathed.

"Yes, I would. Really I would. Now can I go and get the book? I'll go in by the side door."

"All right," said Arrietty absently. Her eyes were shining. "When can I give you the letter?"

"Any time," he said, standing above her. "Where in the house do you live?"

"Well — " began Arrietty and stopped. Why once again did she feel this chill? Could it only be his shadow . . . towering above her, blotting out the sun? "I'll put it somewhere," she said hurriedly, "I'll put it under the hall mat."

"Which one? The one by the front door?"

"Yes, that one."

He was gone. And she stood there alone in the sunshine, shoulder deep in grass. What had happened seemed too big for thought; she felt unable to believe it really had happened: not only had she been "seen" but she had been talked to; not only had she been talked to but she had —

"Arrietty!" said a voice.

She stood up startled and spun round: there was Pod, moon-faced, on the path looking up at her. "Come on down!" he whispered.

She stared at him for a moment as though she did not recognize him; how round his face was, how kind, how familiar!

"Come on!" he said again, more urgently; and obediently because he sounded worried, she slithered quickly toward him off the bank, balancing her primrose. "Put that thing down," he said sharply, when she stood at last beside him on the path. "You can't lug great flowers about — you got to carry a bag. What you want to go up there for?" he grumbled as they moved off across the stones. "I might never have seen you. Hurry up now. Your mother'll have tea waiting!"

Now that Arrietty has been "seen," the quiet, comfortable life of the Borrowers will never be the same. You can find out what happens by reading the rest of Mary Norton's book The Borrowers.

Author

As a child in England, Mary Norton invented stories about tiny people. This childhood fascination led to her four popular books about the Borrowers: *The Borrowers, The Borrowers Afield, The Borrowers Afloat,* and *The Borrowers Aloft.* Mary Norton also wrote *Bed-knob and Broomstick,* which was made into a motion picture.

THE
REAL THIEF
WILLIAM STEIG

Houghton Mifflin Literature

In the selections you have just read from *Facing the Truth*, the characters sometimes had a hard time knowing what was true and what was not true.

Now you are going to read *The Real Thief* by William Steig. In this story, Gawain the goose is in charge of guarding the Royal Treasury. When Gawain is accused of stealing gold and jewels from the Treasury, the *real* thief is forced to face the truth of what he has done.

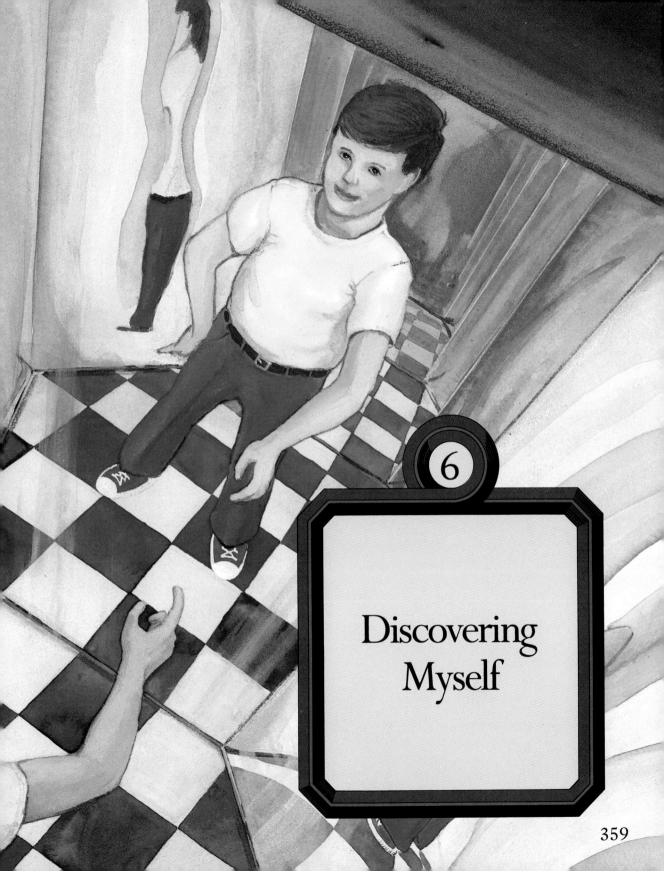

6

Discovering
Myself

The Cabin Faced West

by Jean Fritz

Illustrated by Christa Kieffer

In the early 1780's, Ann Hamilton left her comfortable Gettysburg home east of the Allegheny Mountains. She moved with her parents and brothers to a cabin in Hamilton Hill on the western frontier of what is now Pennsylvania. Ann found herself homesick for Gettysburg. She missed her home and school, her cousin Margaret, and the friends and good times she had had there. She found life hard in the Western Country, where her father had little free time and where good times and special things had to wait for "some day." To amuse herself, Ann kept a diary, and when her friend Andy McPhale went back East, he gave her a deerskin cover for it. Ann often wrote in her diary in a special place at the side of the road that led from Gettysburg, a road that seemed to hold a special promise for Ann.

Ann fitted the new deerskin cover over the diary. It was very handsome, made from the soft underpart of a deer's skin where the brown shades into a honey color. It looked like a real frontier diary now, Ann thought as she stroked it. She began to turn the pages over, re-reading parts she had written. All at once it struck her that on the inside her diary wasn't much like a frontier diary. For the first time she noticed that she had hardly written anything about the Western Country. Most of her entries were about Gettysburg, about Margaret, about her homesickness. If any outsider were to pick up this diary and read it, he might not even know where it had been written. She turned the pages more slowly. She had never mentioned what Hamilton Hill looked like. Ann jumped up. She didn't want to think about Hamilton Hill now. She didn't care if her diary did have a handsome new cover, she didn't feel one bit like writing in it. She went inside the cabin and put the diary up on her shelf.

All day long as Ann went about her chores, she felt out-of-sorts and out of courage. It wasn't only that the McPhales had gone East while she was staying behind. She didn't know what was bothering her, but everything she did went wrong. She cut her finger when she was chopping pumpkin for her mother to make a pumpkin pie. She spilled half a pail of milk as she was taking lunch to the men in the field. She caught her dress on a prickly bush and tore it. And every time she picked up the baby, he cried.

"This just isn't your day," her mother said toward the middle of the afternoon. "Why don't you go on down the road and try to find some grapes? You'll like that. But mind you don't go too far."

It certainly wasn't her day, Ann thought crossly as she took an empty pail and went out the cabin door. But when she reached the road, she wondered. Maybe, after all, something might yet turn the day her way. The road seemed to have more magic to it than she had ever known. The sun's rays slanted down on it as though they were lighting up a stage where something important was going to happen. There was a difference in the mood of the road. It wasn't a happy, dancing mood, nor a mysterious, moonlight mood. Today there was a grandness to the road, as though it were a carpet unfurling over the hill before some glorious secret. As Ann stood in the middle of the road, holding her pail in front of her, two golden

leaves drifted down, turning slowly over and over in the air, and settled in the bottom of her pail. A wild goose dipped low, honking, from the sky, like a herald sent ahead with news.

Ann walked down the hill, captured by the spell of the road. As she rounded each bend, she found herself half expecting something wonderful to be waiting on the other side. She didn't know what, but something. From time to time she stopped to pick grapes that had survived the storm. On all the hill, the only sounds were the plopping of grapes in her pail and the occasional long honk of a passing goose. Ann followed the road as it wound its way down the hill, turning corner after corner, looking for grapes but secretly hoping for something she couldn't even put into words.

Her pail was almost full when she suddenly noticed where she was. She was almost to the bottom of the hill. Almost to the spot her brother David had pointed out as the site for the first church. She had let the road lead her farther than she had ever gone alone. Instead of something wonderful lying around the next corner of the road, there was probably something dreadful.

And then Ann heard hoofbeats. They were coming from the east — not just one horse but three or four, and they were not far away.

Ann ducked down behind some tall grass by the side of the road and made herself into the smallest ball she could possibly squeeze into, wrapping her arms tightly around her knees. She held her breath as the first horse rounded the bend of the road. She must not move — not even a finger. She kept her eyes on the road, counting the legs of the horses as they came into sight. Now there were

two horses . . . three . . . four. If four men were traveling together from the East to the West at this time of
year, they were probably not settlers. They were likely up
to no good. They must be the Doane gang that David had
warned her about.

All at once Ann began to tremble all over. The first
horse had stopped on the road in front of her. Then the
other horses came to a stop. As Ann peeped out between
the tall grasses, all she could see was a forest of horse legs.
From some place way up high above the legs of the first
horse came a deep voice. "Little girl," it said, "I wonder
if you could tell me what your mother is having for
dinner tonight."

The voice didn't sound like the voice of a horse thief.
Slowly Ann lifted her eyes from the legs of the horse to

the boots of the rider. Slowly she lifted them to the place where the voice had come from. Then she found herself looking into the most wonderful face she had ever seen.

It was a strong face, kind and good, and there was something strangely familiar about it. It was as if Ann ought to know this man, as if she almost knew him. No matter what David had said about strangers, somehow Ann knew deep inside that he hadn't been talking about this one. She stopped feeling afraid. She stood up.

"My mother is having peas and potatoes and corn bread for our evening meal," she said, "and she's baking pumpkin pie."

The man smiled. He leaned down toward Ann. "Would you tell her," he said, "that General George Washington would like to take supper with her?"

For a moment Ann could not believe her ears. General Washington on Hamilton Hill! Then all at once she knew it was true. This was the way she had pictured George Washington from what her friend Arthur Scott had said about him. This must have been just how Washington looked, riding among the men at Valley Forge. Suddenly Arthur Scott's words flashed into her mind. "He always seemed to be there just when our courage began to peter out."

Ann swallowed hard. She tried to drop a curtsy but it turned out to be just a stiff little bob. She tried to find her voice, but it didn't turn out any better than the curtsy. It was more like a squeak. "My mother will be pleased," she said. "I'll tell her."

Then Ann found herself and her pail of grapes up on the saddle in front of one of the men in General Washington's party. He said he was Dr. Craik, a friend of the

General's, but Ann didn't pay much attention. She didn't even look at the other men. All she could see was the white horse in front of her and the straight back of General Washington going up Hamilton Hill. The road itself seemed almost to be moving them up the hill in a kind of magic dream. Except it wasn't a dream, Ann reminded herself. It was true — gloriously, wonderfully true. For some unbelievable reason, General George Washington was on the western side of the mountains and he was going to have supper on Hamilton Hill.

Suddenly Ann turned to Dr. Craik. "Why did General Washington come here?" she asked.

"He owns land in this county," Dr. Craik replied. "He's come to check on it."

"He owns land *here* — in Washington County?" Ann repeated.

Dr. Craik smiled. "Yes, he can't move here, but he bought land because he believes in this part of the country. Some day this land will be worth a great deal of money. He wants to do all he can to develop this side of the mountains."

Ann fell silent, her eyes on General Washington. Again she pictured him at Valley Forge. A lot of people hadn't believed in a free and independent country, she thought. But Washington had. And now he believed in the Western Country. It wasn't just fathers and brothers and settlers who believed in it and owned land here. *George Washington did too.*

Ann and Dr. Craik jogged up the hill. The other men called back and forth to each other, but Ann didn't hear them.

Afterward Ann could never remember just how she introduced General Washington and his friends to her mother. When she caught her breath again, they had started on a tour of the farm with David. Ann and her mother were alone in the cabin with supper to prepare.

Mrs. Hamilton's eyes were shining as she stepped away from the door. "Now is the time to use the linen tablecloth, Ann," she said, "and the lavender flowered plates."

Ann was standing in the doorway, her head in the clouds, watching the men put up their horses. At her mother's words, she came quickly down to the world. What a wonderful world it was, she thought, as she flew over to her mother's chest for the linen tablecloth.

"The food is almost ready," Mrs. Hamilton said. "I'll take care of that while you set the table."

Ann spread out the white linen cloth on the table. She smoothed it gently over the rough boards. She pulled it to hang even on all sides. She unwrapped nine flowered plates and placed them around the table. She put knives, forks, and spoons at each place and set new tall candles in the center of the table.

Then Ann stepped back to look at what she had done. Somehow the whole room seemed changed; it seemed larger and more dignified. The clothes hanging awkwardly on hooks along the wall drew back into the shadows. All the light from the fire and from the open doorway fell on the gleaming white party table, waiting for General Washington.

"It's more beautiful than any table we ever set in Gettysburg," Ann whispered.

Mrs. Hamilton looked up from the hearth and smiled.

Later the table looked even more wonderful, piled high with steaming food — hot yellow corn bread, round bowls of green peas, roasted brown potatoes, a platter of cold venison, bowls of purple grape jelly, golden pumpkin pies. It was the same meal that they had had nearly every evening all summer on Hamilton Hill, but tonight with the lavender flowered plates, it managed to look different.

"I hope I look different too," Ann thought as she fingered her two blue hair ribbons and hastily tied the sash of a fresh apron.

She felt different. General Washington and Mr. Hamilton led the others into the cabin, and suddenly Ann found herself feeling strangely shy. All the time they were taking their places at the table, she kept her eyes down. It was not until her father was asking the blessing that she stole her first look up from under half-closed eyelashes. When she saw George Washington's head bowed over the white tablecloth and lavender plate, the peas and potatoes, Ann thought she could hardly bear her happiness.

During the rest of the meal, Ann followed the conversation in a kind of daze. She didn't seem to hear anything that anyone said, except General Washington. Everything he said rang out clear, with a special meaning, it almost seemed, just for her.

"If I were a young man," General Washington said, "preparing to begin the world, I know of no country where I should rather live."

"I am determined to find a way," he said again, "that we can join the waters of the West with those of the East so that the two countries may be close together."

Ann held onto every word, turned them over in her mind, locked them away in her heart. It was after the evening meal, after all the thank-you's had been said and General Washington and his party were preparing to leave that he said what Ann was to treasure forever afterward. He stood at the doorway, looking toward the west, his eyes resting on Hamilton Hill, yet somehow going beyond.

"The future is traveling west with people like you," he said to Mr. Hamilton. "Here is the rising world — to be kept or lost in the same way a battlefield is kept or lost."

General Washington turned to Ann and put his hand gently on her shoulder. "Through the courage of young

girls as much as anyone's. You will live to see this whole country a rolling farmland, bright with houses and barns and churches. Some day. I envy you, Miss Hamilton."

Ann felt her heart turning over within her. Even after General Washington had gone, she went on standing in the doorway, still feeling his hand on her shoulder. She looked out on Hamilton Hill. It seemed to her she had never seen it so beautiful — the trees more stately, the sky closer. She remembered the tea party she and her mother had had in the woods. The hill had been lovely that day, too. And, of course, the part of the hill that went up and down with the road had always been wonderful.

Ann looked at her vegetable garden laid flat by a storm. It seemed to her that again she could feel the rain beating down on her and her peas. She could feel her own helplessness and despair as the vines broke all around her and she had to fish pods out from the muddy water. Suddenly Ann knew what she had not known before. She had cried during the storm, but it was not really because she hated the Western Country. It was because she loved her vegetable garden.

Other thoughts began crowding in on Ann almost faster than she could take care of them. Maybe she had begun to love Hamilton Hill too, without even knowing it. Perhaps that was one reason her thoughts had been so mixed up and she hadn't asked if she could go East.

Ann lifted her chin. Well, she was going to plant another vegetable garden in the spring. It was *important* for her to do it. *She* was important to the Western Country. George Washington had said so. And some day, she thought. . . .

Ann caught herself and smiled. Here she was thinking "some day" just like the others.

David, coming back from the road and seeing General Washington off, caught Ann's smile.

"Here's something else for you to smile about," he said. He pulled a small packet of letters from his pocket and fingered through them. "Dr. Craik was given these letters at Devore's Ferry to bring on to us. They had been left there about a week ago. There's one for you." He handed Ann an envelope. It was a letter from Margaret.

All the excitement and all the happiness of the long day seemed to rush into Ann's feet. She took the letter and she ran — not because she wanted to get anywhere, but just because she had to run. Sometimes, Ann had discovered, there is only one thing to do about gladness and that is — to run. Her two brown braids and blue hair ribbons streaming behind her, she ran to the road, to the crest of the hill where on one side the road dropped away to the west and on the other side it dropped away to the east. Here Ann stopped to catch her breath. She sat down on a rock beside the road and slowly slit open the envelope of Margaret's letter. She didn't want to read it too fast. Letters didn't come often and she wanted to make this first reading last as long as she could.

The sun seemed to follow the path of the road as it rolled west to the evening. Ann read about the new teacher in the Gettysburg school, about the frolic at the Gettysburg Hamiltons'. And then she came to the last paragraph.

"This is the big news," Margaret wrote. "At last I have persuaded Mother and Father to allow me to do what I have wanted to do for so long. They say that in the spring

when someone is going over the mountains, I may go along and spend the spring and summer with Uncle John and Aunt Mary. They have no children, and I am sure I could be a help. Just think how close I will be to you! And I will have a little part in the making of the Western Country, after all — even if it is only for one season."

Ann put the letter down in her lap. She wasn't able to find any words to say, even to herself, all that she was feeling. She looked at the road, gathering up the shadows of the evening. Before her in the distant dusk she could just see the outline of the cabin. A thin spiral of smoke climbed up from the chimney and joined a gray cloud in the sky.

"My cup runneth over," Ann whispered to herself.

That night, in the home of a Colonel Cannon several miles west of Hamilton Hill, before he blew out his candle, General George Washington sat down at a table and wrote this in his diary:

> "September 18, 1784. Set out with Doctr. Craik for my Land on Miller's Run, crossed the Monongahela at Devore's Ferry . . . bated at one Hamilton's about 4 miles from it, in Washington County, and lodged at Colo. Cannon's."

That night in the cabin on Hamilton Hill, Ann took down from her shelf her deerskin-covered diary. Her heart was too full to write all she wanted. Instead she wrote in big letters across a whole page:

> "September 18, 1784.
> GEORGE WASHINGTON WAS HERE."

In smaller letters underneath she added:

> "Margaret is coming."

Tomorrow she would write more.

A Postscript from the Author

If you look in George Washington's diary, you will find his words exactly as they are in this story. On September 18, 1784, he "bated" or took supper with the Hamiltons.

I don't know if Ann really kept a diary or not. Most of what happened to her in this book is just a story, but some of it is true. There really was an Ann Hamilton; she was my great-great-grandmother. As long as she lived, she told the story to her children and her children's children, about the wonderful evening when George Washington rode up Hamilton Hill.

Hamilton Hill is known as Ginger Hill now, but grapevines still grow wild by the side of the road. And the little church is really there, just where David pointed out it would be and where he later helped to build it.

Author

Jean Fritz was born and raised in China, where her parents worked as missionaries. She says that growing up in a foreign country led to her great interest in American history. *The Cabin Faced West,* which is based on the life of her great-great-grandmother, was Jean Fritz's first work of historical fiction. She has since written many others, including *And Then What Happened, Paul Revere?* and *Why Don't You Get a Horse, Sam Adams?*

How Paul Bonjean Became Paul Bunyan

**From the tall tale
by Anne Malcolmson**

Illustrated by Marc Tetrault

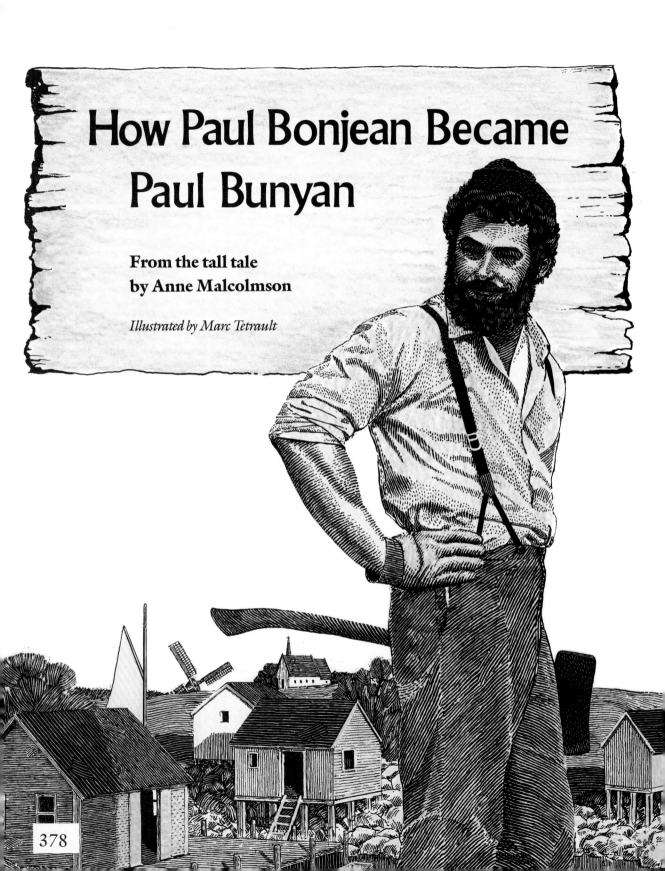

Even before he let out his first baby squall, it was obvious that Paul Bonjean[1] was going to be a hero. He was a large baby, as babies go. Instead of the usual seven or eight pounds, *le petit*[2] Paul weighed seventy or eighty. He was born with a long, glossy black beard and a pair of beautifully waxed and curled mustaches. Furthermore, you could see him grow.

Monsieur[3] Bonjean, his father, nearly burst with pride. Before nightfall, however, he was worried. For the baby had drunk up all the milk that Marie, the cow, could give. The little clothes that Madame[4] Bonjean had made were no longer of any use. The cabin bunk wouldn't hold him. Papa Bonjean wrung his hands in despair.

The neighbors did what they could to help. They gave the baby all the milk from their cows. They gave their sheets for diapers. They spread their blankets in the ox stall for him. Then they went home to bed.

In the morning the whole village gazed in awe at the new baby. He had grown so fast during the night that his chubby little feet and hands stuck out through the doors and windows of the ox shed. The big double sheets were stretched to the ripping point across his tummy. And he was as hungry as a bear. He doubled his little fist and banged it down on the ground, crushing to splinters several racks for drying codfish. He waved his little leg in the air, knocking down two pine trees and a retired sea captain. Something had to be done.

---

[1]**Bonjean** (bōn zhŏɴ′)   [3]**Monsieur** (mə sûr′)

[2]**le petit** (lə pə tē′): The little.   [4]**Madame** (mä däm′)

379

The first problem was food. All the cows in New Brunswick were herded together to give him milk. Several shiploads of cod-liver oil, meant for Boston, were put in storage for him. He had to have three barrels of it every day. The clothing problem was solved by a sailmaker from St. John. He cheerfully donated a pair of mainsails to be made into pants. The Ladies Aid Society offered to do the sewing. A wagon-maker gave a dozen cartwheels to be used for buttons.

Still there was no suitable place for the little fellow to sleep. No hayloft would hold him. Papa Bonjean tried to rent a field from a farmer. "But," objected the farmer, "think of my crops. They will all be crushed and ruined."

At last the problem was solved. A committee was sent to the shipyards in Maine. They found in one the half-built hull of a clipper ship. The ship was to be the largest in the China trade. As yet no decks nor masts had been put in. "The very thing we want!" exclaimed the committee. So they bought it.

They asked the astonished shipwright to line the hold with featherbeds. Then they towed it up to the Bay of Fundy. With the aid of a large steam crane, they hoisted little Paul into his new cradle.

It was a perfect fit. The baby cooed and gurgled to show how happy he was, and soon fell asleep. The gentle rocking of the sea and the slap of waves against the shore were his lullabies. He slept soundly for two weeks, with his little pink thumb nestled against the glossy black of his beard and mustaches.

Unfortunately, when the time came to give him his bottle, he would not wake up. The fishermen rowed out to his cradle and yelled at him. He slept right on. The

lighthouse keeper sounded the fog horn. Little Paul only sighed in his sleep. What to do next? Papa Bonjean went to the mayor. The mayor went to the Provincial Governor. The Provincial Governor went to the Governor General. He had a bright idea. He knew that part of the British Navy was stationed off the coast of Nova Scotia. So he wrote to the Admiral of the Fleet. The Admiral was very fond of children and agreed to help.

He ordered the fleet into the Bay of Fundy. He lined up the ships in battle formation opposite Paul's cradle. Then at a given signal they fired their cannon over the baby's head.

That woke him up! It frightened him, too! He opened his little mouth and screamed *"Maman[5]!"* which is French for "Mama!" His scream was heard in Boston by the Coast Guard Listening Station. Thinking that the whole North Atlantic fishing fleet must be in trouble, the Coast Guard sent out all its ships to see what was wrong.

Furthermore, the child trembled so in his fright that his cradle rocked from side to side, kicking up waves seventy-five feet high. Even after all these years, the water has not calmed down completely. In some places in the Bay of Fundy the tides are still fifty feet or more.

In spite of difficulties which you can well imagine, little Paul grew up. His childhood was a happy one. His parents adored him and he loved them in return. But something bothered him. His clear blue eyes grew dreamy. His thoughts wandered into far places. He seemed to know that some great task lay ahead of him. But what it was, he couldn't tell.

---

[5]**Maman** (mä män´)

He went to school with other children. He was extremely bright for his age. Even so he had his troubles. In penmanship, for instance, he could write only one letter on a page. His geography book was so large it had to be carried by an ox team. Once in a careless moment he sat on his lunch box. When he opened it later, he found the first of his many inventions — hamburger!

He had soon learned all that school could teach him. Although he loved to read, he knew that he must learn other things. He had to find out what it was he had to do in life.

Papa Bonjean suggested that he try fishing. For a year young Paul worked with nets and ships. He was a great help to his father. Every morning at sunrise, he towed a pair of three-masted schooners out into the fishing banks of the Atlantic Ocean. Before breakfast he waded back to the docks, a schooner tucked under each arm. Their holds were jammed with cod and haddock. Fishing was easy, but it didn't satisfy him. It was too easy. Surely this was not the great work he had to do!

Next he tried hunting and trapping. He went up into the Canadian woods to learn from the Indian guides. They taught him to follow the tracks of animals, of moose and bear and caribou. He became so clever at this his teachers were amazed. Once he found the body of a dead moose. From the antlers he judged it to be fifteen years old. Nevertheless, he set out to follow the big fellow's tracks — just for fun. He traced them as they grew smaller and smaller, until they became the tiny hoof-prints of a fawn. He didn't give up until he had reached the moose's birthplace.

The Indians taught Paul Bonjean other tricks, especially how to shoot. In time he became a crack shot. He invented a shotgun with seventy-six barrels to make shooting more interesting. At first it was impossible to sight down all the barrels at once. But Paul's inventive genius helped him out. He rigged up a system of mirrors. The first time he tried out the gun with the mirrors he brought down seventy-six duck.

As great a hunter as he was, Paul was not satisfied that hunting was to be his life-work. Something inside kept urging him on to different fields. He tried one thing after another. Nothing was right. At last the desire to find Something Big to do in a Big Way got to be too much. He became cross and sulky. He wouldn't eat his dinner, not even when his mother fixed his favorite dish — a roasted moose stuffed with wild boar and a dozen wild turkeys.

He had to get away from things. So with a pack of books and provisions on his back, his rifle over his shoulder, he trudged north into the wilderness of Labrador. He was so absent-minded, he stepped across the St. Lawrence River without noticing. On and on he went. At last he found a cave big enough for him, on the coast. Here he settled for the winter.

All winter long he stayed there. He left the cave only to fish and to hunt for food. The rest of the time he lay by his fire, reading and dreaming and trying to figure out just what his life-work was meant to be. He became so interested in his problem that he didn't notice the strange and wonderful snow that was falling on the world. Outside everything was hushed. Forests and thickets, fields and trails, all were being covered with a bright blue blanket. It glistened and sparkled like ground sapphires. It was as blue as Paul's eyes.

Unaware of the miracle, Paul lay dreaming in his cave. Suddenly a great noise made him wake up. He heard the thunder of snow slipping off the roof of his cave. With a rumble and a splash a heavy object tumbled over the cliff and fell into the ocean. Paul rushed out to see what it could be.

Sticking up from the cold black water were the horns and the head of a baby ox. The newborn calf lay still among the icebergs. For a moment Paul thought it was frozen or drowned. He dashed into the sea to pull it out. But it was heavy, much heavier than an ordinary calf. He had to struggle before he could lug it onto the shore and into the warmth of his cave.

When he had finally laid it down before the fire and covered it with his blankets, he had a chance to admire it. The baby ox had bright blue hair the color of the strange snow. It was a big fellow, as big as Paul himself.

"*Ah, Bébé*[6]," he murmured as he stroked its baby head. At that it opened its big blue eyes, and feebly it licked his face with its big pink tongue. For days and nights Paul nursed the little calf back to health. What a remarkable beast he was! Paul himself had to go hungry, for *Bébé* ate everything in sight.

He was strong — fifty times as strong as any full-grown ox should be. He was playful. He loved to play hide and seek. He liked to lie down in the blue snow, which blended perfectly with his hide. His horns stuck up like black trees.

Then Paul would wander about calling, "*Bébé, Bébé,* where are you?" And at last *Bébé,* who had been lying in plain sight all the time, would jump up and charge at Paul.

When spring came, the lovely blue snow began to melt. As the sap began to stir in the trees, Paul's problem began to stir in his mind. Somehow or other, he began to feel that he was about to solve it. Night after night he dreamt the same dream. When he got up in the morning it was gone. All that he could remember was that it had something to do with Real America.

---

[6]**Bébé** (bā bā′)

He decided to go to Real America. Perhaps he could find there the kind of work he was meant to do. One morning he packed a little lunch and called *Bébé*. Together they set out. By evening they had reached the border. Off ahead of them stretched the state of Maine, with its miles of pine woods. As far as the eye could see there were trees, nothing but trees.

Bébé romped on ahead. When a hundred-year-old pine got in his way, he kicked it impatiently with his foot. It snapped under the force of the blow and fell crashing to the forest floor.

And then Paul knew what it was he had to do in life. He had to go to Real America and invent logging. It was his job to cut down all those trees and to make room for all the Real Americans who were coming to plant farms and build cities.

He stepped proudly across the border. He started to call, *"Holà, Bébé"*[7] in French Canadian. But the words wouldn't come. Instead he heard himself shouting a new language — "Hey, Babe!"

He stopped in amazement. He pinched himself all over. He discovered that he was a New Man.

"By my old mackinaw!" he said, and he slapped his knee. "By the great horn spoon! I'm a Real American. And I'll be durned if I'm not goin' to log off this state before you can say 'Jack Robinson.'" With a whoop and a holler he started right in on his new job.

And that is how *Bébé* became Babe, the blue ox. And that is how *Paul Bonjean* became Paul Bunyan!

---

[7]**Holà** (ô lä′)

Author

Anne Malcolmson met a man in New Hampshire who told stories he said he had heard while he worked as a lumberjack with Paul Bunyan. Later she wrote her first book of tall tales, *Yankee Doodle's Cousins,* from which this story of Paul Bunyan was taken.

THE ARRIVAL of PADDINGTON

by Alfred Bradley and Michael Bond

Illustrated by Peggy Fortnum

Cast of Characters

Mr. Brown

Mrs. Brown

Paddington Bear

Refreshment Man

Judy Brown

Mrs. Bird

Jonathan Brown

Props

At Paddington Station:
Cardboard boxes
Sign saying
   "Paddington Station"
Suitcase
Jar of marmalade —
   almost empty
Tea trolley or tray
Cakes on paper plates
Plastic or paper cups
Drinking straw
Cake wrapper

At Number thirty-two,
Windsor Gardens:
Table and chairs
Tray with teapot and cups
Towel
Possibly some cushions
   and anything else that
   helps make the set look
   like the Browns' living
   room.

The play starts on Paddington Station. All that we need is a heap of parcels to hide Paddington, (cardboard boxes will do) and a sign saying "Paddington Station." Paddington wears a floppy bush hat, wellington boots and has a label tied round his neck which says "Please look after this bear. Thank you." In his suitcase, which he takes with him wherever he goes, is a jar of marmalade. When the refreshment man arrives he should have a tea trolley or a tray with several plastic or paper cups and some sticky cakes. (As real cakes may be messy, it is probably best to make your own using shaving cream which will wash off easily.) The sticky cake wrapper can be made out of an ordinary cake wrapper, covered on both sides with double-sided, transparent sticky tape.

When we get to Number thirty-two, Windsor Gardens we will need a table, and some chairs. You can make the splashing and banging for Paddington's shower by hammering on something noisy (an old biscuit tin would do) and by splashing water in a bucket.

Scene One

When the play begins Paddington *is concealed behind an assorted pile of parcels and luggage.* Henry Brown *comes on to the platform, closely followed by his wife.*

Mr. Brown: Well, Mary, after all that rushing about, we're here early.

Mrs. Brown: What's the time now?

Mr. Brown: It's just a quarter past four and Judy's train doesn't arrive until half past.

Mrs. Brown: Are you sure?

Mr. Brown: She told me in her letter and she doesn't usually make mistakes.

Mrs. Brown: I'll just go and check which platform . . .
[goes off]
[Left to himself Mr. Brown *strolls around the platform.* Paddington, *hidden behind the parcels, pops up like a jack-in-the-box and quickly down again.* Mr. Brown *is looking surprised;* Mrs. Brown *returns.]*

Mrs. Brown: It's platform five. And you're quite right, the train doesn't arrive until half past four.

Mr. Brown: Mary, you won't believe this, but I've just seen a bear.

Mrs. Brown: A what?

Mr. Brown: A bear.

Mrs. Brown: A bear? On Paddington Station. Don't be silly, Henry. There can't be.

Mr. Brown: But there is. I distinctly saw it. Over there. Behind those parcels. It was wearing a funny kind of hat. Come and see for yourself.

Mrs. Brown: *[humouring him]* Very well. *[She peers behind the parcels.]* Why Henry, I believe you were right after all. It is a bear!
[Paddington stands up suddenly. He is wearing a bush hat with a wide brim and has a large luggage label round his neck.]

Paddington: Good afternoon. *[He raises his hat.]*

Mr. Brown: Er . . . good afternoon.

Paddington: Can I help you?

Mr. Brown: Well . . . no. Er, not really. As a matter of fact, we were wondering if we could help you.

Mrs. Brown: *[taking a closer look]* You're a very unusual bear.

Paddington: I'm a very rare sort of bear. There aren't many of us left where I come from.

Mr. Brown: And where is that?

Paddington: Darkest Peru. I'm not really supposed to be here at all. I'm a stowaway.

Mrs. Brown: A stowaway?

Paddington: Yes. I emigrated you know. I used to live with my Aunt Lucy in Peru, but she had to go into a Home for Retired Bears.

Mrs. Brown: You don't mean to say you've come all the way from South America by yourself?

Paddington: Yes. Aunt Lucy always said she wanted me to emigrate when I was old enough. That's why she taught me to speak English.

Mr. Brown: But whatever did you do for food? You must be starving.

Paddington: [*opening his suitcase and taking out an almost empty jar*] I ate marmalade. Bears like marmalade. And I hid in a lifeboat.

Mr. Brown: But what are you going to do now? You can't just sit on Paddington Station waiting for something to happen.

Paddington: Oh, I shall be all right . . . I expect.

Mrs. Brown: What does it say on your label?

Mr. Brown: [*reading it*] "Please look after this bear. Thank you."

Mrs. Brown: That must be from his Aunt Lucy. Oh, Henry, what shall we do? We can't just leave him here. There's no knowing what might happen to him. Can't he come and stay with us for a few days?

Mr. Brown: But Mary, dear, we can't take him . . . not just like that. After all . . .

Mrs. Brown: After all, what? He'd be good company for Jonathan and Judy. Even if it's only for a little while. They'd never forgive us if they knew you'd left him here.

Mr. Brown: It all seems highly irregular. I'm sure there's a law against it. *[Turning to* Paddington*]* Would you like to come and stay with us? That is, if you've nothing else planned.

Paddington: *[overjoyed]* Oooh, yes, please. I should like that very much. I've nowhere to go and everyone seems in such a hurry.

Mrs. Brown: Well, that's settled then. And you can have marmalade for breakfast every morning . . .

Paddington: Every morning? I only had it on special occasions at home. Marmalade's very expensive in Darkest Peru.

Mrs. Brown: Then you shall have it every morning starting tomorrow.

Paddington: *[worried]* Will it cost a lot? You see I haven't very much money.

Mrs. Brown: Of course not. We wouldn't dream of charging you anything. We shall expect you to be one of the family, shan't we, Henry?

Mr. Brown: Of course. By the way, if you *are* coming home with us you'd better know our names. This is Mrs. Brown and I'm Mr. Brown.

Paddington: *[raises his hat twice]* I haven't really got a name, only a Peruvian one which no one can understand.

Mrs. Brown: Then we'd better give you an English one. It'll make things much easier. *[Thinking hard]* It ought to be something special. Now what shall we call you? I know! We found you on Paddington Station so that's what we'll call you . . . Paddington.

Paddington: *[savouring it]* Paddington. Pad-ding-ton. Paddington. It seems a very long name.

Mr. Brown: It's quite distinguished. Yes, I like Paddington as a name. Paddington it shall be.

Mrs. Brown: Good. Now, Paddington, I have to meet our young daughter Judy off the train. I'm sure you must be thirsty after your long journey, so while I'm away Mr. Brown will get you something to drink.

Paddington: Thank you.

Mrs. Brown: And for goodness sake, Henry, when you get a moment, take that label off his neck. It makes him look like a parcel.

[Paddington *doesn't much like the thought of looking like a parcel.*]

I'm sure he'll get put in a luggage van if a porter sees him. *[She goes off almost bumping into a* Man *pushing the refreshment trolley.]*

Mr. Brown: *[removing the label]* There we are. Ah! The very thing. Now I can get you something to drink.

[Paddington *puts the luggage label into his suitcase.*]

Man: What would you like, tea or coffee?

Paddington: Cocoa, please.

Man: *[annoyed]* We haven't got any cocoa.

Paddington: But you asked me what I would like . . .

Man: I asked you what would you like, *tea* or *coffee*!

Mr. Brown: *[hastily, trying to avoid an argument]* Perhaps you'd like a cold drink?

Man: Lemonade or orangeade?

Paddington: Marmalade.

Mr. Brown: *[before the man loses his temper]* I think some orangeade would be a good idea — and a cup of tea for me, please.

[The Man *serves them.]*

And perhaps you'd like a cake, Paddington?

Paddington: Oooh, yes, please.

Man: Cream-and-chocolate, or cream-and-jam?

Paddington: Yes, please.

Man: Well, which do you want?

Mr. Brown: We'd better have one of each.

[The Man *puts them on a plate.* Mr. Brown *pays him, and hands the plate to* Paddington.]*

How's that to be going on with?

Paddington: It's very nice, thank you, Mr. Brown. But it's not very easy drinking out of a beaker. I usually get my nose stuck.

Mr. Brown: Perhaps you'd like a straw.

[He takes one from the Man *and puts it into Paddington's beaker.]*

Paddington: That's a good idea. *[He blows through the straw and makes a noisy bubbling sound.]* I'm glad I emigrated. *[Takes a bite from one of the cakes]* I wonder what else there is?

[He puts the plate of cakes on the floor in order to peer at the trolley and promptly steps on the cake. In his excitement he upsets the rest of the cups on the trolley, scattering them in all directions. Trying to steady himself, he knocks Mr. Brown's *tea out of his hand, slips over and ends up sprawled on the platform. As* Mr. Brown *bends to help him up* Paddington *staggers to his feet. They collide and* Paddington's *cream cake ends up plastered all over* Mr. Brown's *face. Just at this moment* Mrs. Brown *returns with* Judy. *All this will need to be carefully rehearsed beforehand.]*

Mrs. Brown: Henry! Henry, whatever are you doing to that poor bear? Look at him! He's covered all over with jam and cream.

Mr. Brown: *He's* covered with jam and cream! What about me? *[He begins to tidy up the mess.]*

Mrs. Brown: This is what happens when I leave your father alone for five minutes.

Judy: *[clapping her hands]* Oh, Daddy, is he really going to stay with us?

[Paddington stands up, raises his hat, steps on the cake and falls over again.]

Oh, Mummy, isn't he funny!

Mrs. Brown: You wouldn't think that anybody could get in such a state with just one cake.

Mr. Brown: Perhaps we'd better go. Are we all ready?

Judy: Come along, Paddington.

[Paddington picks up his suitcase and puts the remains of the cakes in it. The cake wrapper sticks to his paws but he doesn't notice it.]

We'll go straight home and you can have a nice hot bath. Then you can tell me all about South America. I'm sure you must have had lots of wonderful adventures.

Paddington: I have. Lots. Things are always happening to me, I'm that sort of bear. *[He goes off with Judy.]*

Mr. Brown: *[to his wife]* I hope we haven't bitten off more than we can chew.

Man: Well, if you have, you'll just have to grin and *bear* it. *[He laughs loudly at his own joke and goes off.]*

Scene Two

[Number thirty-two, Windsor Gardens. Judy *and*
Paddington *have just walked into the living room.]*

Judy: Here we are. Now you are going to meet Mrs.
Bird.

Paddington: Mrs. Bird?

Judy: Yes. She looks after us. She's a bit fierce sometimes
and she grumbles a bit, but she doesn't really mean it. I'm
sure you'll like her.

Paddington: *[nervously]* I'm sure I shall, if you say so.
[The door opens and Mrs. Bird *appears.]*

Mrs. Bird: Goodness gracious, you've arrived already, and
me hardly finished the washing up. I suppose you'll be
wanting tea?

Judy: Hello, Mrs. Bird. It's nice to see you again. How's the
rheumatism?

Mrs. Bird: Worse than it's ever
been. *[She stops abruptly as she
sees* Paddington.] Good gracious! Whatever have you got
there?

Judy: It's not a what, Mrs. Bird. It's
a bear. His name's Paddington.
[Paddington raises his hat.]

Mrs. Bird: A bear . . . well, he has
good manners, I'll say that for
him.

Judy: He's going to stay with us. He's come all the way from South America and he's all alone with nowhere to go.

Mrs. Bird: Going to *stay* with us? How long for?

Judy: I don't know. I suppose it *depends!*

Mrs. Bird: Mercy me. I wish you'd told me he was coming. I haven't put clean sheets in the spare room or anything.

Paddington: It's all right, Mrs. Bird. I didn't have any sheets in the lifeboat. I'm sure I shall be very comfortable.

[He shakes hands with her. When he lets go, the leftover cake wrapper is sticking to her hand. She tries in vain to get it off, and finally it sticks to her other hand.]

Judy: Let me help, Mrs. Bird. *[Judy takes it from her, but then finds that it is glued to her own hand.]*

[At this moment Mr. and Mrs. Brown arrive with Jonathan.]

Hello, Jonathan. *[She shakes hands with Jonathan and passes the sticky paper on to him.]* You haven't met Paddington yet, have you? Paddington, this is my brother Jonathan.

Jonathan: How do you do?

Paddington: Very well, thank you.

[Paddington shakes hands with Jonathan and collects the sticky paper.]

Mrs. Bird: Whatever's going on?

Paddington: I'm afraid I had an accident with a cake, Mrs. Bird. It's left me a bit sticky.

Mrs. Bird: I think a good hot bath will do you the world of good.

Judy: *[confidentially]* She doesn't mind really. In fact, I think she rather likes you.

Paddington: She seems a bit fierce.

Mrs. Bird: *[turning round suddenly]* What was that?

Paddington: I didn't hear anything.

Mrs. Bird: Where was it you said you'd come from? Peru?

Paddington: That's right. *Darkest* Peru.

Mrs. Bird: Humph. Then I expect you like marmalade. I'd better get some more from the grocer. *[She leaves the room.]*

Judy: *[happily]* There you are! What did I tell you? She *does* like you.

Paddington: Fancy her knowing that I like marmalade.

Judy: Mrs. Bird knows everything about everything.

Mrs. Brown: Now, Judy, you'd better show Paddington his room.

Judy: Come on. It used to be mine when I was small. There's a bathroom as well so you can have a good clean up.

Paddington: A *bathroom.* Fancy having a special room for a bath.

[They leave the room.]

Mr. Brown: I hope we're doing the right thing.

Mrs. Brown: Well, we can hardly turn him out now. It wouldn't be fair.

Mr. Brown: I'm sure we ought to report the matter to someone first.

Jonathan: I don't see why, Dad. Besides, didn't you say he was a stowaway? He might get arrested.

Mr. Brown: Then there's the question of pocket money. I'm not sure how much money to give a bear.

Mrs. Brown: He can have twenty pence a week, the same as Jonathan and Judy.

Mr. Brown: Very well, but we'll have to see what Mrs. Bird has to say about it first.

Jonathan: Hurrah!

Mrs. Brown: *You'd* better ask her then, it was your idea.

[Mrs. Bird *comes in with a tray of tea, followed by* Judy.]

Mrs. Bird: I suppose you want to tell me you've decided to keep that young Paddington.

Judy: May we, Mrs. Bird? *Please.* I'm sure he'll be very good.

Mrs. Bird: Humph! *[She puts the tray on the table.]* That remains to be seen. Different people have different ideas about being good. All the same, he looks the sort of bear who means well.

Mr. Brown: Then you don't mind, Mrs. Bird?

Mrs. Bird: No. No, I don't mind at all. I've always had a soft spot for bears myself. It'll be nice to have one about the house. [*She goes.*]

Mr. Brown: Well, whoever would have thought it?

Judy: I expect it was because he raised his hat. It made a good impression.

Mrs. Brown: [*pouring the tea*] I suppose someone ought to write and tell his Aunt Lucy. I'm sure she'd like to know how he's getting on.

Mr. Brown: By the way, how *is* he getting on?

[*There is a loud gurgling noise from the bath, followed by a tremendous splashing sound. Paddington begins to sing.*]

Judy: Oh, all right, I think. At least, he seemed all right when I left him.

[Mr. Brown *suddenly feels his head.*]

Mr. Brown: That's funny. I could have sworn I felt a spot of water.

Mrs. Brown: Don't be silly, Henry. How could you?

Mr. Brown: *[another drop lands on his head]* It's happened again!

Jonathan: *[looks up at the ceiling]* Crikey! *[He nudges Judy.]* Look!

Judy: *[looks up too]* Oh, gosh! The bath!

Jonathan: Come on!

Mr. Brown: Where are you two going?

Judy: Oh . . . *[pretending to be casual]* We're just going upstairs to see how Paddington's getting on. *[She bundles Jonathan out of the room.]* Quick!

Mrs. Brown: What was all that about, I wonder?

Mr. Brown: I don't know, Mary. I suppose they're just excited about having a bear in the house . . .

Judy: *[calls offstage]* Are you all right, Paddington?

Paddington: Yes, I think so.

Judy: Gosh! Look at the mess.

Jonathan: Why on earth didn't you turn the tap off? No wonder all the water overflowed.

Paddington: I'm afraid I got soap in my eyes. I couldn't see anything.

[*As he is led back into the room by* Jonathan *and* Judy, *he squeezes water out of his hat.*]

It's a good thing I had my hat with me. I used it to bail the water out. I might have drowned otherwise.

Mr. Brown: No wonder I thought I felt some water.

Judy: Now you just dry yourself properly, or you'll catch cold. [*She drapes a towel round him.*]

Paddington: [*proudly as he looks at himself*] I'm a lot cleaner than I was.

[Mrs. Bird *enters.*]

Mrs. Bird: You'd better give me your hat, Paddington. I'll put it on the line.

Paddington: *[puts his hat back on]* I'd rather you didn't, Mrs. Bird. I don't like being without it. It's my special bush hat and it belonged to my uncle.

Mrs. Brown: In that case, perhaps you'd like to tell us all about yourself, and how you came to emigrate.

Paddington: *[sits down in an armchair and makes the most of his audience]* Well . . . I was brought up by my Aunt Lucy. *[He closes his eyes.]*

Jonathan: Your Aunt Lucy?

Paddington: *[sleepily]* Yes. She's the one who lives in the Home for Retired Bears in *[SNORE]*-ima . . .

Mr. Brown: *[puzzled]* In *[SNORE]*-ima! Where's that?

Paddington: It's in Peru, Mr. Brown. *[SNORE] Darkest* Peru.

Judy: Paddington . . . wake up.

[Paddington *gives a longer snore.* Mr. Brown *pokes him gently.*]

Mr. Brown: Well I never. I do believe he's fallen asleep.

Mrs. Brown: [*drapes the towel round him to make him more comfortable*] I'm not really surprised. I don't suppose there are many bears who've had such a busy day!

Jonathan and Judy: [*in chorus*] Especially from [SNORE]-ima.

Curtain

Author

British author Michael Bond wrote his first children's book, *A Bear Called Paddington,* about a small toy bear he had given his wife. Other books about Paddington followed. Alfred Bradley put some of them into play form.

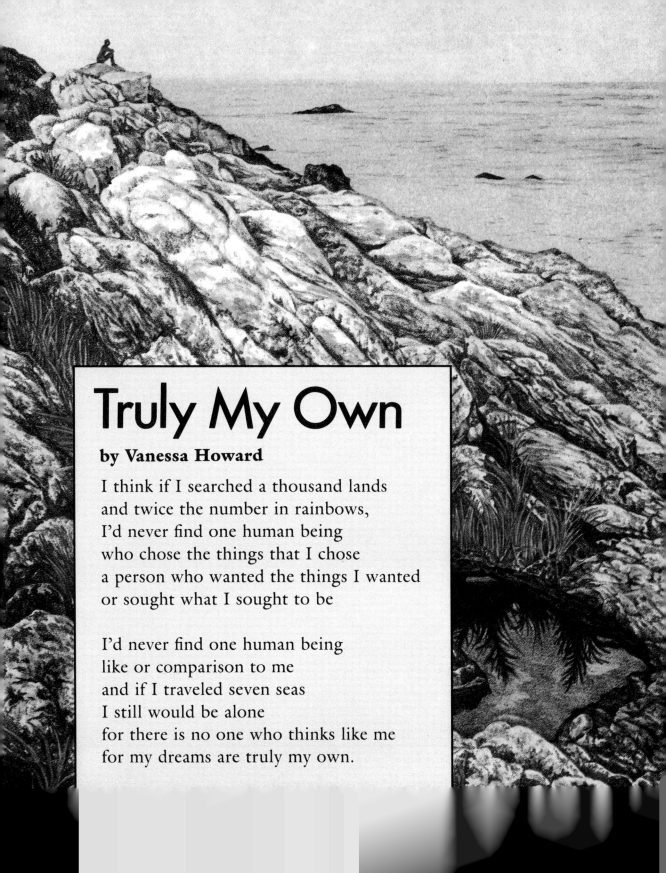

Truly My Own

by Vanessa Howard

I think if I searched a thousand lands
and twice the number in rainbows,
I'd never find one human being
who chose the things that I chose
a person who wanted the things I wanted
or sought what I sought to be

I'd never find one human being
like or comparison to me
and if I traveled seven seas
I still would be alone
for there is no one who thinks like me
for my dreams are truly my own.

An excerpt from

...and now Miguel

by Joseph Krumgold
Illustrated by James Watling

The trouble with Miguel Chavez[1] was that he was too young to do an adult's job and too old to enjoy children's play. He longed for a chance to prove to his family that he was ready to do the work of an adult on their New Mexico sheep ranch. Most of all, he wanted to go with the men and the sheep to the summer pasture in the Sangre de Christo[2] Mountains. When an unexpected storm scattered the flock, Miguel thought his chance to prove himself had come at last. However, Miguel's father would not let him take part in the search for the missing sheep and insisted that he go to school.

---

[1]**Miguel Chavez** (mē gĕl′ chä′ vĕs)

[2]**Sangre de Christo** (sän′ grē də krĭs′ tō)

Juby is my oldest friend. He lives in Los Cordovas[3] where the schoolhouse is. Ever since I can remember doing anything, fishing or playing ball or just talking, most of these things I did with Juby. And as long as I can remember Juby, he's been wearing this same big black hat with a wide brim on it curved up on the sides like the wings look on a buzzard when it circles around, taking things easy in the sky. By now the hat is pretty old and has some holes in it, but it still looks all right on Juby because it would be hard to tell what Juby looked like without it.

He was playing basketball when I came to the yard of the schoolhouse, my sister Faustine and my younger brother Pedro after me. That is, Juby and some of the others were playing just shooting for baskets, and as soon as he saw me, he waved his hand and quit, and came over.

"How're you doing?" he asked me.

I said, "Pretty good," because what's the use telling everybody your troubles?

"D'you folks lose any sheep," he asked me.

"What?" I made one grab at his arm and held tight.

"Sheep," he said. "What's the matter?"

"Now look, Juby," I said. "What's the use talking you and me? How do you know we got missing sheep? What about them?"

"I saw them."

"What?"

"At least I think they're yours. From the shape of the numbers they look like yours." We don't put our brand

---

[3]**Los Cordovas** (lōs kôr′ dō väs)

on the sheep until after we shear them. But our numbers had a different shape to them than any of the others in the neighborhood.

"Where?"

"Then you did lose some sheep?"

"Juby!" I was a little excited. "What's the use, Juby? Just to talk? Where did you see them?"

"Well — you know Carlotta?"

"Who?"

"Our milk cow."

"Cows? What about the sheep?"

"I'm telling you. She got loose last night, Carlotta, and when I went to herd her back I saw these sheep."

"Where? Where? Where?"

"What's the matter with you, Mike? Something wrong?"

"Juby," I said. "You and me, you're my oldest friend aren't you?"

"Sure."

"Then tell me, where are the sheep?"

"Give me a chance. I saw them across the river. Maybe fifteen, ewes and lambs. They looked like they were heading straight for Arroyo Hondo.[4]" It was just in the opposite direction from where my older brother Blasito and the sheep wagon were, from where he looked this morning. "Were they yours?"

"You don't know what this could mean, Juby. That is, for me."

But just then the bell started to ring, and Mrs. Mertian, who is the teacher of our school over there in

---

[4]**Arroyo Hondo** (ə roi′ ō ŏn′ dō)

Los Cordovas, she came to the door and told everybody to come in.

"Let's go." Juby went with the others into the class.

And that's the way things stood.

On one side, Mrs. Mertian with the bell ringing. And on the other side the big mountains, looking very dark and a little mad, if you can think of mountains like they were mad. But that was the way they looked, and at that moment there came thunder from behind them.

And in the middle, I stood. If it ever happened that I came home with the missing sheep? Could anything ever be better?

Mrs. Mertian said, "Miguel."

From the Sangre de Cristo there came thunder, very low.

I did not stand too long. Because there was no question about it! Nothing, that is to say, nothing at all could ever be better.

I headed straight for the other side of the yard.

"Miguel!" It was Mrs. Mertian yelling. I didn't even look back. I jumped into this whole bunch of bushes and started down the hill.

Big champion jumps, every one breaking a world's record, that's the way I came down that hill. With each jump, everything went flying. My books banging at the end of the rope in my hand, swinging all around. My arms, like I had a dozen of them, each one going off by itself. My feet, like I was on a bike, working away to keep my balance. But I couldn't balance. Except by jumping. I couldn't stop. Each jump bigger than the last. I cleared a bush, then a big cracked rock. Then, I wasn't going to make it but I did, a high cactus. Each jump I thought was the last. Each jump was going to end with a cracked head, a split rib, or maybe two broken legs. But it didn't. I don't know why? There was nothing I could do. I came down that hill, like a boulder bumping in bigger and bigger bumps, bumping its way down a cliff. Straight for the river. Until I wasn't scared of falling anymore. I had to fall! Or land in the river. But how? I grabbed a bush. That didn't stop me. And then my books caught, between a couple of rocks. I slipped, grabbed at another bush. Slid a couple of feet, and then took off again. And then I landed. On my face. I landed in a whole piled up bunch of mesquite. No one, I'm sure, ever since that hill was first there, ever came down it so fast.

I wasn't hurt. Except for a scratch stinging near my eye, I was all right. It didn't even bleed. All I needed was to catch my breath. I lay there in the bushes until I did. Breathing and listening for Mrs. Mertian, in case she came to the top of the hill and was yelling down at me. But I didn't hear any yelling. When I looked she wasn't there. The school bell stopped, too. All there was to hear was the thunder, now and then, far off, and the wind blowing quiet.

I got up thinking, I'd done it. After what Juby told me there was only one thing to do, and now I'd done it. Here I was, just me, Miguel, getting the sheep that were lost, all alone. And there would be no one bringing them home but me. All I had to do was to get up there, on the mesa across the river, round up the bunch and march them back to where everyone could see. It would be something worth watching, me herding the ewes and lambs that were lost back into the corral at home. My father would tell me how sorry he was about breakfast, the way he wouldn't let me go help. And I would tell my father, it was nothing, he didn't have to feel sorry.

I felt good. Looking at the mountains, and the mountains looking down at me as if to see what I was going to do next.

I hopped across the river. The easy place to cross was downstream a way, where there were more rocks to jump on. I didn't bother to go to the easy place. I could have made it even if the rocks were twice as far from each other, feeling good like I was, and all in practice from the way I'd come jumping down the hill. I only slipped into the water twice, without much water getting into my shoes at all.

To get up the cliff on the other side was not easy. It was steep in this place and wet and slippery with the rain, the stones high and smooth with nothing to grab on to except sometimes a juniper bush. And besides having the books in one hand. It would be better without the books. But I couldn't leave them around or hide them, seeing they might get wet. I made it all right, pulling and crawling my way up. Steep places and books, that wasn't too hard. Not to find a bunch of lost sheep, it wasn't.

When I got up to the top and looked, I didn't see them. I guess I did expect a little bit they'd be up there waiting for me. But they weren't. I didn't mind too much. The kind of thing I was doing had to be hard. Such a big thing couldn't be too easy. It'd be like cheating. I set out, walking to the north.

Up on the mesa, it looked empty. Like one of those pictures that Pedro draws. One straight line across the middle of the page and big zigzags off to one side which is the mountains. Then dark on top for the clouds, which he makes by smudging up all the pencil lines. And dark on the bottom for the mesa, which he makes with a special black crayon. That's all there is in the picture. And that's why it's a good picture. Because that's all there is. Except for some little bushes, juniper and chaparral and sagebrush. With nothing sticking up, only a high soap-weed or a crooked looking cactus. Nothing else.

Especially, no sheep.

I walked from one rise to the next. Every three or four steps turning all around as I walked. And when I got near to the top of each rise I had to run. Because I thought in the next ten, fifteen steps up top there, sure, I'd see them. The first few times I saw nothing, which I didn't mind too much. And the next few times, I saw nothing, too. Pretty soon I was getting ready to see them, because after an hour or so of walking and turning around and running I figured it was hard enough. Even for something big.

Besides I had a pebble in my left shoe. I felt it down there coming up the cliff. I didn't mind then, because it only made everything even harder. And that was all right with me. But now it was getting to hurt good. And I couldn't sit down and take it out. That would be like giving up.

Besides, I didn't have any time to waste. The mesa spread out, as far as you could see, with many breaks — everywhere little canyons and washes. And it was sure that on top of the next canyon, maybe, I was going to see them, those sheep. If I didn't waste time getting up there. Which I didn't. But all I saw was the same kind of nothing that I saw from the last high place, just this wide straight line stretching right across the middle.

Walking down was harder than walking up. For one thing, walking down on my left heel made the pebble bigger. It was getting to feel like a rock. And for another, walking down, you've already seen what there is to see all around, and there's nothing to look forward to until you start to walk up again. It got so I was running more than I was walking. Running downhill because I wanted to get that part over with, and running up because I couldn't wait to get to the top. And all the time, turning around. I got pretty good at being able to turn around and keep running at the same time.

Except what good was it, getting pretty good at anything? When the only thing counted was to get one look, one quick look at those sheep.

All the turning around did was to get me so mixed up I didn't know whether I was going north, south, east or west. Not that it made any difference, I guess. The sheep weren't particular which direction you went to find them. They weren't in any direction. There were just no sheep. There was all the dark sky, and all this straight flat plain you'd ever want to see. But, no sheep.

And after a couple of hours of seeing no sheep, I would've been glad to see any sheep, even if they weren't ours. I kept trying to see sheep so hard, it was like my eyes got dry and thirsty just to see sheep. To see nothing for two, three hours, especially sheep, it gets hard on your eyes.

It was getting hard on my left foot, too, with that big rock pressing in.

And it wasn't so easy on my hands, either, on account of the books. The books weren't heavy, but when you keep that rope wrapped around your hand it can pinch.

And even if you take it off one hand and put it on the other, it don't take long before it's pinching that hand, too.

Another thing was it got to be hard breathing. Because there was no time to stop and get a good breath. There was always somewhere to go take a look, and you couldn't stop because maybe that very second the sheep were moving away out of sight, and that very second if you were up on a top you'd see them.

After so many hours of it being so hard, I figured it was hard enough by then. It was getting long past the time I ought to find our sheep. Only it didn't make any difference how I figured. They weren't there to be found. Not anywhere.

And after a while, walking, walking, every place started to look like you'd been there before. You'd see a piece of tumble weed. And you were sure it was one you saw an hour before. It didn't help to think that maybe you were just walking up and around the same hill all the time.

Then looking, looking, I thought I heard a bell. I listened hard in the wind. One of the ewes that was lost might have a bell. In the flock there are ten or a dozen sheep with bells. Each one is like the leader of a bunch. I stood still, listening. Then I heard it again, and it was for sure a bell. But it was the school bell, far away, back in Los Cordovas. It must've already become noon, and that was the bell for noontime. Soon the ringing far away stopped. And there was nothing to listen to again, except the quiet wind.

It was never the same, after I heard that bell. It made me feel hungry. Because the bell meant going home to eat. And feeling hungry, I got to feel not so good in the other parts of me. Like lonely. At the beginning being alone was the best part of it, going off by myself to bring home the sheep. But now it was getting to look like I wasn't bringing home any sheep. And that made a lot of difference about being alone, while everybody else was back there going home to eat. The only way I could go home was to find them. It wasn't only so I could bring the sheep back. I had to find them so I could go back, too.

From then on, I got very busy. I didn't stop to walk any more. I ran. Everywhere I went I kept up running, and I did most of my breathing going downhill when I didn't have to try so hard to keep running. There was hardly any breath left over to keep looking with. And that was the hardest part of all, the looking. Because there was never anything to see.

420

And after a long while, I heard the bell again. School was out for the day.

It was hard to figure out what to do next.

I could leave home. That's about all that was left. I couldn't go back without the sheep. Not after what my father said at breakfast, and especially not after the way he looked. And it was clear enough that in all this whole empty place I was never going to find them, those sheep. I could just as well stop, that's all. I could take some time and do a lot of breathing. I could bury my books under a bush. I could sit down and take off my shoe and get rid of that rock with all the sharp edges on it. Then I could go somewhere until I saw a lot of sheep and sit down and look at them, till I got enough again of looking at sheep. And then I could decide where I was leaving home to go to.

Maybe even to the Sangre de Cristo Mountains. On my own, by myself.

But when I looked at the mountains, I knew that was no good. It was impossible. There was only one way to go up into the Mountains of the Sangre de Cristo. And that was to make everyone see you were ready, and then you would go.

Indeed, in order that I should go this way, that's why I was looking for the sheep right now. And if I gave up looking for the sheep, then the idea of going up into the Mountains, I had to give that up, too. I guess if you are going to leave home you just leave home, that's all, everything.

Except, it wasn't up to me anymore. It wasn't a question that I should give up looking for the sheep.

It was just no use.

I could keep running from the top of one rise up to the next, looking, with my eyes getting drier and drier, without any breath, and the bones in my hands like they were cracking, and the heel of my left foot like it was getting torn away, listening to nothing but the wind — I could keep on doing that forever. It wasn't a question of me giving up, it was a question that just everything had given up, me and everything.

So I sat down. I took a deep breath. And I started to untie the laces from my left shoe. And then — what do you think?

I smelled them.

It is not hard to know that what you're smelling is sheep. If only there are some sheep around to smell. They smell a little sweet and a little old, like coffee that's left over in a cup on the table. That's sort of what they smell like.

So when there was this smell, I looked around. I found out from which direction was the wind. And in that direction I went to the top of the next rise, a dozen steps. And no farther away than you could throw a rock, there they were coming up the hill toward me, about fifteen ewes and their lambs, ambling along, having a good time eating, just taking a walk like there was no trouble anywhere in all the world.

"Wahoo!" I took off. Around my head in a big circle I swung my books. Like it was a rope, and I was going to throw a loop on all fifteen at once. "Wahoo!"

The sheep looked up, a little like they were a bunch of ladies in church and they were interested to see who was coming through the door.

I showed them who was coming through the door. Before they knew what was happening they were moving. *Whoosh* — I let my books swing out, and I hit one right in the rump. *Whish* — I kicked another one with my foot that had the rock, so that it hurt me more, I think, than the sheep. I picked up a stone and — *wango* — I let a third one have it in the rear. I got them running right in the opposite direction than they were going.

I kept them going at a gallop. Running first to the one side, then to the other, swinging the books around my head all the time. Yelling and hollering so they wouldn't even dare slow down. They looked scared, but I didn't care. I had waited too long for this. And now I wanted them to know that I was here. I ran them down the hill fast enough to be a stampede. And whichever one ran last, he was the unlucky one. There were a lot of rocks around, and I throw rocks good.

At the bottom of the hill I quieted down. Why was I acting like I was so mad? I had no reason to be mad at the sheep. It wasn't as if they started out to get me in trouble. Indeed, because of them, here I was doing a great thing. I was finding them and bringing them home. If they didn't take it into their heads to go out and get lost, I never would have this big chance.

I quieted down. I stopped and I breathed. The air was good. After the rain it was clean and it smelled sweet, like a vanilla soda in Schaeffer's Drugstore in Taos[5] before you start to drink it with the straw. I took in the air with deep breaths. I sat down and took off my shoe. I found the rock down near the heel. But my goodness, it wasn't any kind of rock at all. Just a little bit of a chip off a stone. In my foot it felt like a boulder. But in my hand it didn't look like anything at all.

I was quieted down. We started off. It was going to be a long drive home. I didn't mind. There were so many

---

[5]**Taos** (tä′ ōs)

good things to think about. What my father would say to me, and my grandfather.

It is no great trouble to drive a small bunch of sheep. You just walk behind them, and if one begins to separate you start in the same direction that it starts and that makes it turn back and bunch up again. It was very little work. So there was much time to think what my uncles would say, and my big brothers. And how Pedro would watch me.

There was much time to look around. At the mountains, not so dark now and not so mad. There was much to see, walking along thinking, breathing, and looking around. How the clouds now were taking on new shapes, the dark ones separating and new big white ones coming up. And on the mesa everything looked fine. I saw flowers. Before when I was looking there were no flowers. Now, there they were. The little pink ones of the peyote plants. And there were flowers on the hedgehog cactus, too, kind of pinkish purple some, and others a real red.

After a little while I had something else to do. One of the lambs lay down. Whether it was tired or why, I don't know. I picked it up, the lamb under my arm, and in the other hand the rope with my books. It was not so bad. Even the rope didn't pinch anymore. And when the lamb got heavy under one arm, I put it under the other.

The number of the lamb was 119. I remembered the morning I put the number on him. That day was one of the best days as far as how many lambs came. When it started we were only using two numbers, around 83 or 84. Then I had to use three irons when we got to a hundred. Before the day was over we were already making numbers in the one-twenties.

Some of the other numbers in the bunch I remembered too. Like 251, and 170 and 582. They were like friends these numbers, that is the ewes with these numbers and the lambs. They were my friends. And I was their pastor.[6] I was the one who put numbers on them. And I was the one who brought them home, now, from being lost.

I felt better, now, than in a long time.

Even when I had to pick up this second lamb which was straggling behind, I still felt good. It was harder this way because now I couldn't use one arm after the other when the lambs got heavy, and there were the books I had to carry in addition. By now though we

---

[6]**pastor:** Shepherd.

were coming down the dry wash that led to the river. There was not much further to go.

They were a good bunch of sheep, all of them. When I brought them to the place in the river that was not so deep, they waded right across without any trouble. As for me myself, I almost fell in but all the way this time. I was balancing myself all right on the rocks going across when 119 started to wriggle like it wanted to shake itself apart. But I held on, and I kept my balance and didn't fall in. I wouldn't have minded, anyway, if I had. If I came to the house with all my clothes wet, that would make what I did look as if it was even harder than it was.

Blasito was the first one to see me.

He was walking across the top of the hill near the corral when I came around the bend from the river.

"Hey, Mickey," he yelled, "where you been? What's those sheep you got?"

"Yours," I shouted back.

"Mine? What do you mean mine? The lost ones?"

"That's what," I yelled. "The lost ones!"

"No! No fooling?" He turned away from me. "Ai

Grandpa. Padre de Chavez. Mira!⁷ Miguel's here, with the bunch that was lost!" He looked back to where I was coming up the hill. "Bravo, Miguelito!⁸ Where'd you find them? How did it happen?"

"I'll tell you." I needed my breath to get up the hill with those two lambs under my arms. "Wait'll I get there."

The two of them were waiting for me, Blasito and my grandfather. Grandpa took one of the lambs from my arms. I let the other one down. Blasito shooed the bunch into the corral. And all three of us talked at once.

"Where did you find them?" asked Blasito.

"How did this happen?" said Grandfather.

"I'll tell it to you all," I said, "from the beginning. On the way to school this morning I started to think."

Blasito interrupted. "Can't you tell us where you found them?"

"But that's what I'm trying to do. It started on the way to school."

"Miguel," my grandfather wouldn't let me talk. "That part you can tell us later. Where were they, the sheep?"

"Well, I'll tell you that first, then. I found them on the way to Arroyo Hondo, about twenty or thirty miles from here. But the way it started — "

"How many miles?" My grandfather looked at me with a smile.

"Oh many miles, many, many. What happened was — "

---

⁷**mira** (**mē′** rə): Look.

⁸**Miguelito** (mē gə **lē′ tō**)

"How come you went north?" asked Blas. "All morning we've been riding toward the Arroyo del Alamo. In just the other way."

"First comes the way I went down the hill," I tried to explain. "With world record jumps."

"Why is it that you don't want to answer your big brother Blas?" asked Grandpa. "How did you know where to look?"

"But why can't I tell it the way it happened? There was much trouble and it's very interesting."

"Later," said Grandpa. "Now, how did you know?"

"Well, I figured it out, and then I kept my ears open to hear things."

"What things?" said Blasito.

"Things people say?"

"Like who?"

"Like Juby."

"He told you?"

"Look," I said to Blasito. "If I can't tell you in my own way, then what's the use? The kind of questions you ask, it makes it all sound like nothing. If I have to tell it this way, just to answer a few little questions, then what's the use my going out and finding the sheep anyway?"

"Use?" Blasito started to laugh. He banged me on the back. "It's a great thing, finding those sheep. I mean it, Miguel. You did fine!"

"What did you say?"

"I said great, fine!"

Grandfather took me by the hand and shook it like when two men shake hands.

"It's the truth," he said. "This that you have done, it was good."

"What?" I asked my Grandfather.

"It was good."

"Better than the rest of us could do," said Blasito.

"What?" I asked Blasito.

"Better than the rest of us!" Blasito shouted so I would hear.

Grandpa still held my hand, and he shook it again. "You brought them in all right, Miguel. Like a real pastor."

"What?" I asked my grandfather. I wanted to hear everything twice.

"A real pastor," Grandpa said again, and we all looked at each other and smiled.

"Anything else?" I asked.

Before anyone could answer, there was a great shout from the house. "Miguel!" It was my father. It was a shout that sounded like thunder. "Miguel, get over here!"

He stood, he and my mother both, they stood in front of the house. And with them was Mrs. Mertian, my schoolteacher. They stood with Mrs. Mertian who had come from the school in Los Cordovas, and they talked together.

My father looked around at us once again. "Miguel!"

Grandpa nodded to me that I should go to my father. "Take off," said Blasito. "You'd better get going."

I went. What else? It was too bad, real bad, my teacher should talk to my father before I even got a chance. I knew now that the things I was thinking about on the way home, of what my father would say to me, I knew that these were probably not the things he was going to say to me now. I walked to the house where they stood, and Mrs. Mertian smiled at my mother and they shook hands, then she smiled at my father and shook hands with him. Then everybody smiled at each other and she left. But when they turned to watch me coming up the path, my father and mother, nobody smiled.

"Where'd you go?" said my father.

"Up there to the Arroyo Hondo. Many miles."

"What's in Arroyo Hondo?"

I knew my father didn't want to know what's in Arroyo Hondo. He knew as well as I. Just a grocery store and some houses. If I told him that then everything would get all mixed up the way it did.

"It was not for what's in Arroyo Hondo. It's that I went after the sheep that were lost."

"This morning at breakfast, didn't we talk about the lost sheep?"

"Yes." I knew what he meant. "And you told me to go to school. And I did, I went to school."

"That is true. But it is only one small piece of what is true. The rest is, you didn't go in."

"Because of Juby. He is my oldest friend."

"And why is it, Miguel, that you will obey your oldest friend? But your parents, who are friends to you even older than your oldest friend, what they say means nothing."

"But Juby told me where were the missing sheep. So I went. I got them. I brought them home."

This is not the way I wanted to tell it at all. It was worse than with Blasito and Grandpa. It didn't sound hard this way, or like a big thing. It was like going down to the spring for a pail of water, no more. But what else was there to do? If things kept up like they were, it could get bad.

"You brought what home?"

"The missing sheep. They are in the corral."

My father and mother looked. Blasito and my grandfather, who were watching us, they pointed out the bunch in the corral.

"Well!" My father, at least, he didn't sound so mad anymore when he looked back to me.

"That's why I didn't go to school."

"Well," my father put his hands in his back pockets and looked down at me. "That's different. But not so different to make too much difference, Miguel. Sheep are important. Sure! But you, too, that you go to school is important. Even more important. Always there has to be something done with the sheep. And if every time something had to be done, you stayed away from school, my goodness, you'd grow up to be a burro. And you tell me, do we need a burro around this place?"

"No. Only mules and horses."

"And even more, what we need is young men who are educated, who have learned to know what is the difference between what is right and what is wrong. Do you understand?"

"I understand. And I promise. I will never miss my school again."

"Good, now get into the house. Mrs. Mertian brought the lessons from today. So go in and do them and write your homework for tomorrow."

My mother took me by the back of the head to go into the house with me. And then my father did a wonderful

thing. He gave me one good spank. And when I looked around up at him, he was smiling.

"It would not be true," he told me, "if I didn't say also I am glad to have the sheep back. How you did it was wrong. But for what you did, I want to thank you."

And then he went off to go to Blas and Grandpa where they were working on the tractor. My mother took me with her into the house.

"Come, Miquito.[9] That's enough for today. Good and bad, you've done enough.

---

[9]**Miquito** (mē kē′ tō)

Author

Joseph Krumgold was born in Jersey City, New Jersey, in 1908, and grew up near New York City. When he was young, his father owned and operated several movie theaters, so it was only natural that Joseph became interested in making movies. This interest eventually led him to Hollywood, California, where he began his career as a writer by writing stories for the movies.

One of the films which Mr. Krumgold wrote and directed was made in New Mexico. It is about real people, the Chavez family, and was filmed while the story actually happened. Mr. Krumgold felt that he had more to say about Miguel Chavez than he could say in the movie, so he wrote the book . . . *and now Miguel.*

In 1954 . . . *and now Miguel* won the Newbery Medal. The award encouraged Mr. Krumgold to write two other books on how a child grows up in different parts of the country. They are *Onion John,* awarded the Newbery Medal in 1959, and *Henry 3,* published in 1966.

PAULA FOX

A LIKELY PLACE

Illustrated by Edward Ardizzone

Houghton Mifflin Literature

In the stories you have just read from *Discovering Myself,* a pioneer girl, a giant lumberjack, and a young boy all discover who they truly are.

Now you will read *A Likely Place* by Paula Fox. In this story, Lewis is tired of everyone telling him who he is and what he should think and feel. Finally, he meets two unusual people who help him find his place.

Glossary

Some of the words in this book may have pronunciations or meanings you do not know. This glossary can help you by telling you how to pronounce those words and by telling you their meanings.

You can find out the correct pronunciation of any glossary word by using the special spelling after the word and the pronunciation key at the bottom of each left-hand page.

The full pronunciation key below shows how to pronounce each consonant and vowel in a special spelling. The pronunciation key at the bottom of each left-hand page is a shortened form of the full key.

Full Pronunciation Key

Consonant Sounds

b	**bib**		p	**pop**
ch	**church**		r	**roar**
d	**deed**		s	**miss, sauce, see**
f	**fast, fife, off,**		sh	**dish, ship**
	phase, rou**gh**		t	**tight**
g	**gag**		th	pa**th**, **th**in
h	**hat**		*th*	ba**the**, **this**
hw	**wh**ich		v	**cave, valve, vine**
j	**judge**		w	**with**
k	**cat, kick, pique**		y	**yes**
l	**lid, needle**		z	**rose, size, xylophone,**
m	a**m**, **m**an, **mum**			**zebra**
n	**no**, sudden		zh	**garage, pleasure,**
ng	thi**ng**			**vision**

Pronunciation key © 1986 by Houghton Mifflin Company. Adapted and reprinted by permission from the *American Heritage Intermediate Dictionary*.

Vowel Sounds

ă	pat		ô	alter, caught, for, paw
ā	aid, they, pay		oi	boy, noise, oil
â	air, care, wear		o͝o	book
ä	father		o͞o	boot, fruit
ĕ	pet, pleasure		ou	cow, out
ē	be, bee, easy, seize		ŭ	cut, rough
ĭ	pit		û	firm, heard, term, turn, word
ī	by, guy, pie		yo͞o	abuse, use
î	dear, deer, fierce, mere		ə	about, silent, pencil, lemon, circus
ŏ	pot, horrible		ər	butter
ō	go, row, toe			

Stress Marks

Primary Stress ′
bi·ol′o·gy   (bī ŏl′ə jē)

Secondary Stress ′
bi′o·log′i·cal   (bī′ə lŏj′i kəl)

437

a·brupt·ly (ə **brŭpt′**lē) *adv.* In a sudden, unexpected way: *We were all surprised when the band stopped abruptly.*

ab·sent-mind·ed (ăb′sənt **mīn′**dĭd) *adj.* Tending to be lost in thought and forget what one is doing.

ac·cus·tomed to (ə **kŭs′**təmd tōō) *adj.* Used to; familiar with; in the habit of: *My cousins, who live in the country, are not accustomed to city noises.*

ac·quaint·ed (ə **kwān′**tĭd) *adj.* Known to each other: *They became acquainted at school.*

ac·ro·pho·bi·a (ăk′rə **fō′** bē ə) *n.* A very strong fear of high places.

ad·just (ə **jŭst′**) *v.* To become accustomed; adapt oneself: *He was not able to adjust to life in the city.*

aisle (īl) *n.* A narrow passage through which one may walk, as between rows of seats in a theater or between counters in a store.

am·a·teur (ăm′ə chŏŏr′) *or* (ăm′ə-chər) *or* (ăm′ə tyŏŏr′) *n.* A person who does something just for pleasure and does not get paid; someone who is not a professional.

a·mid (ə **mĭd′**) *prep.* In the middle of; among.

an·nu·al (ăn′yōō əl) *adj.* Occurring or done every year; yearly: *an annual medical examination.*

an·ten·na (ăn **tĕn′**ə) *n.* **1.** *pl.* **an·ten·nae** (ăn **tĕn′** ē). One of the pair of long, slender feelers growing on the head of some insects. **2.** *pl.* **an·ten·nas.** A device for sending or receiving radio, television, or other signals.

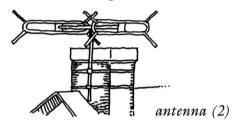

antenna (2)

anx·ious (ăngk′shəs) *or* (ăng′-) *adj.* Having a feeling of uneasiness; worried. — **anx′ious·ly** *adv.*

ap·pe·tiz·ing (ăp′ĭ tī′ zĭng) *adj.* Appealing to the taste: *The food at the picnic looked appetizing.*

Arc·tic (ärk′tĭk *or* är′tĭk) *adj.* Of or relating to the region surrounding the North Pole.

ar·ri·val (ə **rī′**vəl) *n.* The act of reaching a destination or of coming to a place: *The arrival of the plane will be delayed.*

as·sign·ment (ə **sīn′**mənt) *n.* A task or job: *What's the math assignment for tomorrow?*

as·so·ci·a·tion (ə sō′sē ā′shən) *n.* A group of people organized for a common purpose.

ă pat / ā pay / â care / ä father / ĕ pet / ē be / ĭ pit / ī pie / î fierce / ŏ pot / ō go / ô paw, for / oi oil / ŏŏ book / ōō boot / ou out / ŭ cut / û fur / *th* the / th thin / hw which / zh vision / ə ago, item, pencil, atom, circus

asth·ma (ăz′ mə) *n.* An ailment whose main symptoms are wheezing, coughing, and difficulty in breathing.

as·ton·ish (ə stŏn′ĭsh) *v.* To surprise greatly; amaze.

awe (ô) *n.* A feeling of wonder, fear, or respect.

bac·te·ri·a (băk tîr′ē ə) *pl. n.* Tiny one-celled living things that can be seen only with a microscope. Some bacteria cause diseases.

bar·gain (bär′gĭn) *v.* To discuss the terms of an agreement or a price to be paid.

barge (bärj) *n.* A large, flat-bottomed boat used to carry loads on rivers and canals.

bi·lin·gual (bī lĭng′ gwəl) *adj.* Speaking two languages very well.

black·smith (blăk′smĭth′) *n.* A person who makes things out of iron. A blacksmith heats the iron and shapes and hammers it into horseshoes, tools, and other objects.

bliz·zard (blĭz′ərd) *n.* A very heavy snowstorm with strong winds.

break (brāk) *v.* **broke, bro·ken.** To lessen in force or effect; stop: *break a fall.*

brick·work (brĭk′wûrk′) *n.* A structure made of baked blocks of clay called bricks.

brin·dle (brĭn′dl) *adj.* Tan, gray, or brown with darker streaks or spots.

britch·es (brĭch′ĭz) *pl. n. Informal.*

breeches. Short, fitted trousers ending at or just below the knees.

cal·i·co (kăl′ĭ kō) *n., pl.* **cal·i·coes** or **cal·i·cos.** A cotton cloth with a tiny figured pattern printed on it.

cam·pus (kăm′pəs) *n.* The grounds and buildings of a college or school.

can·yon (kăn′yən) *n.* A deep valley with steep cliffs on both sides and often a stream running through it.

cau·tious (kô′shəs) *adj.* Not taking any chances: *You should be cautious when you are crossing a busy street.*

cen·tu·ry (sĕn′chə rē) *n., pl.* **cen·tu·ries.** A period of a hundred years.

chal·lenge (chăl′ənj) *v.* **chal·lenged, chal·leng·ing.** To call to engage in a contest or fight. **— chal′leng·er** *n: The young challenger beat the champion.*

chore (chôr) *or* (chōr) *n.* **1.** A routine or minor task. **2.** An unpleasant task.

cir·cum·stance (sûr′kəm stăns′) *n.* A condition, fact, or event that is related to and may affect something else: *Sickness and bad weather are circumstances that may cause low attendance at school.*

clum·sy (klŭm′zē) *adj.* **clum·si·er, clum·si·est.** Lacking grace or deftness; awkward.

clut·ter (klŭt′ər) *v.* **clut·tered, clut·ter·ing.** To fill or litter in a disordered or confused way: *The room was cluttered with toys.*

com·mit·tee (kə **mĭt′**ē) *n.* A group of people chosen to do a particular job.

com·mo·tion (kə **mō′**shən) *n.* Noisy activity; confusion.

com·mu·ni·ty (kə **myoo′**nĭ tē) *n.* **1.** A group of people living in one area. **2.** The area in which a group of people live.

com·pare (kəm **pâr′**) *v.* **com·pared, com·par·ing.** To study in order to note likenesses and differences: *We compared the habits of bees and spiders.*

con·fused (kən **fyoozd′**) *adj.* Mixed up: *The boy seemed confused by the directions.*

con·science (**kŏn′**shəns) *n.* Inner feelings and ideas that tell a person what is right and what is wrong: *My conscience tells me that it is wrong to cheat.*

con·sole (kən **sōl′**) *v.* **con·soled, con·sol·ing.** To comfort during a time of disappointment or sorrow.

con·tent·ment (kən **tĕnt′**mənt) *n.* Satisfaction: *The director had a look of contentment at the end of the play.*

con·test·ant (kən **tĕs′**tənt) *n.* Someone who takes part in a competition.

con·trib·ute (kən **trĭb′**yoot) *v.* **con·trib·ut·ed, con·trib·ut·ing.** To give or supply in common with others: *contribute time and money.*

cor·ral (kə **răl′**) *n.* A pen or a place with a fence for keeping cattle or horses.

coun·cil (**koun′**səl) *n.* **1.** A group of persons called together to discuss or settle a problem or question. **2.** A group of persons elected or appointed to make laws or rules.

cross (krôs) *or* (krŏs) *adj.* Irritable or annoyed; angry.

curl·i·cue (**kûr′**lĭ kyoo′) *n.* A fancy twist or curl, usually made with a pen.

curt·sy (**kûrt′**sē) *n., pl.* **curt·sies.** A way of showing respect to a person by bending one's knees and lowering the body while keeping one foot forward.

curtsy

cush·ion (**koosh′**ən) *n.* Anything used to absorb or soften the impact of something: *Rubber stripping was nailed around the opening to form a cushion for the door.*

ă pat / ā pay / â care / ä father / ĕ pet / ē be / ĭ pit / ī pie / î fierce / ŏ pot / ō go / ô paw, for / oi oil / oo book / oo boot / ou out / ŭ cut / û fur / *th* the / th thin / hw which / zh vision / ə ago, item, pencil, atom, circus

cus·tom·er (kŭs′tə mər) *n.* A person who buys goods or services.

daugh·ter-in-law (dô′tər ĭn lô′) *n., pl.* **daugh·ters-in-law.** The wife of a person's son.

daze (dāz) *n.* A confused or stunned condition: *The surprising news left us in a daze.*

de·cay (dĭ kā′) *v.* To rot or cause to become rotten: *The wood decayed because of the dampness.*

de·cent (dē′sənt) *adj.* Fairly good; adequate: *He wore a decent shirt to the theater.*

dem·on·strate (dĕm′ən strāt′) *v.* **dem·on·strat·ed, dem·on·strat·ing.** To show, describe, or explain.

de·sert (dĭ zûrt′) *v.* To go away from someone or something one has a duty to stay with or support: *The guards deserted their posts.* — **de·sert′ed** *adj.: a dark, deserted street.*

des·pair (dĭ spâr′) *n.* Lack of all hope: *They gave up in despair of ever winning the game.*

des·per·ate (dĕs′pər ĭt) *or* (-prĭt) *adj.* In a critical or hopeless situation and thus ready to do anything: *a desperate criminal.*

de·spite (dĭ spīt′) *prep.* In spite of: *They won despite great odds.*

de·tail (dĭ tāl′) *or* (dē′tāl′) *n.* A small part of a whole: *He couldn't remember all the details of the trip.*

de·vo·tion (dĭ vō′shən) *n.* Loyalty and affection: *a dog's devotion to its master.*

di·a·ry (dī′ə rē) *n., pl.* **di·a·ries. 1.** A daily record of personal experiences, events, observations, or opinions. **2.** A book for keeping such a record.

dig·ni·fied (dĭg′nə fīd′) *adj.* Elegant or grand in manner: *behave in a dignified manner.*

dis·card (dĭs kärd′) *v.* To throw away: *We cleaned the cellar and discarded all our old magazines.*

dis·ease (dĭ zēz′) *n.* Any condition that keeps the body from functioning normally; illness.

dis·qual·i·fy (dĭs kwŏl′ə fī′) *v.* **dis·qual·i·fied, dis·qual·i·fy·ing, dis·qual·i·fies.** To declare to be unsuitable or unfit to hold a position or win a contest: *The racer was disqualified for pushing.*

dis·tin·guished (dĭ stĭng′gwĭsht) *adj.* Elegant or dignified in conduct or appearance.

dis·turb (dĭ stûrb′) *v.* To bother; to intrude upon: *The loud noise disturbed the baby.*

diz·zy (dĭz′ē) *adj.* Having a feeling of whirling or of being about to fall.

down·cast (doun′kăst′) *or* (-käst′) *adj.* Depressed; sad: *The children were feeling downcast about missing the picnic.*

drum (drŭm) *n.* A barrel-shaped container, as for oil.

ea·sel (ē′zəl) *n.* A stand for holding a painting or displaying a sign or picture.

easel

el·e·vat·ed (ĕl′ə vā′tĭd) *adj.* Raised or placed above a given level. — *n.* A train that operates on a track raised high enough above the ground so that vehicles and pedestrians can pass beneath.

em·bar·rass (ĕm băr′əs) *v.* **em·bar·rass·ed, em·bar·rass·ing.** To feel or cause to feel ill at ease: *I was embarrassed when the teacher called on me and I didn't know the answer.*

em·i·grate (ĕm′ĭ grāt′) *v.* **em·i·grat·ed, em·i·grat·ing.** To leave one's own country and settle in another: *My grandparents emigrated from Italy in 1908.*

en·chant (ĕn chănt′) *or* (-chänt′) *v.* **1.** To cast under a spell; bewitch. **2.** To delight.

en·cour·age·ment (ĕn kûr′ĭj mənt) *or* (-kŭr′-) *n.* The act of giving hope or confidence to: *Your encouragement helped me to win the race.*

e·nor·mous (ĭ nôr′məs) *adj.* Extremely large; huge.

en·vy (ĕn′vē) *v.* **en·vied, en·vy·ing.** To feel discontent at the success or advantages enjoyed by someone else and to desire them for yourself.

ep·i·logue, *also* **ep·i·log** (ĕp′ə lôg′) *or* (-lŏg′) *n.* A short section at the end of a story, which often deals with the characters' future.

e·quip·ment (ĭ kwĭp′mənt) *n.* The things needed or used for a particular purpose: *camping equipment.*

ewe (yo͞o) *n., pl.* **ewes.** A female sheep.

ex·ag·ger·ate (ĭg zăj′ə rāt′) *v.* **ex·ag·ger·at·ed, ex·ag·ger·at·ing.** To describe something as being larger than it really is: *When I said the fish was two feet long, I was exaggerating.*

ex·hib·it (ĭg zĭb′ĭt) *v.* To present for the public to view; display: *The artist exhibited her paintings in a museum.*

ex·hi·bi·tion (ĕk′sə bĭsh′ən) *n.* A display for the public: *an exhibition of paintings.*

ex·traor·di·nar·y (ĭk strôr′dn ĕr′ē) *or* (ĕk′strə ôr′dn ĕr′ē) *adj.* Very unusual; remarkable.

faint (fānt) *adj.* **faint·er, faint·est.** Not clearly seen, sensed, or heard; indistinct: *a faint light.*

ă pat / ā pay / â care / ä father / ĕ pet / ē be / ĭ pit / ī pie / î fierce / ŏ pot / ō go / ô paw, for / oi oil / o͝o book / o͞o boot / ou out / ŭ cut / û fur / *th* the / th thin / hw which / zh vision / ə ago, item, pencil, atom, circus

fa·mil·iar (fə **mĭl′**yər) *adj.* Well known, as from frequent experience: *I heard the familiar voice of the announcer.*

fare (fâr) *n.* The money paid for a trip or ride on a plane, train, bus, etc.: *Pay your fare when you get on the bus.*

fierce (fîrs) *adj.* **fierc·er, fierc·est.** Wild or intense: *The dog had a fierce look when it got scared.*

fig·ure (**fĭg′**yər) *n.* A picture or statue, especially of a person.

foot·hold (**foŏt′**hōld′) *n.* A place to put the foot so that it will not slip, as when climbing.

foul (foul) *n.* In sports, something done that is against the rules of play: *a personal foul in a game of basketball.*

frail (frāl) *adj.* **frail·er, frail·est. 1.** Thin and weak in body. **2.** Easily broken.

fringe (frĭnj) *n.* An edge made of hanging threads, cords, or strips. Fringes are often used on bedspreads and curtains.

fron·tier (frŭn **tîr′**) *n.* **1.** A boundary between countries or the land along such a boundary. **2.** A region just beyond or at the edge of a settled area. — *adj.* of or relating to a frontier: *frontier towns.*

frus·tra·tion (frŭ **strā′**shən) *n.* A feeling of helplessness.

gal·ler·y (**găl′**ə rē) *n., pl.* **gal·ler·ies.** A building or group of rooms for showing artistic works; museum.

gap (găp) *n.* An opening or space; a distance: *The dog ran through a gap in the fence.*

gas·light (**găs′**līt′) *n.* **1.** Light made by burning gas in a lamp. **2.** A lamp that uses gas as fuel.

glit·ter·ing (**glĭt′**ər ĭng) *adj.* Sparkling brightly: *two glittering eyes.*

gog·gles (**gŏg′**əlz) *pl. n.* A pair of glasses worn for protection against wind, dust, sparks, or glare.

grad·u·ate (**grăj′** o͞o āt′) *v.* **grad·u·at·ed, grad·u·at·ing.** To finish a course of study and receive a diploma: *My cousin graduated from high school last year.*

grat·ing (**grā′**tĭng) *n.* A set of parallel bars set across an opening in order to block it; a grate.

great-great-aunt (**grāt′ grāt′** ănt *or* änt) *n.* The sister of one's great-grandparent.

grind·stone (**grīnd′**stōn′) *n.* A flat, stone wheel that spins on a rod set in a frame. It is used to shape, polish, and sharpen tools.

grindstone

guilt·y (gĭl′tē) **1.** Having committed a crime or bad deed: *The jury found them guilty of stealing.* **2.** Feeling deep shame: *I felt guilty about lying to my parents.*

hearth (härth) *n.* The floor of a fireplace and the area around it.

height (hīt) *n.* Often **heights.** A high place or area: *not afraid of heights.*

her·i·tage (hĕr′ĭ tĭj) *n.* Something handed down to later generations from earlier generations: *Freedom of speech is an important part of our national heritage.*

hes·i·tate (hĕz′ĭ tāt′) *v.* **hes·i·tat·ed, hes·i·tat·ing.** To be slow to act, speak, or decide; pause in doubt or uncertainty; waver.

hide (hīd) *n.* The skin of an animal: *Leather is made from hides.*

hin·drance (hĭn′drəns) *n.* Something that gets in the way of or makes very difficult: *Strong winds may be a hindrance to small boats.*

hoist (hoist) *v.* To lift or haul up, often with a mechanical device.

hold (hōld) *n.* A space inside a ship or airplane where things are carried.

hull (hŭl) *n.* The body of a ship, including its sides and bottom.

hul·la·ba·loo (hŭl′ə bə lōō′) *n.* An uproar; great noise or excitement.

i·den·ti·fy (ī dĕn′tə fī′) *v.* To recognize and acknowledge as being a certain person or thing: *I identified my pocketbook by telling what was in it.*

im·pa·tience (ĭm pā′shəns) *n.* The inability to wait patiently or calmly: *his impatience with the whining puppy.*

im·pa·tient·ly (ĭm pā′shənt lē) *adv.* In a way that shows unwillingness to wait calmly.

in·spect (ĭn spĕkt′) *v.* To examine carefully and critically, especially for mistakes or problems: *If you find any mistakes when you inspect the sweater, please let me know.*

in·te·grate (ĭn′tĭ grāt′) *v.* **in·te·grat·ed, in·te·grat·ing.** To bring together different racial or ethnic groups.

in·ter·rupt (ĭn′tə rŭpt′) *v.* To stop the conversation, speech, or action of (someone) by breaking in: *She interrupted the speaker before he finished his lecture.*

in·ves·ti·gate (ĭn vĕs′tĭ gāt′) *v.* **in·ves·ti·gat·ed, in·ves·ti·gat·ing.** To look into or examine carefully in a search for facts, knowledge, or information: *investigate a burglary.*

ir·reg·u·lar (ĭ rĕg′yə lər) *adj.* Unusual or improper: *You have made a highly irregular decision.*

ir·ri·ta·ble (ĭr′ĭ tə bəl) *adj.* Easily annoyed.

ă pat / ā pay / â care / ä father / ĕ pet / ē be / ĭ pit / ī pie / î fierce / ŏ pot / ō go / ô paw, for / oi oil / o͝o book / o͞o boot / ou out / ŭ cut / û fur / *th* the / th thin / hw which / zh vision / ə ago, item, pencil, atom, circus

lan·tern (lăn′tərn) *n.* A case or container for holding and shielding a light, having sides or an opening through which the light can shine.

lantern

lap¹ (lăp) *n.* A single length or turn over or around something, as a racecourse: *Each day I swim another lap of the pool.*

lap² (lăp) *n.* The front part of a sitting person's body from the waist to the knees.

lay·er (lā′ər) *n.* A single thickness, coating, or sheet of material covering a surface: *A layer of dust covered the furniture.*

leg·end (lĕj′ənd) *n.* A story that is often connected with a national hero or historical event and that may be based in truth.

length (lĕngkth) *or* (lĕngth) *n.* The distance from one end of a thing to the other: *the length of a boat.*

lin·en (lĭn′ən) *n.* Strong, smooth cloth made of flax fibers.

loft (lôft) *or* (lŏft) *n.* An open space under a roof, often used for storage: *a loft full of old furniture.*

log·ging (lôg′ing) *or* (lŏg′ing) *n.* The work of cutting down trees and moving logs to a mill.

lug·gage (lŭg′ĭj) *n.* The suitcases, bags, and boxes taken on a trip; baggage.

lum·ber (lŭm′bər) *v.* To walk or move with clumsiness and often great noise: *Twenty elephants lumbered slowly into the arena.*

mack·i·naw (măk′ə nô′) *n.* A short coat of heavy woolen material, usually plaid.

mackinaw

mag·nif·i·cent (măg nĭf′ĭ sənt) *adj.* Very grand and fine; large and beautiful.

mar·ma·lade (mär′mə lād′) *n.* A jam made from sugar and the inside and the tough outer covering of fruits.

mar·vel (mär′vəl) *v.* **mar·veled** *or* **mar·velled, mar·vel·ing** *or* **mar·vel·ling.** To be filled with surprise or wonder: *We marveled at the beauty of the sunset.*

mas·sive (măs′ĭv) *adj.* Very large and heavy; huge.

may·on·naise (mā′ə nāz′) *n.* A thick dressing, as for salad, that is made of beaten raw egg yolk, oil, and lemon juice or vinegar.

me·sa (mā′sə) *n.* A hill with steep sides and a broad, flat top.

min·i·a·ture (mĭn′ē ə chər) *or* (mĭn′ə chər) *n.* Something that is much smaller than the usual size.

mis·er·a·ble (mĭz′ər ə bəl) *or* (mĭz′rə-) *adj.* very unhappy. — **mis·er·a·bly** *adv.*

moist (moist) *adj.* Slightly wet; damp: *The soil was moist.*

mon·o·logue (mŏn′ə lôg′) *or* (-lŏg′) *n.* A long speech given by one person.

mo·tion·less (mō′shən lĭs) *adj.* Not moving.

muf·fler (mŭf′lər) *n.* A scarf worn around the neck for warmth.

mul·ti·col·ored (mŭl′tĭ kŭl′ərd) *adj.* Having many colors.

munch (mŭnch) *v.* To chew (food) in a noisy, steady manner: *They found our cow munching away in a neighbor's pasture.*

mus·tache (mŭs′tăsh′) *or* (mə-stăsh′) *n.* The hair growing on the upper lip.

mustache

noose (no͞os) *n.* A loop in a rope with a knot that lets the loop tighten as the rope is pulled.

nudge (nŭj) *v.* **nudged, nudg·ing.** To push or poke gently: *He nudged her with his elbow.*

ob·vi·ous (ŏb′vē əs) *adj.* Easily noticed or understood: *The student made an obvious mistake in the subtraction problem.*

pan·ic (păn′ik) *n.* A sudden, overwhelming terror.

par·cel (pär′səl) *n.* Something wrapped up in a bundle; a package.

par·tic·i·pate (pär tĭs′ə pāt′) *v.* **par·tic·i·pat·ed, par·tic·i·pat·ing.** To join with others in an activity; take part: *She wanted to participate in the hockey game.*

pat·tern (păt′ərn) *n.* A diagram used in cutting out garments to be made, consisting of separate pieces, usually of paper, cut to a certain size and style.

pence (pĕns) *n. British.* A plural of **penny.**

perch[1] (pûrch) *n.* **1.** A branch or rod that a bird grasps with its claws while at rest. **2.** Any resting place. — *v.* To rest or sit as if on a perch.

ă pat / ā pay / â care / ä father / ĕ pet / ē be / ĭ pit / ī pie / î fierce / ŏ pot / ō go / ô paw, for / oi oil / o͝o book / o͞o boot / ou out / ŭ cut / û fur / *th* the / th thin / hw which / zh vision / ə ago, item, pencil, atom, circus

perch² (pûrch) *n., pl.* **perch** or **perch·es.** Any of several mostly freshwater fishes often used as food.

pheas·ant (fĕz'ənt) *n.* A large, often brightly colored bird with a long tail.

pheasant

plank (plăngk) *n.* A thick, wide, long piece of wood that has been sawed.

plot (plŏt) *v.* **plot·ted, plot·ting.** To plan secretly; scheme.

pneu·mo·nia (nŏō mōn'yə) *or* (nyŏō-) *n.* A serious disease of the lungs.

pol·ish (pŏl'ĭsh) *n., pl.* **pol·ish·es.** **1.** A substance used for polishing. **2.** A smooth and shiny surface; shine.

por·cu·pine (pôr'kyə pīn') *n.* An animal covered with long, sharp spines called quills.

porcupine

pre·cious (prĕsh'əs) *adj.* Of high price or value: *Gold and silver are precious metals.*

pri·vate (prī'vĭt) *adj.* Owned by a person or group of persons rather than the public or government: *private property.*

pro·vi·sions (prə vĭzh'ənz) *pl. n.* Supplies of food and other necessary items: *The guide packed the provisions for the river trip.*

pul·ley (pŏŏl'ē) *n., pl.* **pul·leys.** A device having a freely turning wheel with a groove around its edge through which a rope, chain, or cable runs.

pu·ny (pyŏō'nē) *adj.* **pu·ni·er, pu·ni·est.** Small or unimportant in size, strength, or value; weak: *That puny horse is not big enough to run in the race.*

pur·pose (pûr'pəs) *n.* The intended or desired result; a goal; aim; intent: *The yacht club's sole purpose is to promote the sport of sailing.*

quea·sy (kwē'zē) *adj.* **queas·i·er, queas·i·est.** Sick to one's stomach: *The rocking of the boat made her feel queasy.*

quiv·er (kwĭv'ər) *v.* To shake with a slight vibrating motion; tremble: *My voice quivered with excitement.*

re·con·sid·er (rē'kən sĭd'ər) *v.* To think about again, especially with the possibility of making a change.

rec·ord (rĕk'ərd) *n.* The best performance known, as in a sport: *the world record in swimming.*

re·flec·tion (rĭ **flĕk′**shən) *n.* **1.** An image or a likeness. **2.** A thought; idea.

re·main (rĭ **mān′**) *v.* To be left: *Only three peas remained on my plate.*

res·er·va·tion (rĕz′ər **vā′**shən) *n.* An area set aside by the government for a certain purpose: *a wildlife reservation.*

re·u·nite (rē′yo͞o **nīt′**) *v.* **re·u·nit·ed, re·u·nit·ing.** To bring or come together again.

rheu·ma·tism (ro͞o′mə tĭz′əm) *n.* A disease that causes swelling of the muscles, tendons, bones, or joints. It also makes them stiff and causes pain.

rig·ging (**rĭg′**ĭng) *n.* The system of ropes, chains, and tackle used to support and control the masts, sails, and yards of a sailing vessel.

right·eous (**rī′**chəs) *adj.* Morally right; just: *a righteous cause; a righteous person.*

roam (rōm) *v.* To travel over or through (an area) without a fixed goal; wander: *She loved to roam about a new city.*

rud·der (**rŭd′**ər) *n.* A movable, flat piece of metal or wood at the rear of a boat. The rudder is used for steering the boat.

rung (rŭng) *n.* A rod or bar that forms a step of a ladder.

sat·is·fy (**săt′**ĭs fī′) *v.* **1.** To fulfill or gratify: *We ate just enough to satisfy our hunger.* **2.** To set free of doubt; convince.

scaf·fold (**skăf′**əld) *or* (**skăf′**ōld) *n.* A platform that is used to support people who are constructing or repairing a building.

schoon·er (**sko͞o′**nər) *n.* A ship with two or more masts and sails that are set lengthwise.

schooner

sculp·tor (**skŭlp′**tər) *n.* An artist who makes sculptures.

sculp·ture (**skŭlp′**chər) *n.* **1.** The art of making figures or designs that have depth, as in wood, stone, or metal. **2.** A work of sculpture.

seed·ling (**sēd′**lĭng) *n.* A young plant that has grown from a seed.

sense (sĕns) *v.* **sensed, sens·ing.** To be aware of; feel: *The animal sensed that its enemy was nearby.*

sen·si·ble (**sĕn′**sə bəl) *adj.* Showing good judgment; reasonable: *a sensible decision.*

sep·a·ra·tion (sĕp′ə **rā′**shən) *n.* The act of separating or the condition of being separated.

ă pat / ā pay / â care / ä father / ĕ pet / ē be / ĭ pit / ī pie / î fierce / ŏ pot / ō go / ô paw, for / oi oil / o͞o book / o͞o boot / ou out / ŭ cut / û fur / *th* the / th thin / hw which / zh vision / ə ago, item, pencil, atom, circus

set·tler (sĕt′lər) *n.* A person who makes his or her home in a new region. *The settlers appreciated the kindness of their new neighbors.*

shab·by (shăb′ē) *adj.* **shab·bi·er, shab·bi·est.** Run down; worn out.

ship·wright (shĭp′rīt′) *n.* A carpenter employed in the construction or maintenance of ships.

shock·ing (shŏk′ĭng) *adj.* Causing great surprise and emotional disturbance; astonishing: *a shocking event.*

shoot (shoot) *n.* A plant or plant part, such as a stem, leaf, or bud, that has just begun to grow, sprout, or develop.

shrewd·ly (shrood′lē) *adv.* In a clever and sharp manner: *The lawyer spoke to the jury shrewdly.*

sketch (skĕch) *v.* To make a rough drawing or painting: *She sketched the baby.*

skim (skĭm) *v.* **skimmed, skim· ming.** To move, pass, or glide lightly and swiftly over (a surface): *The sailboat skimmed the lake.*

slav·er·y (slā′və rē) *or* (slāv′rē) *n.* **1.** The condition of being a slave. **2.** The practice of owning slaves.

sleigh (slā) *n.* A light vehicle or carriage with runners, usually pulled by a horse and used for traveling on ice or snow.

slith·er (slĭth′ər) *v.* To move along by gliding: *The snake slithered across the road.*

slops (slŏps) *n.* Waste food fed to animals.

snor·kel (snôr′kəl) *n.* A breathing device used by skin divers, consisting of a plastic tube curved at one end and fitted with a mouthpiece.

snorkel

sol·id (sŏl′ĭd) *adj.* **1.** Having a definite shape and volume; not liquid or gaseous. **2.** Not hollowed out: *a solid block of ice.*

sports·man·ship (spôrts′mən-shĭp′) *n.* The qualities and conduct suitable to a person who observes the rules of a contest and accepts victory or defeat without behaving boastfully or angrily.

sprawl (sprôl) *v.* To sit or lie with the body, arms, and legs spread out: *We were so tired from the hike, we sprawled out on the grass and took a nap.*

sprout (sprout) *v.* To begin to grow; produce or appear as a bud, shoot, or new growth: *The newly planted corn sprouted after the rain.*

square (skwâr) *n.* **1.** An open space surrounded by streets on all sides. **2.** A figure having four sides that are the same length.

squat (skwŏt) *v.* **squat·ted** *or* **squat, squat·ting.** To sit on one's heels.

stage (stāj) *n.* A level, degree, or period of time in the course of a process; a step in development: *a disease in its early stages.*

stam·pede (stăm **pēd'**) *n.* **1.** A sudden violent rush of startled or scared animals, such as horses, cattle, or buffalo. **2.** A similar sudden or headlong rush of people.

sta·tion (stā'shən) *v.* To assign to a position: *The soldier was stationed in Germany.*

steep (stēp) *adj.* Rising or falling sharply: *We climbed a steep hill.*

stee·ple (stē'pəl) *n.* A tall tower rising from the roof of a building.

steeple

stern (stûrn) *adj.* **1.** Serious and severe: *a stern talk on manners.* **2.** Strict, firm: *stern discipline.*

stow·a·way (stō'ə wā') *n.* A person who hides on a ship, plane, train, etc., to get a free ride.

strand (strănd) *v.* To leave in a difficult or helpless position: *They were stranded on the mountain when their car broke down.*

strug·gle (strŭg'əl) *v.* **strug·gled, strug·gling.** To make a great effort: *The team struggled to win.*

stub·born (stŭb'ərn) *adj.* Not willing to change a purpose or opinion in spite of urging or requests from others: *The stubborn child refused to wear boots.*

stu·di·o (stoo'dē ō' *or* styoo' dē ō') *n., pl.* **stu·di·os.** The place where an artist works.

stump (stŭmp) *n.* The part of a tree trunk left in the ground after the tree has fallen or been cut down.

stump

suc·ceed (sək **sēd'**)·*v.* To follow or come next in time or order; to replace (another) in an office or position: *The princess will succeed her mother to the throne.*

sulk·y (sŭl'kē) *adj.* **sulk·i·er, sulk·i·est.** Quiet because of one's ill temper or bad mood.

su·per (soo'pər) *n. Informal.* A person who supervises or is in charge of something, such as an apartment or office building; a superintendent.

sup·ply (sə plī') *n.* Often **sup·plies.** Materials or provisions stored and used when needed.

ă pat / ā pay / â care / ä father / ĕ pet / ē be / ĭ pit / ī pie / î fierce / ŏ pot / ō go / ô paw, for / oi oil / oͦo book / o͞o boot / ou out / ŭ cut / û fur / *th* the / th thin / hw which / zh vision / ə ago, item, pencil, atom, circus

sur·round·ings (sə **roun′**dĭngz) *pl. n.* The things, circumstances, and conditions that surround a person: *peaceful surroundings.*

sus·pi·cious (sə **spĭsh′**əs) *adj.* **1.** Causing suspicion. **2.** Tending to suspect; distrustful.

swerve (swûrv) *v.* **swerved, swerv·ing.** To turn or cause to turn quickly or sharply: *The car swerved off the road and onto the sidewalk.*

ten·e·ment (**tĕn′**ə mənt) *n.* A cheap apartment building that is found in the poorer sections of a city.

ter·race (**tĕr′**ĭs) *n.* A paved, open area next to a house; patio.

ter·ri·fy (**tĕr′**ə fī′) *v.* **ter·ri·fied, ter·ri·fy·ing, ter·ri·fies.** To fill with terror: *Heights terrify some people.*

thought·less (**thôt′**lĭs) *adj.* **1.** Not thinking; careless: *It was thoughtless of me to forget to lock the door.* **2.** Not showing consideration of other people's needs and feelings.

till (tĭl) *v.* To prepare land for growing crops by plowing and fertilizing.

tim·id (**tĭm′**ĭd) *adj.* Easily frightened; shy.

tow (tō) *v.* To pull along behind with a chain, rope, or cable: *A truck towed the damaged car.*

trag·ic (**trăj′**ĭk) *adj.* Very unfortunate; disastrous.

treach·er·ous (**trĕch′**ər əs) *adj.* Dangerous.

trem·ble (**trĕm′**bəl) *v.* **trem·bled, trem·bling.** To shake from or as if from fear or cold; quake; shiver; quiver.

trol·ley (**trŏl′**ē) *n. Chiefly British.* A cart.

trough (trôf) *or* (trŏf) *n.* A long, narrow box or other container. It is used for holding water or feed for animals.

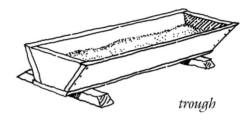

trough

trum·pet (**trŭm′**pĭt) *v.* To give forth a loud sound.

trun·dle bed (**trŭn′**dl bĕd) *n.* A low bed that can be rolled under another bed when not in use.

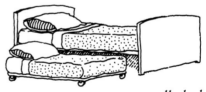

trundle bed

trust·wor·thy (**trŭst′**wûr′thē) *adj.* Dependable; reliable: *a trustworthy secretary.*

tur·bu·lent (**tûr′**byə lənt) *adj.* Violently agitated or disturbed; stormy: *The turbulent waters made the boat sway back and forth.*

un·furl (ŭn **fûrl′**) *v.* To spread or open out; unroll: *He was unfurling the flag.*

urge (ûrj) *v.* **urged, urg·ing.** To plead with: *I was urged to accept the job.*

vain (vān) *Idiom.* **in vain.** Without effect; to no use or purpose: *Their work was all in vain.*

vast (văst) *adj.* Very great in area, size, or amount: *The ship sailed the vast ocean.*

ven·i·son (věn′ĭ sən) *or* (-zən) *n.* The meat of a deer, used as food.

vic·to·ri·ous (vĭk tôr′ē əs) *or* (vĭk- tôr′ē əs) *adj.* Of or resulting in winning: *a victorious cheer.*

whine (hwīn) *v.* **1.** To make a high, shrill sound or cry: *The electric saw whined as it cut the wood.* **2.** To complain in a childish, annoying way: *Don't whine about your homework.*

width (wĭdth) *or* (wĭth) *n.* The measurement of something from side to side: *Our living room is ten feet in width.*

will (wĭl) *n.* An official paper that tells what a person wants done with his or her property after death.

wound (wo͞ond) *v.* To hurt by cutting or breaking body tissue.

yam (yăm) *n.* **1.** The starchy root of a climbing vine that grows in the tropics. The yam is eaten as a vegetable or ground into flour. **2.** A sweet potato having reddish flesh.

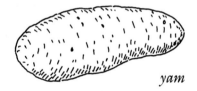

yam

ă pat / ā pay / â care / ä father / ě pet / ē be / ĭ pit / ī pie / î fierce / ŏ pot / ō go / ô paw, for / oi **oil** / o͝o **book** / o͞o **boot** / ou **out** / ŭ **cut** / û **fur** / *t h* **the** / th **thin** / hw **which** / zh **vision** / ə **ago, item, pencil, atom, circus**

Continued from page 2.

"Bicycle Rider," slightly adapted from *Bicycle Rider* by Mary Scioscia. Copyright © 1983 by Mary Hershey Scioscia. Reprinted by permission of Harper and Row, Publishers, Inc.

"The Borrowers," adapted from *The Borrowers*, copyright 1952, 1953, © 1980, 1981 by Mary Norton. Reprinted by permission of Harcourt Brace Jovanovich, Inc.

"The Cabin Faced West," by Jean Fritz, adapted and reprinted by permission of Coward, McCann and Geoghegan from *The Cabin Faced West* by Jean Fritz, copyright © 1958, copyright renewed © 1986 by Jean Fritz.

"Carving in Stone," from *The Stone Menagerie* by Shay Rieger. Copyright © 1970 by Shay Rieger. Reprinted by permission of the author.

"Chester Cricket's Pigeon Ride," a selection from *Chester Cricket's Pigeon Ride* by George Seldon, illustrated by Garth Williams. Copyright © 1981 by George Seldon and Garth Williams. Reprinted by permission of Farrar, Straus & Giroux, Inc.

"Child of the Silent Night," adapted from *Child of the Silent Night* by Edith F. Hunter. Copyright © 1963 by Edith Fisher Hunter. Reprinted by permission of Houghton Mifflin Company.

"Ernie and the Mile-Long Muffler," adapted from *Ernie and the Mile-Long Muffler*, by Marjorie Lewis. Text copyright © 1982 by Marjorie Lewis. Reprinted by permission of the author.

"The Gift," from *The Gift* by Helen Coutant, illustrated by Mai Vo-Dinh. Text copyright © 1983 by Helen Coutant. Illustrations copyright © 1983 by Mai Vo-Dinh. Reprinted by permission of Alfred A. Knopf, Inc.

"Hope," by Langston Hughes. Copyright 1942 by Alfred A. Knopf, Inc. and renewed © 1970 by Arna Bontemps and George Houston Bass. Reprinted from *Selected Poems of Langston Hughes*, by permission of Alfred A. Knopf, Inc.

"How Paul Bonjean Became Paul Bunyan," adapted from *Yankee Doodle's Cousins* by Anne Burnett Malcolmson. Copyright 1941 by Anne Burnett Malcolmson. Reprinted by permission of Houghton Mifflin Company.

"How the Forest Grew," from *How the Forest Grew* by William Jaspersohn. Illustrated by Chuck Eckhart. Text copyright © 1980 by William G. Jaspersohn. Reprinted by Greenwillow Books (a division of William Morrow).

"The Hundred Penny Box," from *The Hundred Penny Box* by Sharon Bell Mathis. Copyright © 1975 by Sharon Bell Mathis. All rights reserved. Reprinted by permission of Viking Penguin, Inc.

"Maria's House," condensed from *Maria's House* by Jean Merrill. Text copyright © 1974 by Jean Merrill. Reprinted by permission of the author and Curtis Brown, Ltd.

"Mary McLeod Bethune," by Eloise Greenfield. (Thomas Y. Crowell). Text copyright © 1977 by Eloise Greenfield. Reprinted by permission of Harper & Row, Publishers, Inc.

"Oliphaunt," from *Adventures of Tom Bombadil* by J.R.R. Tolkien. Copyright © 1962 by George Allen and Unwin, Ltd. Reprinted by permission of Houghton Mifflin Company and George Allen & Unwin (Publishers) Ltd.

"The Once-a-Year Day," adapted from *The Once-a-Year Day* by Eve Bunting. Copyright © 1974 by Eve Bunting. Reprinted by permission of the author.

"So Will I," from *River Winding* by Charlotte Zolotow (Thomas Y. Crowell). Text copyright © 1970 by Charlotte Zolotow. Reprinted by permission of Harper and Row, Publishers, Inc.

"Stone Fox," an excerpt adapted from *Stone Fox* by John Reynolds Gardiner. (Thomas Y. Crowell). Text copyright © 1980 by John Reynolds Gardiner. Reprinted by permission of Harper & Row, Publishers, Inc.

"Truly My Own," by Vanessa Howard, from *The Voice of the Children* collected by June Jordan and Terri Bush. Copyright © 1968 by The Voice of the Children, Inc. Reprinted by permission of Henry Holt and Company, Inc.

"Two Big Bears," adapted from pp. 101–116 of *Little House in the Big Woods* by Laura Ingalls Wilder, illustrated by Garth Williams. Copyright, 1932, as to text, by Laura Ingalls Wilder. Renewed © 1959 by Roger MacBride. Pictures copyright 1953 by Garth Williams, copyright © renewed 1981 by Garth Williams. Reprinted by permission of Harper and Row, Publishers, Inc.

"Why Mosquitoes Buzz in People's Ears," by Verna Aardema, illustrated by Leo and Diane Dillon. Text copyright © 1975 by Verna Aardema. Illustrations copyright © 1975 by Leo and Diane Dillon. Reprinted by permission of the publisher, Dial Books for Young Readers.

453

"Wilbur's Escape," adapted from Chapter III of *Charlotte's Web* by E.B. White. Pictures by Garth Williams. Copyright 1952 by E.B. White; text copyright renewed © 1980 by E.B. White, illustrations copyright renewed © 1980 by Garth Williams. Reprinted by permission of Harper and Row, Publishers, Inc.

"The Wish at the Top," by Clyde Robert Bulla, illustrated by Chris Conover (Thomas Y. Crowell). Text copyright © 1974 by Clyde Robert Bulla. Illustrations copyright © 1974 by Chris Conover. Reprinted by permission of Harper and Row, Publishers, Inc.

"The Wright Brothers," condensed by permission of Random House, Inc. from *The Wright Brothers* by Quentin Reynolds. Copyright 1950 by Random House, Inc.

Grateful acknowledgment is made for permission to reprint for the Glossary, the pronunciation key and adapted definitions from *The Houghton Mifflin Intermediate Dictionary*. Copyright © 1986 by Houghton Mifflin Company. Adapted and reprinted by permission from *The Houghton Mifflin Intermediate Dictionary*.

Credits

Cover Design: James Stockton & Associates

Illustrators: 10−27 Nancy Edwards Calder **29−50** Chuck Eckart **51** Sue Thompson **62−74** Garth Williams **75** Leo and Diane Dillon, Linda Medley, Melinda Sullivan **76−77** Tim Jones **78−94** Mai Vo-Dinh **96−111** J. Brian Pinckney **112−121** Garth Williams **122−142** Higgins Bond **143** Thomas B. Allen **146−165** Chris Conover **166−190** James Watling **191−206** Sandra Spiedel **208−218** Garth Williams **220−221** Robert Stein III **222−243** J. Brian Pinckney **244−265** Eileen McKeating **274−287** John Holder **288−289** Lorinda Cauley **290−304** Dee De Rosa **305** Imero Gobbato **306−307** Ruth Flanagan **308−317** Leo and Diane Dillon **318−333** Mai Vo-Dinh **335−356** Pat and Robin DeWitt **357** William Steig **358−359** Robert Stein **360−377** Christa Kiefer **378−389** Marc Tetrault **390−408** Peggy Fortnum **409** Cecilia von Rabinau **410−434** James Watling **435** Edward Ardizzone

Photographers: 8−9 Willard Clay/Click/Chicago **28** F. Brown Brothers **52** Bruce Coleman, Inc. **53** George H. Harrison/Grant Heilman Photography **54** Luis Castanada/The Image Bank **55** Peter Davey/Bruce Coleman, Inc. **56** David Huges/Bruce Coleman, Inc. **57** M.P. Kahl/Bruce Coleman, Inc. **59** (top) Adrienne T. Gibson/Animals, Animals, (bottom) R.S. Virbee/Grant Heilman **60** Peter Davey/Bruce Coleman, Inc. **61** Sveno Lindblad/Photo Researchers **95** Bill Binzen **144−145** Jim P. Garrison/Rainbow **207** Martin Rogers/Stock Boston **220−221** Jeff Persons/Stock Boston **266** Guy Gillette/Photo Researchers **267** (silhouettes) T. Goodale, (detail) Bruce Coleman, Inc. **269** (top) Lee Boltin, (bottom) Dr. E.R. Degginger/Animals, Animals **270** (left) Bruce Coleman, Inc., (right) Lee Boltin **271** © Robert Maier/Animals, Animals **272** (left) Tad Goodale, (right) Bruce Coleman, Inc. **273** © Shay Rieger **334** David Ellis/The Picture Cube